A BEAUTIFUL TAPESTRY

TWO ORDINARY WOMEN, ONE AMAZING GOD, MANY LIVES TRANSFORMED

TRACY WILLIAMSON
WITH MARILYN BAKER

Foreword by Jennifer Rees Larcombe

T0352130

Authentic

First published 2020 by Authentic Media Limited,
PO Box 6326, Bletchley, Milton Keynes, MK1 9GG.
authenticmedia.co.uk

British Library Cataloguing in Publication Data
A catalogue record for this book is available from the British Library.
ISBN: 978-1-78893-156-4
978-1-78893-157-1 (e-book)

Cover design by Rados 777
Printed and bound by CPI Group (UK) Ltd, Croydon, CR0 4YY

'This extraordinary account tells of two remarkable women who, despite severe difficulties, have blessed tens of thousands of people, including me. It is a story of both enduring faith and of a God who can be trusted. This book will give you a faith-lift.'

J.John, minister, speaker and author

'To read this book felt like a privilege to be a witness to Tracy and Marilyn's journey of friendship through joy and heartache. This book points people to the source of all comfort, showing the impact Jesus can make in every season of our lives. Uplifting, compassionate and hope filled.'

Patrick Regan, CEO, Kintsugi Hope

'The subtitle for this dual autobiography is "Two ordinary women, one amazing God, many lives transformed" but perhaps it should read "One amazing God makes two amazing women"! I joke sometimes that we Christians use the word "amazing" too often and too easily, but it's the word that comes to my mind time and time again as I read this book, together with its synonyms: astonishing, incredible, surprising, wow! To travel through Marilyn and Tracy's stories is to wonder with awe at what God can do with his children, often against all the worldly "odds".

'Their lives are like two streams: each begins in a hidden and narrow place, emerging with difficulty through oppressive rocks and entangling vegetation, trickling over stony beds, flowing on a little stronger, sometimes through pleasant sunny landscape but then meeting midstream obstacles and disruptive eddies that cause diversions from the intended course. At last the two streams meet and flow together, becoming a strong and life-giving river transforming the landscape through which it moves, bringing beauty and abundance.

'To go on this journey with them is to experience the tears, pain, laughter, disappointments, thrills and delights of two lives handed over to God for his glory and the building up of his church.'

Jill Rattle, former Editor of Day by Day with God *(BRF)*

'This story of two emotionally scarred and physically disabled women shows how the power of God can take the ordinary and weave it into something beautiful, something that impacts and transforms the lives of many others. And it brings healing to your spirit as you laugh and cry with them as they travel the world, cope with the trials and enjoy the journey together.'

Revd Penelope Swithinbank, Ministries by Design

'As a teenager, I remember hearing a story about a blind singer, a deaf assistant and hair dye (read the story in this book). Years later, I came across MBM and learned about Marilyn and Tracy's ministry. God uses them together for his glory; I could see that. What I didn't see was the other side of this "beautiful tapestry": the background to it, knots and all.

'I have the privilege, now, of calling Tracy and Marilyn friends. I know something of their backgrounds, but reading this book showed me things I didn't know. Marilyn and Tracy write courageously and movingly – with honesty, humour and humility – as they share difficult times, as well as joy-full ones.

'Of their first meeting, Tracy comments: "We didn't mention God once, but I've never been in a social situation in which God has been more present." God is not mentioned in every sentence of this book, nor on every page, but it is hard to think of a book in which God is more present.

'*A Beautiful Tapestry* will, amid laughter and tears, inspire and gently challenge. Through walking with Tracy and Marilyn on their life-journeys so far, we are drawn into an experience of what it means to live each moment with God. We are encouraged in the reality of following where God leads, however unlikely it may seem. And we glimpse God at work in amazing ways.'

Emily Owen, author and speaker

'A Beautiful Tapestry is everything that I would have expected from Marilyn and Tracy. I have known them at work and at play, two places where much laughter and a smattering of tears are pretty well inevitable. Their story, told with typical honesty, compassion and literary flair, will warm the cockles of your spiritual heart. A joy to be in their company as always.'

Adrian Plass, author and speaker

'I first met Marilyn because I was asked to do a songbook with her. She proved to be quite exacting and was impressed at how accurate my transcriptions were (phew!). Subsequently we did a number of albums together and she was always a delightful mixture of open and fiercely rigorous, as worried about the reverb on the snare as she was about the feel of a vocal take. She is in that sense a sensitive music producer as well as a superb artist. I loved working with her.'

Christopher Norton, composer and producer

'This wonderful book is the story of the lives and friendship of two of the most honest, vulnerable, yet "fun-infectious" people you could meet. All those who have been touched by their joint or separate ministries will enjoy meeting the real people behind the work, as they share moments that have made them cry, laugh, bad tempered and joyful. However, A Beautiful Tapestry is more than their story as another story also shines through. This is the unending, relentless love of God for his broken children, and the tenderness with which he seeks to bring us all home.'

The Revd John Ryeland, Director,
The Christian Healing Mission

'This beautifully crafted memoir of two remarkable women and the friendship that God began in them, and then increased and strengthened through years of ministry, is a book that will bring you closer to the Father heart of God. Our culture often strives to lessen those who live with disabilities and place them in unhelpful categories, and sadly Christian culture can be similar at times with its insistence that to be "useful" to God you must be whole in every way. Tracy and Marilyn turn this narrative upside down and reveal the topsy-turvy nature of God's kingdom, where the first are last and the last are first.

'In their endearing stories of life together on the road and at home you will find a place of stillness as you watch the tapestry God weaves take on its chaotic and wonderful life. You will laugh at some of the stories they tell, and cry at others. Tracy's prophetic voice is a beautiful reminder of how much you are loved, and will speak directly into many lives.

'I'm grateful for this book which is more than an autobiography: it draws the reader into a bigger story, a story that God weaves over all our lives, a story that might look jumbled and unexpected at times, and often painful, yet the strands of his loving work in us are evident as we turn more and more to him, and rest in his love.'

Liz Carter, writer, poet and author

Copyright Acknowledgements

Contents

Authors' Note

For the sake of confidentiality, names have sometimes been changed. This story spans several decades and involves many, many people and events. It is not written as an accurate, chronological, factual history but as an overall picture focusing on highlights and themes rather than on a set order. We have inevitably and sadly had to leave many stories out, but they are just as vital to our history, even though not shared on the printed page. Similarly, many people have come alongside us on our journey to where we are today; some just for a short period of time, others for years. As much as we would have loved to, it's not been possible to share each person's story; some we haven't mentioned at all, and yet all have played an invaluable part – we want to thank you with all our hearts for the giving of yourselves into our lives and ministry. For your interest, a timeline is included, starting from 1979 when Marilyn released her first album, chronologically showing how God has led and provided for us, including team changes, up to the present day.

May God bless you all richly.

Tracy and Marilyn

Joy in God's wonderful faithfulness – Marilyn and Tracy, August 2020

About the Authors

Tracy Williamson is an author and speaker working for MBM Trust, an itinerant ministry of music, teaching and prayer, based in Hadlow, Kent. MBM is headed up by blind gospel singer/songwriter Marilyn Baker whose first album was released in 1979. Marilyn's twenty-first and twenty-second albums, *Joy of My Heart* and *Hallelujah Christmas* were released in 2019.

Tracy met Marilyn in 1985 when they became great friends. They started working together in 1986.

With Tracy's deafness and partial sight and Marilyn's blindness, they form an unlikely ministry partnership that spans more than thirty-four years. Tracy has a hearing dog, Goldie, and Marilyn is currently awaiting a new guide dog.

A Beautiful Tapestry will be Tracy's eighth book and the first that Tracy and Marilyn have written together.

Acknowledgements

Our first thanks must go to our publisher, Authentic Media, who have been incredibly supportive and patient as Marilyn and I have tried to get our story down, and in the process have kept moving the goalposts as to submission deadlines! Thank you Donna Harris, Charlie Cuthbert, Becky Fawcett and Rachael Franklin for your belief in us, understanding and prayers. You are amazing.

Also, thanks to Sheila Jacobs, whose committed editing has enabled us to cross the t's and dot the i's. A vital part of every publication.

This whole story is a thank you to the many people, friends, influential contacts, prayer supporters, team, conference centres and organisations that have believed in our ministry, helped us take steps, supported us by offering themselves and their gifts into the work and prayed, and been there for us as we've put this story together. Thank you with all our hearts. Specific thanks to our many trustees over the years, both in Watford and Tonbridge. Your 'behind the scenes' managerial and guiding work has enabled MBM to keep going, and your prayerful care and support have been so enriching. Thanks to our present trustees, Andrew and Val Meade and Ron Seale, who have stood with us now for many years.

Thank you, too, to all you amazing people who have willingly sent in your stories, anecdotes, photos and testimonies; some have gone into the book, others have richly blessed us as we've revisited memories together. We would have loved to include them all, but in the end there just wasn't room. We are so grateful for how you have enriched our memories and our story.

I, Tracy, would love to thank you, Marilyn, for your belief in me from the beginning and for your patience as I've spent so many hours trying to work out how to do this book. Thank you, too, for sharing the story of your early years and all your amazing contributions to the stories of our years together.

Most of all, thank you to God, Father, Son and Holy Spirit, without whose amazing love and works of grace in our lives, this story could never have happened.

Foreword

Over the last few days, I've very slowly been reading this book – I loved it so much I didn't want it to finish! Tracy and Marilyn make it all so real that I feel I have been travelling with them and sharing their adventures.

In the first two parts of the book they each tell us their own stories – up to the dramatic moment when they first met. For different reasons, in early childhood they were both disabled, and it is fascinating to read how they gradually came to the realisation that their physical challenges made them different from other children. They seemed to accept these differences, but it was the way that other children and adults reacted to them which makes for fascinating – but painful – reading. The traumas they experienced, like bullying at school and the lack of understanding and support at home, could have damaged them emotionally for the rest of their lives. Yet something amazing happened to them both when they met Jesus, Marilyn at 15 and Tracy at 18. Not only did he help them both find healing for their invisible wounds, but he also used the scars to give them understanding and compassion for others who struggle with the effects of different kinds of pain. In fact, they have both devoted their lives to helping people find hope and realise how greatly they are loved.

After the point when they meet and begin to work and travel together, the book changes in structure. They each give us their own perspective on some of the events they have shared and amazing adventures they have been through together. The book begins to feel more like an enthralling and hilarious conversation round the fire with old friends!

It has always astonished me how two disabled women could dare to travel round the world, singing and speaking. This would be a tough lifestyle for able-bodied people, involving constant adjustment to new people, surroundings, different beds, food; getting on and off planes, buses and trains; adjusting to unfamiliar audiences, languages and venues. How Marilyn and Tracy, with their complex challenges, have successfully managed all this for so many years is nothing short of miraculous!

I've heard them both speak hundreds of times over years of working with them, but what makes this book totally unique is that they share some of the more private aspects of themselves that were new to me and which most of us have never been given access to before.

I first 'met' Marilyn through listening to her songs in the early 1980s, lying in hospital, seriously ill. I remember playing one particular track over and over again, 'He gives joy to the hopeless, peace to the weary and He binds up the broken hearted.'[1] 'This person knows exactly how I feel,' I used to think, 'and she knows just what I need – I would so love to meet her one day.' When we actually did meet, a decade later, I was so awestruck at talking to someone so famous, I just didn't know what to say. The awe didn't last long once I realised how gloriously ordinary, fun-loving and down-to-earth Marilyn and Tracy both are. Once, when we'd all been running a five-day healing retreat together, we went back to Marilyn's house so she could cook us a meal. While she was out in the kitchen fetching the dessert, I was so tired I fell fast asleep with my head on my placemat! There are not many friends you can do that to in the middle of their dinner party.

Over the thirty years that I have known, loved and worked with Marilyn and Tracy, what I most admire about them both is their complete dependence on the Lord and their ability to be exactly the same 'on stage' or off it. I hope you will enjoy this book as much as I have.

Jennifer Rees Larcombe
Author, speaker and director of Beauty from Ashes

Preface

Tracy

When Authentic Media contacted Marilyn in 2019 to ask if she'd be interested in writing her memoir, Marilyn asked if I could help and make it a joint story of our lives together, with me doing most of the writing. I thought it was a lovely idea but little realised what a marathon it would be! Just the logistics of how to put the book together and then trying to recall stories and choose which to include . . . Plus the rollercoaster of remembering our childhoods and the joy of thinking of all the amazing things God has done.

One day the phrase 'A Beautiful Tapestry' dropped into my mind, and I realised that is what the book is. It is a tapestry of threads woven together by God; a tapestry of stories, both our own and other people's; so many examples of God speaking, acting, comforting, inspiring, providing, anointing and enabling. One thread on its own may not look much, but when all the threads are woven together the tapestry comes into being, a beautifully complete and unique picture. That is what this story is: a glorious mix of anecdote, testimony, struggles, pain, achievements and joy. You may laugh on one page and cry on another, but it's our hope that through this beautiful tapestry you will encounter the God who loves you so much, and be blessed.

Marilyn

I have been recording and ministering now for over forty years, and for at least thirty-four of them, I have worked with my lovely friend and partner in ministry, Tracy. The way God has woven our lives together has been amazing, and it is with great joy that we now try to tell some of our story: how a deaf person and a blind person do life and ministry together. We hope you will find it insightful, inspiring and also entertaining.

I want you woven into a tapestry of love, in touch with everything there is to know of God. Then you will have minds confident and at rest, focused on Christ

Col. 2:2 (*The Message*)

We would like to dedicate *A Beautiful Tapestry* to all who, through your friendship with us and the ministry of MBM, are adding beautiful and unbreakable threads into this picture of transforming love that God is constantly weaving.

Part 1

Marilyn's Story

Beginnings

He formed me in my mother's womb, even then, even then I was in His hands

Marilyn Baker[1]

I was born in Birmingham in 1950. It was a time when everyone was looking for new beginnings, trying to recover from the dark days of the war and bravely hoping for a brighter future to emerge.

Dad's business was thriving and my parents moved into a brand-new house they'd built themselves. But the one thing lacking for them was that they had no children. They had longed to start a family but it felt like a dream that would never come true. But out of the blue, just after the move, Mum realised she was pregnant. At last it was happening, and they knew that their child would be the best, their pride and joy, and would have everything they could possibly give it.

Mum was 38 and because of fears for her health, they induced her labour a month prematurely and, at last, after all the years of waiting, baby Marilyn was born. Such joy! But I was whisked away immediately as Mum needed serious medical attention. We were both kept in hospital while she recovered and I was bottle-fed by the nurses. One day while feeding, I choked, and because I was premature, they immediately put me in an incubator and gave me oxygen. When Mum was well enough, we went home, and there was great excitement among our family and friends. Little did anyone know that something devastating had occurred.

A new pattern of life began for our family, and at first all seemed to be going well. Then after about seven months, Mum noticed I had developed a squint. She took me to the hospital and to her shock they said they would keep me in for tests. When she came to collect me, she had no idea what was about to happen. The surgeon told her that I was going to lose my sight and would be completely blind for the rest of my life. It turned out that it was because I'd been given too much oxygen. This was happening to lots of babies at that time, but it was only discovered that oxygen was the cause in the early 1950s.

My mum could hardly take it in. She came home on the bus holding me and sobbing, her world turned upside down. The news had the profoundest effect on my parents. My dad had already been through deep struggles in his life, having suffered abandonment as a child. From having nothing he'd pulled himself up and become a successful businessman, but those experiences had created a deep mistrust of others and, indeed, of life. Now this news of my blindness overwhelmed him and made him lose even more hope. His way of coping was to bury himself in his work. He became bitter as he imagined my future as a blind person. What would I ever achieve in life? All he had hoped to show me, the things he wanted to do with me, would never come to anything. He would just have to make sure that I'd always have enough to be secure.

My mum's reaction was very different, and after the initial shock she tried to make the best of things. She loved me dearly and believed I could learn to do many things that sighted children did. Nevertheless, she felt anguish as she saw each day how I was losing more and more of the tiny amount of sight I had. She later told me how I would sit, staring up at the sky, trying to catch the last glimmer of light.

Mum was determined I would get enjoyment out of life and began to think of ways that could happen. So whenever she left me in my pram in the garden, she would put the radio on. Maybe this accounts for me showing a great deal of interest in music at an early age! As I began to talk and walk, although she had no support or advice, she could see that I was entering into life, and somehow she knew I would be able to do far more than even she could imagine.

In the winter, Mum used to take me out on a little toboggan in the woods that backed on to our garden. She would guide it and I would sing to her at the top of my voice. I adored playing in the snow. If Dad was hammering something together, I would want a hammer too, and one day even sold some bits of wood that I had cobbled together to our neighbours, saying I was learning to make furniture. They played along, giving me a penny for each strange creation, much to Mum's embarrassment!

When I was nearly 5, Mum told me I would soon be starting school, and an important lady was coming to see if I was suitable to attend a special school for blind children in Bromsgrove. I wanted to impress her, and remembered how on Saturdays Mum and Dad would go out to their club and Mum would always get herself dolled up with beads, bangles and make-up, so I decided that's what I needed to do. I crept into Mum's bedroom and got everything out. I was determined to look the part. When the lady arrived I wasn't quite ready, so when Mum called me, I yelled, 'I'm coming in a minute. I'm just making myself look posh.' Then I proudly descended the stairs waiting for their gasps of delight. To my consternation they both screamed and burst out laughing. What had I done? Didn't I look the tops? Mrs Williams immediately pronounced I could certainly go to the school.

The day soon arrived for me to start school. I knew it would be great as Mum had kept telling me so. But when she left me with the teachers, on that first day, I remember feeling utterly lost and alone. At home I had felt secure, but now I was surrounded by the noise of lots of children rushing around. Before that I hadn't even been to a nursery school or a playgroup. I don't remember much about those early days, but I do remember missing home and my mum so very much. The school had a very strict, almost Victorian, regime and we were made to sleep in set positions in our beds with our two hands under our left or right ear. I couldn't sleep like this and would stay awake for hours till they had finished checking on us. At last I could get into my usual curled-up position and drop off to sleep.

Ideas about education in the fifties were very different from what they are now, and it was thought better for us to only have limited contact with our parents. So the school didn't let us go home for a whole weekend, but just for Saturdays. I was always heartbroken when I had to return to school after only a few hours. My parents felt this was ridiculous and fought for me to spend the whole weekend with them, returning to school early Monday mornings. This caused a rumpus but they won the day, and in the end the rule was changed for the whole school.

Soon after starting school I began piano lessons with a blind teacher, but she never remembered what we'd covered previously, so I just kept repeating the same pieces. Eventually, the school realised I was not getting on well and changed me to a different teacher who was much more on the ball, and I began to learn more quickly.

My friends at home would often talk about riding their bikes. I remember saying that I wanted my own bike, so Dad had a special guide put on a tricycle so that Mum could guide me as I pedalled. When I came home at weekends, I loved this new adventure and always wanted to go out on my bike.

As a young child I had always enjoyed playing in the garden. Often during lunchtimes Dad would push me hard on the swing he'd put up in the outbuilding. I found this exciting and although I was half-afraid, I would laugh with delight. I had no thought of self-consciousness when moving around, but at school I began to have problems. I became particularly frightened when climbing onto boxes in PE lessons. I felt clumsy and the other children seemed much more agile than me. The thrill of heights turned to terror, especially on the climbing frame. Unfortunately, the teachers didn't understand and just told me to try harder, saying I would soon get used to it.

Because the school seemed so huge, I felt generally anxious and unsure of myself. I had difficulty in finding my way around the school buildings and grounds and was often late for lessons because of being left behind by the other girls. We all had a set time to practise music and I became afraid of being left alone in the music building. I used to hurry my practice time and shout for the other girls to wait for me, but very often they didn't. It was all fun to them, but to me it was a nightmare.

It transpired later that my confusion about direction was due to the oxygen damaging certain brain cells, which affected my concept of shape and sense of direction as well as my sight. At that time no one realised this, and so all similarly affected children were told off for being slow and not managing to keep up.

Because everyone in my school was blind and my parents didn't talk about my disability, it never occurred to me that anyone would find it a problem. But when I was 9, a customer came to visit my dad, who owned a garage. Dad enthusiastically introduced my mum: 'This is my wife, Marion.'

'Hello, nice to meet you,' he said, shaking hands.

'And this is my daughter, Marilyn.'

'Lovely to meet . . . oh . . .' his voice fizzled out. 'I didn't realise, I'm so sorry.'

Sensing his embarrassment, it began to dawn on me that he saw me as different to everyone else and found it hard to relate to me. For the first time in my life I felt ashamed of my blindness, and self-conscious about how I appeared to others. Until then, I'd been happy, but now I was seeing something different: the effect my disability could have on other people.

The older I got, the more I could tell how disappointed my dad felt about me. When friends came over, he would chat animatedly with them, but if I asked what he was showing them, he would reply that I wouldn't understand. This hurt me deeply. I wanted my dad to affirm me and, most of all, to believe in me. We all need to experience true validation from those who are closest to us, to enable us to grow into the confident adults God designed us to be, but I felt cast aside.

Though I was his daughter, I could tell that he was bitter about my blindness. Nothing I did, including practising hard on the oboe because I knew he loved it, ever drew out a 'Well done'. He would always say, 'You could have done better.'

As I entered my teenage years, I sensed with deep sadness that I would never be good enough for him, and I felt the gnawing longing for his approval growing ever deeper.

2

Chorleywood College

Do you know the difference that Christ can make to you?

Marilyn Baker[1]

My parents were keen for me to gain good qualifications so that I'd be able to get some kind of job. So they urged the headmaster to put me in a special class for pupils who wanted to try for the 11 plus to enable them to go to Chorleywood College, the one grammar school for blind girls in the country. Only selected pupils could sit the entrance exam and this made me feel under pressure. Dad often said to me, 'If you're going to get anywhere, you've got to do better than the average sighted person.' I felt I owed it to my parents to pass, but I completely lost my nerve and gave stupid answers to simple questions – when asked, 'What is the feminine for bull?' I wrote 'Bulless'! This was the first real exam I had taken and what a mess I made of it.

Mum and Dad were very disappointed, but in a way I was relieved, as it meant that I wouldn't have to leave my friends. There would be another chance for me in twelve months' time, and during that year I was specially tutored to prepare me for the exam.

Amid all this extra studying, I was getting ready for something which I found far more exciting. I'd started learning the oboe, and after a year my teacher said, 'My father runs a youth orchestra in Blackpool and I would like you to play as their guest soloist.' This was a great privilege and I had to learn a concerto by Pergolesi for the occasion. Mum came with me to the Winter Gardens in Blackpool, but to Dad's disappointment, he couldn't come. After my performance, the applause was terrific and being only 10 years old, I lapped up the attention. When asked by reporters how it felt being famous, I replied, 'Wonderful!' Mum and Dad thought my career was set fair – I was almost a child prodigy.

The time soon came round for me to retake the Chorleywood College entrance exam. I felt calmer than before as I knew more what to expect. Fortunately, all my hard work paid off, and I passed.

I had mixed feelings about going further away from my parents, so when I started my first term, I was both excited and frightened. My first impression was of a huge, complicated building and grounds. I felt panicky and wondered how on earth I would learn my way around.

At first the teachers were understanding, but because of my problem with direction, I was much slower than many of the others. There were two drives in the school and one dreadful day the headmistress asked those of us in the first year to go down the front drive and back again. I had never mastered which was the front drive and which the back, and consequently I went the wrong way – the others didn't!

The head was very cross with me. 'You've been here two months now, Marilyn, and you don't know the difference between the front and back drive,' she shouted.

This really knocked my confidence: I still thought my problems with direction were due to my stupidity rather than to damaged brain cells, and I was ashamed of my failure. I made a special effort to learn my way around the school and several months later I repeated the test and was successful.

I found it very difficult to settle at Chorleywood. I was used to being at the top of the class, but now I was struggling, which left me feeling insecure and inferior. The school was much larger than my previous one and I didn't feel like an individual any more; I was just one child among many. I became desperate for people to take notice of me.

My biggest disappointment was that I had to stop my oboe lessons as the headmistress felt that my first year would require a lot of me, and since no one else was learning the oboe, the school didn't have a teacher.

I also missed my weekends at home, and although Mum and Dad came once a month, we could only spend a few hours together. Mum always brought a picnic and we'd sit in the car on Chorleywood Common to eat it.

After my first year I won a prize for progress because I had improved in all aspects of my work. Mum and Dad were still very keen for me to go on with the oboe and in recognition of my achievement, the headmistress decided it was time to find me a teacher.

Miss Fisher was excellent. She told my parents I was so gifted she thought I might one day become a professional oboist, so they invested in a more expensive oboe to help me. Academically I was rather slow, but I shone in my music studies.

Like most young people, I wanted to be popular but generally had a low sense of self-esteem, so I acted the class fool, pretending to be more gullible than I was: putting on silly accents and getting myself into trouble to give everyone a laugh. The class played along, daring me to do more naughty things. We did have fun, but deep down I always felt an inner loneliness.

One of my happiest memories was meeting a lovely girl called Susie who'd come to the school from New Zealand. We became really close friends and did everything together. But she could only be there a short while and I was heartbroken when she left.

Around the same time, my nan, whom I loved very much, was taken ill. She looked after me during school holidays and weekends at home, when my parents went out, and she was like my confidante. We used to tell each other our special secrets. One day, Mum told me off after I crept up to Nan when she was asleep and put a furry glove on her face. She jumped violently and Mum told me I could have given her a heart attack.

We missed each other now I was so far away, and I really looked forward to seeing her again in the holidays. But on this occasion, when I got home for Christmas, Mum said, 'Love I've got something to tell you. Your nan is very poorly. She's had a stroke and is in hospital, but she wants to see you.'

A cold shudder went through me. It was the first time I had come into contact with serious illness, and I felt lost and unsure how to cope. Nan couldn't speak but she could hear, so I told her to squeeze my hand once if she wanted to reply 'Yes' and twice for 'No', and that was how we communicated. It made me feel a bit more connected to her, but it was difficult to hold back the tears. I felt as if my heart was breaking with sadness. Her rattling breathing frightened me, and I realised how much I hated frailty and old age. It was obvious that she was slipping away from me, and I found it so hard that I could do nothing about it. Soon she would be gone and I wouldn't be able to share my secrets with her any more.

Nan died just after Christmas, and her funeral service was one of the bleakest experiences of my life. The vicar tried to comfort us and quoted words from the Bible which seemed irrelevant and old-fashioned. Where was she now? Did we just exist for a moment, then disappear? As we made New Year's resolutions at the beginning of 1964, I felt that the coming year would be the worst I would ever have to face. Returning to school, those deeply felt questions started me on a search for real meaning, for somehow I felt there had to be more to life. Sundays were boring at school and so was the compulsory church attendance, but deep inside I felt that God ought to be more important.

I had never been to Sunday school, though Mum would read me snippets from a children's Bible story book. My friend Judith, whose parents were missionaries in Zambia, started a club called YPF. I said, did that mean Young Poultry Farmers? But it stood for Young People's Fellowship, and it was a Christian club. Out of curiosity, I went along with my friend Sue. I was amazed when Judith talked about Jesus as if he was alive. I was puzzled. Surely he had died a long time ago and though he'd obviously been a good man, he was just someone famous in history. But I continued to go along to the club.

Soon after I joined, Judith's brother was tragically killed. She was devastated and couldn't cope with leading the YPF and asked me to lead it instead. That was a challenge indeed, but I never like to see a good thing end, so I tried my best.

On Sundays, Judith had been visiting a couple connected with her parents' church and she asked me if I would like to visit them in her place. I was very happy as it would mean getting away from school. I could tell immediately that there was something different about Doris and Denis Bannard-Smith. They treated Sunday as a special day, and when they said grace they talked to God as if he was really there. One evening they invited me to their church. It was very different to anything I'd experienced before. The hymns were lively and people prayed as if they were talking to a real person. I was invited to the young people's meeting after church, and again the singing was lively – people were clapping their hands and really enjoying themselves. They spoke of their everyday problems and how they could talk to Jesus about them. I was amazed at their certainty. To me, Jesus had always been someone in a stained-glass window, an historical character with no relevance for today. These people seemed sure that he was more than just an ordinary man. But could they prove this? Why did Jesus die? I wondered, and how could he have come back from the dead? I really wanted to find out, but I had no idea where to find the answers.

Then two amazing things happened. First, I found a Braille book in the school cellar called *The Transforming Friendship* by Leslie Weatherhead.[2] It ignited a hunger within me to know this friend he was talking about. I remember saying, or rather, praying, 'God, I can believe in you, but I can't believe that Jesus was more than an ordinary man. Show me the truth about him.' To my astonishment, the next day a Braille booklet from America arrived in the post for me called, *The Overwhelming Proof of the Divinity of Jesus*.[3]

A Braille Bible takes up nearly 2 metres of bookshelf space, with many volumes to search through, but in this booklet, everything was made clear. It detailed prophetic words that had been written centuries before Jesus' birth describing what he would do and even how he would die. I was amazed, and as I read my certainty that Jesus was truly God began to grow.

One day I and interested friends from school were invited to go to a Billy Graham Crusade at a local church. The preacher, one of Billy's team, seemed to answer all my questions, and at the end when he said, 'If you want to be saved, raise your hand,' I did, and I prayed the prayer to commit my life to Christ. Immediately afterwards, we were all whisked back to school, but I knew that something real had happened. I woke the next morning feeling a joy deep inside that I'd never experienced before, a sense that I would never be alone again. I told my friends, but they didn't get it, yet I knew it was real. I had a lot to learn and had my ups and downs, but that day, I started to come to know my heavenly Father and experience his everlasting love.

I tried to tell my parents about my new faith, but they didn't understand and felt it was a religious phase I was going through. My dad had no time for religion and had always instilled in me his own life's motto: look after number one because nobody else will. He kept reminding me that he'd had to fight for everything in life. He'd never experienced unconditional love, so found it hard to trust, and told me that to believe in God was a total waste of time. He even said once that no one's opinion was worth listening to but his. This made me feel very small, believing that my opinions would never be worth anything. So instead of sharing things with him, I would clam up. I'm sure he had no idea of the crushing effects of his dictatorial manner.

Now I was entering into a new era; becoming a Christian had given me wings, and I felt a new joy. Friends would ring wanting to take me to church or out for a meal, and I felt freer than ever before. But one day Dad dealt the hardest blow of all. He told me not to keep asking people for lifts because I would just make myself a nuisance to them. This word went right into the very depth of my being, as I started to believe that I really was a nuisance. It began to seriously shape the way I viewed myself, and I would hardly ask anyone for favours in case I would be a nuisance. In the years to come this false way of thinking would rob me of the very freedom I had only just stepped into – to know that I was loved as myself.

3

The Sighted World

O we must trust in the Lord with all our hearts, and not rely on our own understanding. Every promise of God is true ...

Marilyn Baker[1]

When I was 15 the school asked me what kind of career I was thinking of taking up. I replied that I would like to become a professional oboist. As I was the first blind pupil to have such an ambition, they felt that a second opinion was needed. My oboe teacher, Miss Fisher, knew the famous oboist Terence McDonough, who played with the BBC Symphony Orchestra, and she wrote to ask if he would listen to my playing. He graciously agreed. My music teacher, Jean Coates, would accompany me on the piano. Jean and I had spent many happy hours playing music together, and felt such a oneness in it; so, despite my nerves, I thoroughly enjoyed playing for him, and amazingly he commented positively, saying that I should definitely continue with the oboe.

In 1966, when I was 16, Miss Fisher left to join the Hallé Orchestra and I was once again without a teacher. The school wrote to Terence, asking if any of his students could teach me, and he replied to say that he would come himself! I could hardly believe it as he was a highly acclaimed oboist. He came monthly and I felt it a great privilege to be taught by such a genius.

In the sixth form I achieved grade eight oboe with distinction, which qualified me to enter for the special scholarship offered by the Associated Board of the Royal Schools of Music. Jean Coates told me there was little chance for me because of the hundreds of people entering. I had to play an extremely difficult piece for the oboe by a composer called York Bowen. This taxed me to the limit, but it was also very satisfying to get to grips with it. Jean was amazed when I reached the semi-final, and although I didn't win, it gave my confidence a real boost. Later I took the entrance exam for the Royal College of Music and was given an interview. I was delighted, and so were my parents, when I was accepted and given a grant.

Though life for me was exciting, for my blind friend Penny Cooze, this was a difficult time. I discovered that she had taken an overdose, and later on, she confided in me that she had been feeling so desperate that she had tried to end it all. I suddenly became aware that I had been living in cloud-cuckoo-land. I had never realised that anyone could be as unhappy as that and it awakened me to my responsibilities as a Christian. I saw how important it was for Penny to find the love of God for herself.

Penny started to come along with me to St Andrew's Church, Chorleywood, and I began to pray earnestly that God would help me to show her what it meant to become a Christian.

Chorleywood College was an excellent school, but there is no doubt that it was a sheltered environment, and the first real contact I had with sighted teenagers was when I went on an Inter-School Christian Fellowship camp run by Scripture Union for blind, partially sighted and sighted girls. I learned such a lot at that camp, and many of the people involved became good friends.

In 1968 I left Chorleywood and entered into the sighted world. It was a massive change. I had hoped to be given accommodation in the hostel nearest the Royal College of Music, but they didn't want the responsibility of having a blind student because some previous students had become depressed, and one had committed suicide, so trying to deal with a blind student was thought to be too much of a challenge. For the first time I had to face the fact that people were fearful of having a blind person in their care, and it hit me hard. I was deeply disappointed and almost felt God had let me down. After much searching I found a place that would be willing to have me. But it was half-an-hour's walk from the college and very daunting, as I'd never had to manage such difficult routes before with my white stick. The traffic was so fast, and everything so noisy, that I felt overwhelmed at the prospect.

When September arrived, Mum and Dad drove me to the hostel, where I found I was to share with some foreign students. Mum told me afterwards that she was heartbroken at leaving me alone in the hostel. Both she and Dad were worried about how I would cope, but they knew that I needed to be independent, so neither of them communicated their concern to me. I didn't want them to know how frightened I was, either, but when we said goodbye and they drove off down the road I felt very alone, left in this strange place surrounded by strange people.

There was a common room downstairs and the other girls asked me to go down and join them, but I wouldn't because I thought people would be watching me in a critical way. I sensed a kind of silence as the path was cleared for me as I walked around, and this made me feel self-conscious and awkward. I was now the odd one out and that was something I'd never had to deal with before.

On the first day of term I walked to the college with another girl and arranged to meet her for the return trip at half-past four because, although I had done the route many times with my old music teacher Jean, the thought of walking it on my own still filled me with apprehension.

We were taken on a guided tour of the college, and it seemed so big that I wondered how I would ever manage to find my way around. At the end of the day my mind was spinning, and I made my way down to the canteen to meet my companion for the return home. I was tired and overawed. One of the canteen staff brought me a cup of tea and I waited at the table. Twenty-five to 5 . . . twenty to 5 . . . ten to 5 . . . 5 o'clock and there was no sign of this girl. The loneliness of my situation swept over me and I was almost paralysed with fear. I didn't know what to do. There was chattering and laughter all around me, but I wasn't part of it – I was alone.

This was the time to put my Christian faith to the test. I had not had to rely on God much before, but now I needed him, and I prayed desperately, 'Lord Jesus, if you are real, then please come and help me right now.'

Just then somebody sat down opposite me. He asked me if I was one of the new students and introduced himself as Martin, the president of the Christian Union. I was overjoyed to meet him, and told him about my predicament. God was certainly with me and had provided an answer to my prayer almost before I had asked him. Martin decided the best thing was for him to follow me rather than walk with me, so that he could watch me do the route on my own. I managed this successfully and so regained my confidence.

I had known there was a Christian Union at the college because the Bannard-Smiths had told me they would write and tell the president I was coming. So it was really good to meet Martin on my first day. The Christian Union took me under their wing. They were so good to me, and I soon began to blossom under their kindness and practical care. I began to grow in my Christian faith, and eventually became the prayer secretary for the group.

After a year in the first hostel, I was asked to leave by the Greek owner, who said that having a blind person walking into their premises using a white stick was turning away trade. Of course, today that would be gross discrimination, but I just felt I didn't want to be anywhere I wasn't wanted, so I left with no fuss. But I felt very concerned about finding somewhere to live. No hostels had responded positively when they heard about my blindness, and I was beginning to despair. Then some friends suggested I try their hostel at a convent in Kensington. The rules seemed awfully strict, but I thought I'd give it a go, and the nuns gave me a very warm welcome. I spent two very happy years there, and my confidence grew as I entered into convent life, enjoying good times with both the nuns and students and making some wonderful friends. In my third year I was invited by a dear friend, Sally, to share a flat with her. I was amazed she chose me, but she had, and I felt so happy.

It was when I was part of the Christian Union that I began to go with the other Christian students to sing at Christian youth events. But our music was classical and far from modern. I felt that I wanted to have a go at writing an upbeat song that would be more appealing to our young audiences. I prayed earnestly that the Lord would inspire me, and later that week I came up with the first gospel song I ever wrote, 'He's My Saviour, My Friend and My Lord'. I felt shy about sharing it with the others, but when I did, they really loved it and we all enjoyed getting into the swing of it. When we sang to the young people, they loved it too.

I didn't try to write any more, though, until I heard one of the students from the college, Lou Hayles, singing songs she'd recently written. Lou's life had been in a mess because of a rebellious lifestyle, but she'd become a Christian, and when I heard her songs I was moved to tears. They sounded so rooted in life, and they came right from her heart. I asked how she wrote such incredible stuff. She told me she'd given her musical gift to God and asked the Holy Spirit to anoint her to write songs that would speak about his amazing love. I'd never thought of giving him my musical gift, but when I got back to my hostel that night, I did just that, and over the next few weeks, something wonderful happened.

I'd been studying composition as part of my course, and one day my harmony professor told me that, although my previous efforts had been rather boring, something had changed, and he was excited about what I was writing now. I knew this was the power of the Holy Spirit bringing anointing to my musical talent.

Over the Christmas of my first year, romance began to bud. I had always been shy of boys and subconsciously felt that I wouldn't be attractive to someone sighted. The college held a Christmas ball, and a young man in the Christian Union called David, who had been particularly kind all term, invited me to go with him. Others in the CU encouraged us and we eventually started going out together.

David had a quiet, caring personality and had been a real friend from the beginning. He would often come to the canteen with me and help me get some lunch and find a seat, which I always found difficult. He lived in an all-boys' hostel and was a clarinettist. Friends told me that he was handsome and I was very pleased, although looks don't really matter to me as much as they do to people who can see.

I felt great when David came to collect me at the hostel in the evenings, especially when I heard the call, 'Marilyn, your boyfriend's here.' He took an interest in my appearance and commented on the type of clothes he thought suited me, which made me take more interest myself in how I looked. David and I became close friends, and I shared with him all my problems, knowing that he understood. It was a new experience for me and a marvellous time in my life.

After David and I had been seeing each other regularly for a while, we started to talk about marriage. When my parents met him, they really liked him, and I think they held out great hopes for our future. I went to stay with his parents in Chelmsford and initially, because I wasn't on familiar territory, must have given them a negative impression. It wasn't easy for them to think of me as a future daughter-in-law, but once we got to know each other better they accepted me more.

Mum and Dad encouraged us, but even though I loved David as a friend, I knew deep down that I didn't care for him enough to marry him. In the end, by mutual consent, we agreed to end our relationship. It was very difficult for a while. It wasn't that I was heartbroken, more that I felt lonely, as we had been so close and enjoyed doing things together. When David started going out with someone else almost straight away, I found that really painful.

A few weeks later at a special service, a speaker talked about relationships, and afterwards David came and apologised for any hurt he'd caused, and I said sorry too. From that time on it was great; we remained really good friends. In fact, some people thought we were still going out together.

A crowd from the Christian Union decided to go to hear American evangelist Jean Darnall, and David urged me to go. He said that she was filled with the Holy Spirit and had a lot to teach us. We went along, and as Jean talked, there was a depth to her words which made me hungry to have what she had. I went forward to be prayed for, but as far as I was concerned, nothing happened, and I went home feeling frustrated. Why couldn't I speak in tongues, this special heavenly language?[2] Why didn't I have this bubbling joy? What was wrong with me? I went through a few months of intense spiritual anguish. In the end a friend said, 'Marilyn, you've got to be much simpler and just receive it as a love gift.' I realised that God was saying, 'Be childlike when you come to me; just thank me that I am giving you what you asked for.' As I began to accept that God had heard my prayer, a deep joy, peace and real assurance began to fill my heart, and ultimately, I did start speaking in tongues too. I felt a new desire to be close to Jesus, and the Bible became more real than ever. I was being wrapped more and more in his love.

Testimonies

Marilyn and I were great friends at school but went our separate ways afterwards. We met up after we had both graduated and Marilyn had moved to Watford. I was in a state of depression, lost and feeling alone, uncertain of the future. Marilyn, on the other hand, seemed full of hope and joy and excited about her future.

She sang a couple of songs that she'd composed which spoke of God's love for me as his child and his plans for me. This was deeply moving and kind of unsettling . . . how could this love apply to me? And I began to question life even more. Six months later I committed my life to Jesus and now, when I'm feeling down or stressed, Marilyn's music brings me peace and hope and puts me together again. Thank you, my special friend.

Margaret

Please will you thank Marilyn for me? I have quite an old cassette called *Overflow of Worship* which has ministered to me in a stressful, disturbing situation. Marilyn's ministry helped me to sleep last evening and was such an enormous blessing. A God-anointed tape.

Thank you.
A grateful listener

4

Stepping into God's Plans

God has a plan for you, something only you can do. You are so valuable to Him

Marilyn Baker[1]

At the end of my third year at college, I was offered a job as an oboe teacher at Watford Grammar School for Girls because the head of music there was friends with the head of music at Chorleywood College and knew my capabilities. This was a wonderful career break for me, and I was also asked by the Royal College of Music to teach oboe to a young man, who was in fact an emerging pop star, Peter Gabriel.

These were great opportunities, so when it came to leaving college, I chose to make my home in Watford. My dad decided to buy me a house so I would never have to face being asked to leave rented accommodation again. I wanted God to guide where I lived, but Dad was not into praying, so I asked my heavenly Father to be Lord over my dad's choices.

I loved the little two-bedroom house that Dad found for me in West Watford. Mum and Dad stayed with me, and there seemed a lot to do, buying furniture and mundane things like tea towels, pots and pans and wastepaper bins. They had just bought themselves a new lounge suite, and their old one fitted into my house nicely. Mum made curtains and soon the new house became a real home.

It was a complicated route to and from the girls' grammar school. I had to travel by bus, train and on foot, and so while dad went home, Mum stayed longer to help me master the route, and when I came home in the evenings I appreciated knowing that she was there waiting for me with a cooked meal ready. It was so lovely to have this special time together with Mum.

My dear spiritual parents Doris and Denis introduced me to St James Road Baptist Church (SJR) in Watford, which became my spiritual home. I joined the youth group there and met a lovely girl who was looking for somewhere to live. Hilary Ellwood soon moved in with me, and a wonderful friendship began. She was a very gentle, warm person with a deep faith. She taught me a great deal about how to show God's love to people in practical ways. She was the kind of person who could always see when people were lonely and would invite them home for a meal.

As she had been in the church for a long time, she helped me get to know a lot of people, and our friendship developed into one of the deepest of my life.

Hilary and I went to a weekly house group meeting where we learned more about worship and the gifts of the Holy Spirit. The teaching at these meetings enabled me to centre my mind upon my heavenly Father, rather than on my own problems.

Rita and Neil, who ran the house group, regularly invited wonderful speakers to help us go deeper, and one night the speaker came round to pray for each of us individually, giving us personal prophecies. This was new to me, and I didn't know if I even wanted it! When he reached me, he seemed very accurate in his knowledge, so I relaxed. He then prophesied that one day I would become a musical missionary and would travel to the nations. I had no idea what this could mean. I had only written one song; how could I become a musical missionary? Though I didn't understand, I was determined not to miss anything God had planned for me, so kept it in mind.

Other local schools asked me to join their staff, and soon there were five that I was teaching at regularly. I enjoyed teaching very much, but travelling to different schools was challenging because the routes were difficult to navigate using my white cane, and the schools were hard to find my way around. So I decided I needed a guide dog. I applied, and only six weeks later I got a call to say that I could go to Forfar in Scotland to train.

It was a very long journey and I stayed at the centre for a month. It was there I had a go at playing the bagpipes too! My dog was called Susie, a sweet little black Labrador. There was under-floor central heating in our rooms, and she loved lying under my bed, but I just couldn't get her out in the mornings. I had to crawl under it myself to get her up, which made me late for breakfast. It sounded a rather feeble excuse when I said that my dog didn't want to get up!

I had to learn to follow Susie's every move through the harness as she guided me round obstacles and stopped at kerbs. Eventually we completed the course, and I arrived back at Watford to be met by my parents. The first thing Dad said was that Susie looked too fragile to last long as a guide dog. I felt upset as I was very proud of her. She made my life as a peripatetic teacher much easier and the pupils adored her, but I began to notice that any loud noise frightened her.

One day when we were out, there was a loud crack of thunder; Susie swerved and I hit my head hard on a post. I was taken into a fish and chip shop and given a cup of tea, and someone drove me home. I contacted the trainers, and after observing Susie, it was decided that, sadly, she would have to retire as she had developed noise shyness. She went to live with a dear friend in the country. The trainers realised I needed a more robust dog, and soon Yuma, a boisterous yellow Labrador, came on the scene. She would eat anything she could find, including chops from the butcher and expensive cakes from the baker! But she was an amazing guide, and one memorable winter's day, she got me home through thick snow despite there being no paths to follow. Snow is like fog to a blind person, but Yuma stopped at every crossing and we arrived home safely.

Hilary and I loved living together, but after about two and a half years she had some tragic news. Her brother's wife had died unexpectedly, leaving him with two young children. Somehow, I knew she should go to help them, and she did too. But it was heartbreaking to see her go, because we shared so much together.

Hilary shares . . . after moving to her brother's

While looking after the little ones, I was listening to Marilyn's new song, 'God Wants to Give You a Glorious New Life'. Tears were streaming down my face, knowing that God knew what he was doing with my life, and I was learning to submit to his purposes. Even before her songs had been recorded, I knew they were going to minister to people in a very powerful way.

After Hilary left, I urgently needed to find a new housemate. A young person, Carol Franklin, who was training at London Bible College, had been assigned to our church to work with the Girls' Brigade. I was also an officer, and so we became friends. The Lord spoke to her, and I could hardly believe it when Carol said she felt God wanted her to take Hilary's place. God had it all in hand and was providing people to come alongside me. Little did I know then how important this new friendship would be.

I still loved playing the oboe and sometimes had the joy of doing recitals in London. Carol was very musical and loved accompanying me to these events.

Carol shares

These days we all think of Marilyn as a singer and keyboard player. But when I shared her house in the mid-seventies she would say that piano playing was the least of her musical skills. As a peripatetic music teacher, she taught many young people to play the piano, clarinet and flute to a high level. But her principal instrument was the oboe, which she played to a professional standard. To hear Marilyn playing the oboe stirred my soul so deeply that I would cry. I went with her to Armitage Hall in London, and when she played the oboe you were drawn into the story and emotion of the piece, and you were touched so deeply that your heart was torn. Marilyn had a God-given gift to share her heart and soul with yours through her music; a rare and very special talent.

Carol had a lovely singing voice, and when I heard her sing, something stirred within me, making me want to write beautiful worship songs to suit her clear, expressive style. One day Richard Harbour, our minister, asked Carol and me if we could do a musical item in church. I usually played the piano for the worship, but the very day he asked us, I had just written a song I wanted Carol to try singing. It was like God speaking the words to us directly:

> My love will never fail you,
> My peace will be your guide;
> My grace will always keep you,
> Yes I am close by your side.
> My strength is here to help you,
> And my arms are open wide.
> Let me show you how I love you;
> Yes I am close by your side.[2]

We shared it in the service on Sunday morning and people were deeply touched. I felt inspired to write more, and Shirley, Richard's wife, suggested we make a record together. How on earth would we do that? Amazingly, a man who worked for Christian Audio Visual Services came to the church to look at its PA system. Shirley asked him to listen to Carol and me and, to our delight, he agreed to make a record for us. He came to our house with his recording equipment. Yuma kept barking, and we had to turn the boiler off because of its clicks and bangs, but in the end we finished. I played the piano, Carol sang the melody lines and I harmonised with her. We used mainly well-known choruses, but I included a few I had written.

The album was called *Open Our Eyes Lord*, but I was shocked when I was told I had to purchase 500 copies to make it worth manufacturing. What would I do with them all? Richard said he would try to get us one or two meetings in local Baptist churches to share the songs. In the end we sold 1,500 of them, and we received reports from people who were being very blessed, including a lady who said she'd been healed from claustrophobia through experiencing God's love for her as she listened. We were staggered that our simple, home-grown offering was having such an effect and knew it was the anointing of God.

I began to write more songs, as I longed to share with others the amazing love of Jesus through music. Although people wouldn't always listen to a sermon, I thought they might listen to a song, especially if it touched their hearts, but I realised that I couldn't write such songs without the anointing of the Holy Spirit. As I prayed, inspiration began to flow. I would be walking along the high street with Yuma and suddenly a melody would pop into my mind, something beautiful, almost as if I was hearing it from heaven, and I knew I had to find words to fit it. This happened with my song 'Jesus You are Changing Me'. I felt depressed about my life, not seeing the changes I so longed for, and suddenly these words came:

Jesus You are changing me,
By Your Spirit You're making me like You.
Jesus You're transforming me,
That Your loveliness may be seen in all I do . . .[3]

I didn't believe this could be true for me and argued with God. He showed me 2 Corinthians 3:18 and seemed to be challenging me to trust his Word and his power within me, rather than my feelings. So I wrote it, telling people to sing it in faith, as I was learning to do myself.

With all the new songs, Shirley got so excited that she decided to introduce us to a minister friend in Watford who was also a recording artist, Len McGee. After hearing us he suggested to David Payne, head of Pilgrim Records, that he did a recording with me. David wasn't that sure but, on Len's recommendation, decided to give it a go.

It was just at that time that Carol told me she felt called to move on to work for Torch Trust, an organisation reaching out to bring God's love to blind and partially sighted people. I felt so sad that I was losing another very precious friend and musical partner. Who would share my home with me now?

A lady called Marjorie, who was also part of Girls' Brigade and who worked locally as a nurse, needed accommodation and so came to share my house. God had provided again and Marj loved Yuma too.

As plans started to be made for the new album, Carol came back to help me with the recording. I could not sing high notes like Carol and needed to write songs that suited my range. At school they used to call me Mr Baker because my voice was so low, but the Lord assured me he wanted to use my singing to communicate his amazing love.

The studio recording was challenging, as I had never worked in that kind of environment before, and at times we thought we would never finish it. But after some huge struggles, the album called *He Gives Joy* was born.

It went on sale in 1979 and became very popular. Because of its success, I started to receive requests to sing at different churches and my new friend Marj would take me to the venues.

After two years of sharing my home, Marj left to go to Bible college and I was faced once again with the emotional upheaval of saying goodbye to someone I'd grown close to. It was at that time, in 1980, that I got to know a fun-loving 17-year-old girl called Penny Misselbrook. Her parents were farmers and she would invite me there to have lovely home-cooked meals along with her big family. I adored it, and soon she decided she wanted to move in with me. God had provided again.

In 1981, I recorded my second major album, *Whispers of God*. I wondered if this would be as well received and was delighted when it clearly was.

About a year after Penny moved in, Pam Chance who worked for CTVC – a Christian television company – rang, wanting to talk to me about making a film. She explained that the company were doing a series called Celebration about people who had different talents and believed that God inspired them. Having heard my new album, Pam wanted to do a documentary about my life as a blind person, showing how my faith affected everyday living. It was to be called *Marilyn*

Baker Songwriter. I was amazed that this was happening to me and when I told my parents they were very excited and happily agreed to be interviewed.

For several months the camera almost ruled our lives; the film crew filmed me feeding Yuma, cooking with Penny, giving music lessons, and generally doing the routine things of life. One scene shot at Chorleywood College showed me playing the oboe and Jean Coates accompanying me.

A two-hour concert was arranged with me singing to an invited audience at the Christian Television Centre in Bushey (near Watford), so that flashbacks from it could be put into the twenty-eight-minute documentary. Carol came to sing with me and it was super to be together again. I wore an Indian-style dress and performed with a group of instrumentalists brought together for the occasion. It was a wonderful experience to be involved in a television production. The company were very good to us and treated us like stars. One scene showed Penny and me driving home after a late concert, and from then on, her Ford Escort was nicknamed 'the film star banger'.

The congregation at SJR were included too and Richard was interviewed. I was very touched by some of the things which were said by my friends but when Penny was asked, 'What is she like to live with?' I wondered what she would say. 'Marilyn's a hilarious person really,' she replied.

Carol told them I had an artistic temperament. I wasn't sure how to take that! When the film was finished it was shown on various Independent Television channels and sometimes repeated because of the demand. The biggest thrill, though, was when it won a bronze medal at the New York Film Festival. Some of the studio concert was put onto a separate film called *Marilyn Baker in Concert* and was also shown on TV.

Soon after that, to my great surprise, David Payne, the manager of the record company, came to see me. He said he had underestimated what I was doing, and had not put his heart into recording the first albums, but now wanted to help me by becoming my manager. He added, 'I will do it free of charge, and my wife, Marilyn, will deal with all the bookings.' What a gift! I was staggered and knew this could only be God.

In the early spring of 1982, David and his friend John Pac, who had produced *Whispers of God*, came to see me and suggested that I think seriously about leaving teaching and going into full-time Christian music ministry.

Well, that was taking it too far. I loved teaching; surely that was what I was born for? But with travelling to bookings, it was getting more difficult to fit in both things, and somehow I knew I had to make a choice. I said I would pray, but really I had no intention of giving up my teaching. But I thought I'd better check with God. 'Lord, please show me what you want me to do,' I prayed. To my amazement, over a period of time, and through many confirmations, I realised he was indeed calling me to leave teaching and all its security to step into full-time ministry.

I had no idea where my earnings would come from, and no bookings to constitute a career change. I prayed with Richard and Shirley, and they encouraged me, so at the end of the summer term I gave my notice in at the various schools, and almost immediately regretted it. My parents, especially my dad, said I was foolish to throw away the career I'd successfully built up, but just a few days later, David informed me that I'd been invited to sing in New Zealand and Australia that September. How had they even heard of me? This was a huge confirmation that I'd made the right decision.

I knew that with increased travelling I would need someone to join me in the work, and to my joy, Penny felt it should be her. How amazing that God had brought this wonderful friend to come alongside me at just the right time. One very hard thing was that I knew I would need to give up my guide dog, Yuma, and therefore my independence. As she was near retirement, she went to live with my mum and dad, so I was glad I'd be able to see her whenever I went home, which was a comfort.

Our trip to Australia and New Zealand drew near and we needed lots of different vaccinations, partly because we were stopping off at Jakarta. I had just had an injection for cholera when I went to sing at a ladies' meeting. As I reached the climax and was saying, 'God has a plan for your life . . .' the piano stool collapsed and I was sprawled on the floor surrounded by hymnbooks. When some alarmed ladies rushed to help me, all I could think of was the pain after my jab and I shouted, 'Get off my arm.' After that it was difficult to finish the meeting with any dignity!

Penny and I loved our time in New Zealand and Australia. Due to a mix-up about dates, we were booked to do a concert on the evening of our arrival at the home of Pearl and Peter Sumner, who were directors of an Australian organisation for the blind. I really don't know how we got through it, and I can clearly remember the floor rocking! We then travelled from Sydney to Brisbane to sing at an evening event arranged by Youth for Christ. It was in Brisbane that we went to a wildlife park, and I had my photograph taken cuddling a koala bear. His fur felt soft as he snuggled into me, and I was surprised at how heavy he was and how sharp his claws were.

The whole tour across Australia and then New Zealand was awesome. We met incredible people and experienced so much kindness and the evidence of God's provision. We hadn't known how things would work financially, but we sold so many records that in the end the tour financed itself. We returned home full of expectation about the future.

Testimonies

Marilyn,
Just to let you know that your song 'Jesus You are Changing Me' is still as inspiring today as it was so many years ago. We played it to our Sunday school class the other week when we were talking to them about 'change' and using the vision that Jeremiah had of the potter moulding the clay. As the song was played, the class was amazingly attentive, and we know that they really understood that God could mould their lives if they were willing for him to do it. Thank

you for your wonderful God-given ministry that continues to inspire so many of us.

Katherine

Marilyn, yours are the CDs I go to when I'm feeling stressed, concerned, anxious, even crying out! God always speaks to me, calms me, reassures me and strengthens me through the words He's given you! Thank you!

An MBM supporter

5

Rest in My Love

Rest in my love, relax in my care, and know that my presence will always be there

Marilyn Baker[1]

Penny and I loved travelling together and meeting so many amazing people. In New Year, 1983, we toured with Prepare the Way, a nationwide presentation to prepare people for Billy Graham's Mission England. It seemed strange to be working alongside people I had always held in high esteem in the Christian world. The whole idea of being a full-time Christian singer and much more in the public eye was still new to me, and sometimes I found the responsibility a little frightening. It was hard to believe that people really took notice of things I said, commenting, sometimes months later, on what I had sung or spoken about during concerts.

Songs were still coming to me, and one that has always had a deep impact on people, even today, was 'Rest in My Love'. One day a beautiful melody came into my mind. It was full of peace and tranquillity, creating an atmosphere of calm and safety, but I had no words for it. I played it to Shirley and she said she would write some words, but although she tried, I knew they weren't right. Weeks later I went to visit Hilary, now married and living in Aylesbury. It was a complicated journey involving two bus changes. I was anxious about getting the connecting bus but eventually sat down on it feeling very relieved. Then an incredible conversation started up between me and the Lord. He said, 'You didn't need to be so worried. Didn't you know that I was watching over you all the time? You could have relaxed!' As I absorbed this, the most beautiful prophetic words slipped into my mind.

Rest in My love,
Relax in My care,
And know that My presence
Will always be there.
You are My child,
And I care for you,
There's nothing My love and My power cannot do.[2]

I was awed when I realised how wonderfully these words fit the melody that had been part of me for weeks. Later I added another verse and this beautiful little song was born, all through God speaking to me when I was anxious about a bus journey!

Not long after that I was in the middle of recording my new album *Refresh Me Lord*, when my dad rang me with some very sad news. My dear mum was very ill and had been taken to hospital. I was crying as I went to record. I needed more than anything that day to rest in his love. John Pac, the producer, was very kind and prayed with me for Mum to be held safe in God's love. That did help, but I was full of fear.

After recording *Refresh Me Lord* I was booked to sing at Royal Week, a family holiday conference in Cornwall. I rang Dad most nights, but it was very hard being so far away and unable to see Mum.

Although I had sensed that she was seriously ill, it was still a staggering blow when I heard that she had been diagnosed with leukaemia. I wept bitterly and a doctor on the team tried to console me, saying that leukaemia is often treatable. Several people from my church were also at Royal Week and were very supportive, but inside I felt devastated. She was my best friend and my greatest encourager in life. I couldn't bear to lose her. I cried, not knowing how to cope. Although people tried to help, they couldn't get inside me or understand my inner anguish. Feeling as I did, it was very difficult to sing some of my songs.

During this time, Penny came to realise that she'd need to stop travelling with me at the end of 1983 because of poor health. We were very sad, and knew that I had to find someone else to join me in the ministry, although Penny would still share my home. We advertised and a lovely young lady called Morfudd Bowen applied for the job. She lived in Cheshire but moved down and was offered accommodation in one of the church houses. She was well qualified for her new role, being a good organiser, very practical and also very musical, with a lovely singing voice.

Although I was feeling far from well, I didn't want her to know, so I tried to put on a brave face, but that probably made it harder for her. I felt I had to be strong, not wanting to load Morfudd with my sadness.

Because I woke each morning about 2.30 and couldn't get off to sleep again, I became very tired and found it extremely difficult to relax. I kept trying to appear as if I was coping, but it was obvious that I wasn't. After a bit of persuasion, I went to my GP who prescribed some mild tranquillisers, which actually didn't work. They made me go from one extreme to another, laughing or crying all the time.

During Morfudd's first week she had to drive me to East London to sing at a mother and baby hospital. She had not long passed her driving test and had never driven in London, so she was very nervous, especially as she also had to navigate. It was pouring with rain and we had a slight bump. This upset Morfudd, but all I could do was laugh, which wasn't very helpful! We eventually arrived at our destination feeling fraught, but managed to do the concert. Pat Wright, one of the helpers, led us to the motorway afterwards and we were very grateful.

It was a real joy to work with someone as musical as Morfudd. She was a good singer and played both the guitar and piano. In concerts, she would harmonise with me and even sing solos occasionally.

In June 1984, we were due to tour in South Africa. Mum's health had picked up, so I felt much better in myself and I was eagerly looking forward to travelling to another continent. I felt a tremendous expectancy about what God could do among his people there, but there were certain cultural aspects which bothered me. We met some Christians whom I would call 'spiritual casualties', who felt that they had let God down because they hadn't had enough faith to be healed. Great emphasis was being placed on the healing power of God, and many felt it was their fault that they were still ill. They had lost sight of the other beautiful things God was doing in their lives. I knew the Lord was using me to show these dear people that he accepts them just as they are, not because of what they can or can't do.

We met some fantastic people that month, and because we couldn't get a flight back at the end of it, we stayed on an extra week and went to the Kruger National Park. Although I couldn't see the animals, I could certainly hear them! I bought a cassette of the different sounds including lions, elephants and monkeys. We also enjoyed many barbecues, called 'braais'. These were great fun.

Later in 1984, Penny left Watford to work with David Payne in Hampshire. She had lived with me for four years and we knew it was time for her to move on. I needed a friend to share again and another sighted person seemed the obvious choice. I was surprised, therefore, when I felt God saying to me very clearly that it should be my blind friend from Chorleywood College, Penny Cooze.

I rang Penny and told her my feelings and she sounded stunned, and explained that she'd been praying that she'd be able to move nearer London. Within a week she decided that she would share my home, even though we were both uncertain as to how it would work out, as I'd always shared with sighted friends before.

The timing wasn't good because Penny and her guide dog, Isla, moved in five days before I was due to go to Nashville in America with Morfudd to record a new album. Penny had not looked after a house on her own before and certainly didn't know the local routes and shops. I was very apprehensive about leaving her alone, but the Lord assured me as I prayed that I could trust him to look after her, as she would be safe in his care.

So Morfudd and I went to Nashville. We didn't know anyone outside of the studio and one day, feeling a bit isolated, I tuned into a Christian radio station where they encouraged people to call if in any need. I called them and explained we were visitors from England and this lovely church group took us under their wing and gave us a great time. The musicians I worked with there were awesome, and the whole experience for both of us was mind-blowing.

When I returned home, Mum's health had deteriorated again because of a bad chest infection and over the next few months she was constantly in and out of hospital to have treatment or chemotherapy. I was amazed to see how bravely she coped, as she felt very sick. I visited her in hospital as much as possible and, as she had a room on her own, she welcomed my company. I would sit close to her bed as we talked about what I was doing and where I had been. Because Mum had always been so fit, Dad had relied on her to look after the domestic things, so it was particularly hard for him to keep things going at home. Dad and I found it difficult to communicate our fears to each other, and it really was a traumatic time.

One day when I was alone with her, Mum said, 'I just don't know what is going to happen to me when I die.' I had been asking the Lord to give me a real opportunity to talk about eternal life, so I told her how much he loved her and wanted her to be with him forever. She found it hard to think he could accept her. I reassured her, talking about the cross and his forgiveness, and to my great joy, she suddenly prayed out loud a very simple but heartfelt prayer, giving herself to him. She didn't end with 'amen' because that wasn't in her normal vocabulary. Instead, she said, 'OK, God,' and I believe he said back to her, 'OK, then.'

Mum struggled for two years, becoming more and more ill. Poor Dad could hardly cope with visiting, but I prayed that somehow I would be with her at the end. One Thursday we went for our usual half-hour slot, and within ten minutes she went peacefully to be with her heavenly Father. The timing was incredible, but my loss was immeasurable.

In the days that followed I could hardly function and had a kind of breakdown. Watching Mum suffer and the emotional seesaw of her recovering from an infection only to dash our hopes by deteriorating again, put my body, mind and spirit under huge pressure. I felt so broken, and although I tried to keep going so as not to let people down, I could hardly get out of bed each morning, as my whole body was shaking. Eventually I told David Payne and he was very supportive, saying I needed a complete break. So I took time out from travelling, cancelling all my bookings, and he arranged with a group called Lovelight, who were based in Dorset, to take some of them for me. The group was made up of Pete Emberley, Sharron Pearcy and Ian Shears, and they and their families were so lovely and full of fun. We became great friends and later did joint tours all over the country. We still meet up most years when I go to Bournemouth to lead conferences.

Friends helped me to gradually recover, coming alongside me and praying. During this time of deep depression, Penny Cooze became a great support. Because of her own brokenness, she understood mine, and believed God wanted to heal me of the emotional scars from difficulties I'd experienced in life. God showed Penny that he would restore and make me much stronger emotionally and spiritually.

It was after this traumatic time that I gradually began to see God my Father in a new way too. A counsellor friend, Mary Pytches, said that now I had lost my greatest source of affirmation, God wanted to replace her voice of encouragement with his own. She suggested I journal my conversations with him and start bathing in his nurturing presence, listening for his sustaining words. My times with her were life-changing and brought me into a depth of relationship with Jesus I had never previously known. This also became reflected in my songwriting, as I wanted my listeners to hear his affirming voice too.

Gradually we started travelling again, and after a couple of months we were back to our usual schedule. It was around this time that Ian Valkeith, who had joined us as sound engineer some months before, helped us to invest in our own amplification equipment. This was a huge step, as it was expensive and we now had three team members to provide for. I'd been worried how we would cope financially, but God provided then and always has done. David Payne stepped down as manager, and my church leaders felt that we should become a charitable trust with a board of trustees from our own and local churches. So Marilyn Baker Ministries Trust (now MBM Trust) was born, and with the increase in bookings I was so thankful for Ian and his expertise, which meant the concerts could be done far more professionally than when I was just relying on what the churches could provide.

As 1985 progressed, Morfudd began to feel tired and decided that she would leave after Christmas that year. I was also very tired. It wasn't just travelling, for I loved meeting people, but it was giving out spiritually day after day, wanting so much to hear the Lord's heart for each event and trying to pray for all those who needed a special touch from God. I was weary and began to long for a spiritual soul mate, someone to share the load. But I couldn't seem to find anyone to replace Morfudd. Surely, if the Lord wanted me to continue, he would provide someone like Morfudd who could drive, sing and organise the events? Our trustees felt that God was going to do something new. One shared a verse, Isaiah 43:19 (ESV UK): 'Behold, I am doing a new thing . . . do you not perceive it?' I didn't know what it meant or how it applied to this situation, and when after much advertising no one suitable could be found, I even wondered if I was meant to give up travelling.

But all the time God was at work to bring the most amazing plan of all to pass, for me to make friends with a young lady called Tracy who was to become a wonderful soulmate in the work, bringing me immense comfort and consolation.

Testimonies

This morning, and at a few other very significant times, the Lord has brought back into my mind, as him speaking to me, the words of 'Rest in My Love'. Through these words he reassures, soothes, encourages and strengthens me.

Thank you for allowing him to use you, even after many years, to bless me.

Rosemary

Part 2

Tracy's Story

6

The Curveball

When you're feeling lonely, when your heart is aching; when something happens that makes you doubt my love

Marilyn Baker[1]

I was born in London in June 1964. My dad worked as a machine minder for the *Evening Standard* and my mum, who'd had several clerical jobs since leaving school, was now at home. My sister Lorraine was 3, and we shared a home together with my dad's parents. My mum and dad both had two siblings, so I had cousins on either side. There was a lot of love and commitment in all branches of the family to provide stable, happy homes and do their best for their children.

My mum had an easy labour with me and I was, in her words, 'A good baby who gave no trouble.' From photos taken at that time, I looked a chubby, contented baby, but all I can remember from those earliest years is me crawling into a room in the middle of the night and putting a potty on my head!

My first real memory is quite vivid and is of when I was aged 2 and a half and became ill with measles. I caught it from my sister and remember lying in my bedroom and my mum rubbing a special pink cream all over me. One night I had a very bad headache, and in the morning she found I was completely limp and floppy like a ragdoll. The doctor immediately called an ambulance. I went to hospital and was eventually kept there for about three months. It was thought that I had polio. I was given a lumbar puncture and was eventually diagnosed with encephalitis – inflammation of the brain from the measles. I was put into a small annexe off a ward with two adult polio victims in iron lungs.

Although I don't have many conscious memories of this time, I have had enough fleeting ones to know that it was a traumatic experience and had a defining influence on me as I grew up. With the measles, I was in my own bed with my family around me. Now all that was familiar was gone, and I was too young to put words to my fears. As an adult you recognise that you are in hospital, but what is hospital to a 2-year-old? I had no concept of it. It was just a stark, frightening place full of strange-looking people; a hubbub of sound and terrifying experiences. I lost control over my body at an age when I had just mastered walking, feeding myself and toileting, and I felt completely lost. My mum says I wasn't in pain, but in my memories I was, and I also remember being scared of the iron lungs and the noise they made, especially at night when in the darkness their gurgling, chomping sound terrified me. It is likely my hearing was already affected, as I can remember a roar of grinding, clashing sound, which was probably the beginnings of the damage I sustained to the aural nervous system. Probably no one realised what was happening in my brain to distort sound, and what to everyone else was a relatively quiet room, to me was like being abandoned in hell.

I also remember a nurse who was always angry. Mum and Dad came at set times and this nurse would get cross when they were not there. I couldn't feed myself but remember once being given beetroot and it fell all over the bed. This nurse was screaming at me, and I was so scared I wet the bed. One day something happened to do with my many toys. My limbs had become very jerky, so maybe I accidentally threw some toys from my cot. I remember this nurse shouting, she may even have smacked me, such is my memory of distress. She was probably just stressed, but I was 2 years old and without any resources to understand. As I look back, all I can sense is the total lack of any lasting comfort.

There were happy moments when Mummy and Daddy or other family members visited and I would enjoy being cuddled and loved, only to have all that stripped away the moment they said goodbye. It was an adult ward and the hospital was Victorian in design. Nowadays children's wards are bright and cheerful, and rightly so, as the children need all the encouragement they can get. So the brighter the walls, and the more toys around, the better. But my ward in 1967 was very different. I was in a cot with high iron bars, probably to prevent me falling out. Any visitors would have to lean over the bars, and without warning, I would suddenly see their faces above me. When those faces belonged to family it was a supremely happy moment, but on so many occasions, it was the red, angry face of the nurse. I couldn't tell if footsteps were approaching the bed, so I had none of the usual clues, just a mass of unidentifiable confusion.

A great deal of fear came into my life through this experience, but after I had been there a few weeks, I believe something else really bad happened, as I have buried feelings of fear and terrifying half-memories that have at different times risen overwhelmingly to the surface. Because of these flashbacks and further insights that have come through prayer, I believe that there were some things that happened of an abusive nature when I was alone and helpless at night.

The time I spent in hospital was a long time for a 2- to 3-year-old to be separated from her parents. Mum says I was never in danger of dying, and the fever did subside. However, my coordination was badly affected, so I was given a wheelchair. For the first year after I returned home, Mum pushed me everywhere, and I had to go to hospital regularly for physiotherapy. Maybe it was because all the attention was focused on whether I'd be able to walk properly again that my hearing loss was sidelined?

I had astigmatism in my right eye and had to wear a patch over it before starting to wear glasses at 5. But lots of kids wore glasses, and I don't think anyone really knew how bad my sight really was because the problem, as with my hearing, was with the brain, not the eyes. As far as my hearing was concerned, although it was probably acknowledged that I had a loss, no action was taken till I was 12, a full 10 years after my illness. This had huge repercussions, which I still battle with today.

But for my family there was great relief. The crisis was over and I was recovering. Yes, I was a bit different to other children. I walked jerkily and was generally clumsy. I seemed a little slow at understanding and was a lot quieter than before. But I was home; I was nearly better. No one knew, least of all me, that my unusual type of hearing loss would mean that despite hearing most of the sounds around me, I would be increasingly unable to comprehend what those sounds meant. I would forever be like an alien in a foreign land but with no means of learning the language.

The night trauma I experienced was never shared, for how could I at the age of 3 put into words something like that? There were too many other things happening, and when I got home, the relief was so overwhelming that I forgot the terrors. But although forgotten, they were still there deep inside me in a heavy box chained and padlocked with a sign saying 'do not open'. And that box was to stay closed for another thirty years. But with sealing these things away, part of 'me' was sealed away too. And from the time of the illness, that part of me was disconnected. I was living, growing, having fun, developing talents, happy, sad, struggling, achieving, like every child, but always with a part of me missing and locked away.

Like any child, there were many facets to my personality because, as I've discovered since becoming a Christian, I was created by God himself. As Psalm 139:13,14 declares:

> For you created my inmost being; you knit me together in my mother's womb. I praise you because I am fearfully and wonderfully made; your works are wonderful, I know that full well.

Despite the trauma of my illness, there was a mischievous streak in me. I was curious and loved to test the boundaries of what I could do. I remember one day realising that the shelves in the tall kitchen larder looked like a ladder, so I decided to climb up and see what was at the top. I can still see myself clinging on to the shelves, which of course were full of jars and packets, and climbing as high as possible. I think I was holding the top shelf when it suddenly came out of the wall. I crashed down onto the floor together with jars, bottles and containers of all kinds. They burst open and I was lying in a sticky mess when my mum rushed in. She wasn't too pleased, especially when she saw that a tiny jar containing my sister's tonsils which she'd recently had out, had also broken. The tonsils had rolled under the fridge and I can still see Mum on her knees scrabbling to find them! Amazingly I wasn't hurt, but it did teach me to save my climbing aspirations for the playground.

7

Mixed Memories

O tell me, where can I go from Your Spirit?

Marilyn Baker[1]

When I was 4, the houses in our road were to be demolished. With the cash settlement, my grandparents paid the deposit for a four-bedroom house in Walthamstow that they would share with us for the rest of their lives. Dad took out a mortgage and we moved in a year after I came out of hospital. The house was in a residential street, with the main road in one direction and in the other, residential roads leading to what we came to fondly call 'The Forest' – part of the original Epping Forest. In the coming years The Forest would become a place of great escape for me and I would grow to treasure the fact that despite living in a town in North East London with all its rough estates, we had these woods right on our doorstep.

I can't remember much detail from that time but there are lots of flashes of memory, especially of holidays in the Isle of Wight where my dad hoped one day to retire. We would travel down to Southampton on the train and queue to go on the ferry. I remember standing at the railing and staring over the miles of grey-green water, eagerly anticipating the adventures ahead. We always stayed in holiday camps, and I loved the intoxicating smell of brightly coloured plimsoles and bouncy beach balls. I would hold onto Mum, Dad or Nan's hands and run and skip. Here, the constant noise and confusion that my hearing had become didn't seem to matter, as it was all sucked into the bigness of the sea and sand and the joy of discovery and play.

In the evenings we would go to the club and Mum would dress us up in pretty frocks with lace at the neck and cuffs. My long, fine fair hair would get into terrible knots and Mum would spray it with a product called No More Tangles before tackling it with a comb. I would scream and try to twist away, to no avail. From when I was about 6, Mum created quite an odd hairdo for me. It was a kind of bun on the top of my head above my fringe and the rest of my hair flowing loose. I hated it and was very jealous of my sister's more pliable hair.

I loved the evenings at the camp, where all the kids would run around the clubhouse. There was always country dancing going on, and I would get into hilarious muddles because I couldn't hear the music properly and was so uncoordinated. Adults and children would stand in rows facing each other and would take steps back and forth, or twirl around to a new partner. I would get terrible giggles, as I never knew what I was supposed to be doing. On each holiday we would make a night-time trip to the theme park Blackgang Chine, which was thrillingly scary in the dark with its dinosaurs and pirate ships. Once Dad bought us all ice creams, and it seemed strange eating them in the dark. I stood behind Nan so that she could block off the slight wind, but she must have been closer than I realised, and when she turned suddenly, her jacket caught my ice cream and the whole of it went down her back. No one had seen, so I moved away and pretended I was still eating my ice cream, but every time I saw the big white blob on Nan's back, I got the giggles.

One place we visited had a strong effect on me – it was the wax-works museum in Brading. It was scary, as apart from small pin lights the whole museum was in darkness. I remember creeping round and jumping as we suddenly came upon bats and other strange animals. One exhibit was called the Chapel of Rest and was a room with a closed coffin in the middle of the floor. An organ stood at the back with a skeleton playing an eerie piece of music. I remember watching its bony fingers jerking over the keys and as the music reached a crescendo, I suddenly noticed that the coffin lid was opening and a skeletal hand was coming out. I screamed and ran out of the museum, convinced that terrifying dead things were coming to get me!

Dad's brother, Uncle Keith, had two boys, Tony and Lee. Tony was a year younger than me, and Lee, three years younger. They were great fun and quite naughty. Sadly, their mum left the family when the boys were very young, so Uncle Keith was bringing them up as a single dad. They lived in Tottenham, and Nan, who was Keith's mum, would often go over to their flat to help look after the boys. Dad's sister Aunty Audrey and Uncle Ken lived in Hounslow. Their son John was a year older than me. I have happy memories of Audrey, Ken and John accompanying us to the Isle of Wight and us floating in the sea in John's huge rubber tyre.

My cousins on my mum's side were older than Lorraine and me. Every Christmas on Boxing Day, Mum's brother Uncle Len and Aunty Hetty and their children Lynn and Carol, and Mum's sister Aunty Betty and Uncle Ron and their children David and Christine would come to ours for Boxing Day tea. I felt in awe of them all as they seemed very grown up to me, even as children.

Mum's parents, Nan and Grandad Sturgeon lived in a rented ground-floor flat in Wood Green. They were quite poor and Nan suffered with lots of health issues. Mum, Lorraine and I would go there shopping most Saturdays and then make our way to Nan and Grandad's to spend the afternoon with them. I remember sitting on the top of Grandad's armchair and playing with his hair! He was a man of few words but was pretty patient to tolerate me doing that.

I started school at 5, still wearing my eye patch, which would soon be replaced by NHS children's glasses in pale pink plastic. My coordination was still very poor, but the authorities felt I would benefit more from being in mainstream than special school. I made some lovely friends at school: Jennifer, who lived about ten minutes' walk away from me, became my best friend and I was also close to another Tracy, remaining good friends with her right until I left Walthamstow to go to college.

There was never any indication given at school that my teachers were aware of how little I could hear. All I knew was that I felt constantly confused about what I was meant to be doing. I would see the teachers standing at the front and hear them giving instructions but it was just the sound of their voices, I had no idea what the instructions actually were.

The rest of the class would get into groups around different tables and I would sit looking on. One teacher was very kind and would always come and take me to the table I was supposed to be on and show me what to do, but I still felt different. Where the other children were learning to chat together and develop into little cliques, I felt constantly alone. I must have tried to compensate for not hearing by watching to see what the others did and copying them, but that didn't always work.

Once, the class was creating a huge mural of a peacock and other colourful birds. Each child was assigned a different part to work on and we made it by scrunching up tiny bits of coloured tissue and pasting them onto the appropriate sections. The problem was that I hadn't heard that it was meant to be a picture of birds. I thought we were just having fun sticking coloured balls onto card. I was supposed to be working on the peacock's chest so should have been using the blue and green tissue paper, but I was adding in balls of pink, orange and yellow too! The children near me got very upset, as they thought I was deliberately messing up their work.

On another occasion, the entire school from infants to top juniors were making Easter hats and there would be a prize for the best hat in each year. Our teacher told us to use our imaginations and make our hats as decorative as possible. I felt excited as I could already visualise how I wanted mine to look. It would be pink, my favourite colour, with paler pink and purple ribbons and blue, pink, purple and cream flowers around the edge. I could envisage how beautiful it would be, but I didn't know how to make it. The teacher had demonstrated and given us instructions but her words and actions meant nothing to me. Nevertheless, I set to and cut out the parts but had no idea how to fit them together. I looked around, but Mrs Roberts was busy and all the others seemed to know what they were doing. I tried to watch the girl next to me, but she sensed my gaze and covered her work with her hands.

There was nothing for it but to try my best. I could hear sniggering behind me and decided to just concentrate on making it look pretty, so spent ages sticking glitter and balls of tissue on to make the flowers. Attaching the ribbons was a problem, so in the end I just stuck them on in a circle under the flowers.

Suddenly Mrs Roberts clapped her hands 'You need to put your hats on now and try parading them round the classroom before we do it in the big assembly,' she said.

One by one I watched the others parade their hats. With my surname I knew I would be near the end and began to feel sick with apprehension. At last Mrs Roberts turned to me. 'Come on, Tracy, let's see yours.'

Picking up my beautifully coloured and be-glittered 'hat', I tried to balance it on my head as I walked forward. Despite all my efforts it was still totally flat and with my very uneven walk I'd only taken a step before it fell off and floated sadly to the floor. The sniggers turned into open laughs as Mrs Roberts bent to pick it up.

'This is useless, Tracy,' she said, crossly. 'You obviously didn't bother to do a single thing I told you. That's not a hat, it's just a waste of good card.' She screwed it up and looked around the giggling children as she tossed my lovely creation into the bin. 'Suzanne, your hat was excellent,' she said. 'You obviously *did* listen to me, unlike Tracy. See if you can rush something together so she's got something to wear in the assembly.'

I watched miserably as Suzanne picked up a plain white sheet of card and, with only ten minutes to go before the bell, cut it roughly into shape and glued the parts together. She made no move to colour or stick anything on it and when I went over to stick on some petals, she pushed my hands away and crammed her misshapen creation on my head. I was nearly crying as the bell rang and Mrs Roberts called us all to line up for the assembly. I felt stupid. Why couldn't I understand what I was meant to be doing when everyone else could? Gritting my teeth I 'buried' the memory of the pretty hat I'd so happily envisaged making. This was just one more thing to shut away deep inside me.

8

Tough Times

*Can anybody find that true peace of mind, a peace that won't depart,
that satisfies the heart...?*

Marilyn Baker[1]

As I progressed through school, although I had good friends, I would
still often be the butt of teasing. 'Spastic', 'Four Eyes', my classmates
would chant as they followed me in the playground, mimicking my
movements. I tried hard to control my steps so that I'd look more normal, but the teasing continued. Once, in a PE lesson, Mr Johnson asked
us to climb to the top of the climbing frame and down the other side.
The class did it in twos but, typically, with my name being Williamson, I
was the last to go. Going up was OK, but when I got to the top, I froze.
I had no idea how to get over and down the other side. Mr Johnson
called instructions, but I couldn't hear so just hung there unmoving. I could see the others pointing and laughing, but my legs just
wouldn't work.

I probably wasn't stuck for long because Mr Johnson climbed up to
help me, but the whole episode was another 'proof' that I didn't match
up. Despite all this, I still enjoyed going to Jenny's house to play, and as
she wore glasses too, I didn't feel quite so different when I was with her.

When I was about 6 it was decided that we would get a dog, and
one afternoon my dad went with Lorraine to bring one home. I sat in

Nan's front room eagerly waiting for their return. At last I saw them coming! I charged downstairs and was so excited as Dad showed me the tiny golden puppy. 'She's a Welsh corgi,' he said proudly, 'like the Queen's dogs.'

'What shall we call her?' asked Mum.

I was expecting Lorraine to choose, being the eldest, but without thinking I said, 'Oh, she looks like a tuppenny bit!'

To my surprise Dad liked that, and soon 'Penny' was settled into her new bed. I loved her, and she was to prove a great comfort to me as I grew up. One day, maybe a year after she'd arrived, our class had a 'knowing our pets' day. Most of the children showed pictures of their hamsters or cats and I felt very proud that I had a 'royal' dog to talk about! Penny definitely improved my status with the other children.

When I was 7, my dad became ill. He had been laying some crazy paving in our front garden and suddenly collapsed with terrible pain in his spine. The doctor thought he had slipped a disc and Dad had to lie flat on his back, but the pain didn't improve and in the end he was sent for tests. It was a great shock to Mum when the consultants said that Dad had cancer and there was nothing they could do. They told Mum he might have a year or two and they would do all they could to help him.

I didn't understand why Dad was suddenly away for long stretches of time. When he was in hospital, Lorraine and I would go with Mum to visit him. Although it was strange seeing him lying in a hospital bed, I just accepted it. Similarly, when he eventually came home and Mum had a bed put into the lounge, it never occurred to me that he was too weak to get upstairs. I just felt sad that he needed to sleep so much.

One evening in January 1972, Dad was sleeping again while Lorraine and I were playing, when he started making a strange, choking noise. The next moment Mum rushed me upstairs. I struggled as I hadn't kissed him goodnight, but Mum wouldn't let me go near him. She ran out, shutting the door. I was confused. Why had I been sent upstairs? What had I done? Why hadn't Lorraine been sent up too? Something in Mum's face stopped me from going down again so I climbed into bed, but I couldn't get to sleep. When Lorraine came up much later, I was still awake but I didn't move as she climbed the ladder to get into the top bunk. I could hear her crying and was scared.

When I went down the next morning my uncle Len was there, and he and Nan and Mum were all crying. Mum hugged me and said, 'Daddy's gone to heaven,' but I only heard that he had gone somewhere and didn't understand what she meant and why everyone was so sad. I'd never experienced death before and had probably missed things in conversations and stories that help children learn about dying. All I knew was that I'd been sent to bed early, which I associated with punishment, Daddy had gone and everyone was sad. Where was Daddy? I must have done something so bad that I'd sent him away.

I went to school that day as I wanted to hide from all these confusing things at home. But somehow all I could think of was that something awful had happened. At playtime when the children went outside, my legs wouldn't move. I felt weak and dropped my head onto my arms. I didn't want anyone to see me, but of course my teacher knew I was there and came over.

'Daddy's gone to heaven,' I told her.

Mrs White seemed shocked at my matter-of-fact tone. She immediately phoned Mum and soon I was on my way back home.

Losing Dad and then his dad, my grandad Willie, just a few months later left a huge void in our family. With two young children to support, my mum went back to work and Nan took us to school. Although I did come to understand that Dad had died, I still felt guilty deep down. Soon I forgot many of the circumstances of Dad's death, just like I forgot the trauma of being in hospital. But inside I felt more and more empty. I'd been sent to bed early and then Daddy had gone. It must have been my fault.

A couple of years later, Mum started going to a widowed and divorced club with her friend Avril. Avril's son Neil was a bit younger than me and we were great friends. I was happy to visit the club, as it meant I could play with Neil and several other children. While our parents did their thing, we kids would chase each other around.

Mum and Avril both met someone special quite soon. For Mum it was a divorced man a bit older than her. Bert seemed big compared to my memory of Dad. He had black, slicked-back hair, a florid complexion and a loud voice. He was OK, and when he started to visit each Saturday, I was happy enough. He always brought Lorraine and me a bag of chocolate bars each, and being a great lover of anything sweet, I began to look forward to his visits.

Reading had become my favourite thing and I could curl up with an Enid Blyton book or a Chalet School[2] story and be lost to the world for hours. Somehow the confusion of sound that always surrounded me never mattered when I was reading. I understood what was being said and the plotlines of the stories without any problem. But at school, and therefore in my own heart too, I was constantly found lacking, and I became more and more afraid of exasperating the teachers. I felt in a vacuum, always watching from the sidelines but never knowing quite what was being said or what I was meant to be doing. With the school presuming that I was slow learning, no one ever seemed to question how it was that I had picked up reading so quickly and so well, reading all of J.R.R. Tolkien's works by the time I was 9! It was a secret achievement that was never applauded until I mentioned it to Marilyn after we became friends, and she was amazed.

Of all my friends, I was the only one who had no daddy. I knew he was in heaven, but I missed him being in my life. My uncles and aunts on both sides were very caring and really tried to come alongside us as a family and to make sure we were coping OK without Dad, yet I always felt an ache of loneliness inside. Bert had started staying overnight when he visited on Saturdays and would then be with us for Sunday lunch too. One Saturday I felt particularly low. When Mum sent me up to bed, I noticed Bert's coat hanging off the banister, and almost without thinking, I dropped a little kiss onto its collar and whispered, 'Please may you be my daddy.' I had never been to church or Sunday school and had no concept of God, but to me that little kiss was a sign of my heart's desire. I wanted a daddy and I was happy for that daddy to be Bert.

Some time later, Mum told us that Bert had grown very fond of us all and wanted to come and stay during the week as well as on Saturday nights. 'It will be as if we are all a family together,' she said. 'And because he hasn't got children of his own, he loves you two.'

Lorraine was quiet but I was OK; maybe it would mean more chocolate bars?

The next day he was there after school, moving about in the kitchen as Mum got dinner. I'd been going to ask if he had any chocolate, but a nervous feeling came over me. He was talking very loudly, almost shouting and his face looked even redder than usual.

When we sat round the table for dinner, the strange tense atmosphere was even stronger. I looked at Mum but she seemed on edge. Lorraine wasn't looking at anyone. Bert was talking loudly, going on and on. As always, the words were unintelligible to me, but the grating sound of his voice made me anxious. Mum was a good cook and dinner looked as lovely as always, but suddenly I had no appetite. I reached out for my drink. I was still very clumsy in my movements, and maybe because I was nervous, my hand jerked just as I went to pick up my glass. I knocked it over and Ribena spread an ugly red stain all over the tablecloth.

With a roar, Bert slammed his hand on the table and started shouting and swearing. 'Look at her, she's mental, she can't even hold her glass . . . Look at the mess she's made.' On and on he shouted, his voice so loud that I understood the words. Mum jumped up to get a cloth, but I was so shocked I just sat frozen, staring at him. His face was red, his mouth working. Mum tried to say something, but his shouting overrode her words. I started to cry.

'What's she crying about now, then?' he shouted, seeming even more enraged by my tears. 'She's just pathetic.'

I didn't know then, that what happened that dinnertime was the beginning of years of fearful tiptoeing around this man that I'd 'prayed' in all innocence would become my new daddy. His moods became the god of my adolescent and teen years. He remained generous, always giving Lorraine and me nice birthday and Christmas presents, and treats of chocolates each weekend. I loved Granny Smith apples and often he would come up with a lovely shiny green apple and plonk it in front of me as I sat reading. Once he bought me an entire set of an old publication of Dickens' works that he'd found in a car boot sale. I accepted these gifts and feel now, after many years of healing, that they were signs of the real, kind, giving man that God had created him to be. But sadly, those moments were far overshadowed by his manic rages and totally over-the-top reactions.

As I moved into my senior school years, I would sometimes go to friends for tea, and it made me cry when I realised how easily they could chat with their dads. There would be real conversations, and it wouldn't matter if their opinions weren't the same, they were just enjoying chatting. For me that was unimaginable, as the moment I began to speak, Bert would launch into a diatribe: 'What's she saying now, then?' he would shout. 'She's just stupid, lazy, mental . . .' Sometimes things seemed peaceful and relaxed; I'd be getting on with my homework and suddenly would hear banging and a roar of noise going on and on. Usually I would hide up with Nan, not wanting to be drawn in, but other times I couldn't avoid it and would see him in the hall by the lounge, slamming the door again and again.

In my anxiety, I began to wake up very early and started slipping out of the bedroom into the lounge. At first I just read, enjoying the rare quietness, but then for some strange reason I devised a game, trying to get around the entire lounge without touching the floor. I pulled chairs closer together and moved a pouffe, and it was great fun jumping from one piece of furniture to the other. I can't remember now why I did it, but it was probably very good for improving my balance! This was a private time of achieving something fun and unseen by anyone else.

But one day that all changed. It was probably about 6 a.m. and I was on my third circuit round the lounge. I was enjoying the snap of pleasure every time I succeeded in reaching the next piece of furniture without touching the floor. I had just turned to head towards the door again and froze. Bert was there, watching me; standing just inside the door, silent. My legs went weak. How long had he been there? I muttered hello then sat on the settee and picked up my book. Maybe he'd just go? But then he sat beside me and still without saying anything, took my hand, making me drop the book. My heart began to pound. Was he going to start shouting? But no, instead he put his hand on my leg. I sat very still. What was he doing? All I knew was that I hated it. I thought the shouting and banging were the scariest parts of my new life, but this was different. This was shrivelling.

That was the morning when I, as a growing girl, began to shut down on the inside.

9

God at Work

He became all that we were, so we could become like Him.

Marilyn Baker[1]

As I entered adolescence, life remained difficult, but I still had a mischievous streak and loved the weekends that Uncle Keith brought Tony and Lee over to see Nan, or when I would travel with her to their flat in Tottenham. I also loved taking Penny for walks to The Forest and, in minutes, being in another world of huge old trees, secret paths and green fields.

Every August, Mum, Lorraine and I would go for a week's holiday to Eastbourne, staying in a small hotel with lots of other mums and their children for a free holiday organised by Dad's work, the *Evening Standard* newspaper – a policy to help the families of any employees who died. It became a lovely week away, enjoying the beach, jumping in the sea, indulging in cream cakes . . . These holidays were oases that I looked forward to all year.

During my childhood the only spiritual content I ever received was when we attended the odd wedding or funeral. I vaguely believed in God, but I had no concept of what faith really meant. And yet, somehow, looking back I can see that my heart was pulled towards God. Once, not long after Bert began to show his true colours, I crept into the lounge late one night. I couldn't sleep and didn't want to wake

Lorraine with my fidgeting. Deep inside I felt a hunger, but for what I didn't know. I went to the bookcase and found myself drawn to the big old Bible. I opened it randomly at the start of a chapter. I tried to read, but the print was so tiny that I gave up. It seemed old and irrelevant, but as I went back to bed, I felt sad. I'd been hoping for something more.

During one Easter, *Jesus of Nazareth* was on TV. I was upstairs watching it with Nan and her friend. After a while, Nan turned it off saying it was boring and religion didn't mean anything nowadays. Unusually, I heard that remark and felt very upset, shouting out, 'Well, it means something to me!' and then slamming out of the room. What was happening? Somehow God must have been stirring my heart ready for finding faith later.

When I was 11, I started attending secondary school and began walking there on my own instead of with Nan. Mum was working so hard to make sure she could provide a lovely home life for Lorraine and me. Bert had intermittent jobs but had left his main work because of heart problems, so he was often there when I got home from school. I always dreaded that time between me getting home and Mum returning from work. Jenny and I had grown apart but I did make some other really good friends, and looking back now, feel thankful that throughout those years I always had a friend in my life. But despite that, I still felt very lonely.

It was around this time that I was finally officially diagnosed as being hard of hearing and was given two hearing aids. My teachers no longer mocked me as being slow-learning and some even took active steps to help me. However, the hearing aids didn't work for me as they just changed the quieter-sounding uproar that was my hearing into an overwhelmingly noisy one! Everyone had presumed I would be OK now I had hearing aids, but what wasn't understood was that my deafness was caused by neurological damage, not damage to the ears. So hearing aids would never help me and in fact made my ability to comprehend a lot worse!

I had become very thin, and as I was shooting up in height, I must have looked an ungainly beanpole. Through the terrifying times at home, I began to feel a deep hatred of my body. Bert had added 'perverted' to his list of crushing names and I knew it must be true. It must be my fault these awful things were happening. I couldn't tell anyone and he seemed all-powerful.

Girls at school were becoming interested in boys, but I felt cut off from all their giggling talk. Where they were always comparing their bodies, I just wanted to hide and was determined never to grow curvy. One day after a games lesson, the teacher was called away suddenly. We were all in the changing rooms and I had just showered and was walking with my towel wrapped round me back to the bench to dress. Suddenly I realised I was surrounded by some of the toughest girls in my class. I tried to press through but Stacey blocked my path, with Dawn close behind her. 'Where are you going, Willibum?' Dawn sneered. 'Are you looking for Miss? She's not here, is she?'

I mumbled something and tried again to press through, but suddenly the girls grabbed me, ripping at the towel. Someone snatched my bag of clothes and they threw it from one to the other, laughing as they pulled out my vest and knickers and tossed them in the shower. I was still too flat-chested to wear a bra and Stacey mocked as she thrust her own well-developed chest at me, trying again to pull down the towel. It began to slip and I clung on frantically. Hands were tearing at the towel, shouting that I was a pathetic lump of snot, a boy pretending to be a girl. Someone tugged it from the bottom and I screamed as it was jerked out of my grip. I stood there naked, crying. I hated my body. The girls were right, I was scum.

I can't remember how I got out of that situation, as my clothes had been stamped on, tossed and hidden. What I do remember is that it was soon afterwards, when I was walking in The Forest, that I found myself at the top of the hill where a concrete platform supported a bridge over the motorway. I sat for ages staring down at the frantic anonymity of the hurtling traffic. Suddenly I was crying out, 'Are you there? Do you care about me?' There was silence, nothing. I shouted again: 'If you exist, you'll have to show me,' and flung myself down the hill, rolling at a tremendous pace. I felt complete abandonment. I didn't care what happened and the speed felt exhilarating. I knew nothing could stop me, I was rolling too fast. I could hear the roar of the traffic and closed my eyes, bracing for the impact, but was totally shocked when I came to a sudden, jarring stop yards away from the road. I lay panting, feeling the weight of the steep gradient. What had stopped me? My face was squashed into the prickly grass. Eventually I turned my head and opened my eyes. No one was there. All I could see was the blue sky and dirty green grass. Yet someone or something must have stopped me. What that was, I had no idea. All I knew was that I was alive. But life was still a dark pit with no way out.

Over the next few years my struggles intensified, yet like a seed thrusting its way up through the rocks, the awareness that something had saved me that afternoon grew inside me, a kernel of truth entering my heart. Someone had heard my cry and answered. I wasn't just an invisible speck. I mattered.

As I went through the school system, I began to achieve more despite still being in the bottom groups (even though it was now understood that I had a hearing loss, I was trapped in the streamed system and there was little expectation that I would do well). This was just before the changeover to GCSEs so the higher achievers were in GCE groups and the lower achievers in CSE. If a person received a CSE grade 1, that was equivalent to GCE, but generally the expectation in my groups was that students would only get grades 2 to 4. I was determined that I would get as many grade 1s as possible, so from the beginning of my fifth year I set up a complicated reading and revising plan, realising that I needed to do a lot more background reading as I could hear so little in the lessons. I wanted to go on to take A levels and then go to university. I was already sitting two GCEs, English Language and Latin, and knew that if I passed those and got at least three grade 1 CSEs that I would be able to take A levels.

In my late teens, I started a desperate battle to secure a good Saturday job, like my sister and many of my friends. Lorraine was working in the library, and with my love of reading that seemed a fantastic job. I'd even wondered about making a career in librarianship. I did get an interview at the same library, but this was in the days of card indexing and when they set me a test to file replacement cards, I was far too slow, so I was never properly interviewed. I went into all the small shops down our local high street to no avail. Eventually I looked further afield and to my joy was offered a six-week contract in Marks & Spencer's. During the training I couldn't hear any of the instructions but thought it would be simple enough to pick up. I was put on the till at the men's underwear department, but my poor vision let me down. At that time you had to enter in the item's code number and then the till would register the correct price; but the numbers were blurry so I often charged people wrongly. My supervisor was patient to begin with, but after one Saturday when nearly every customer complained that I'd overcharged them, she told me I couldn't stay on the till and I was relegated to the plant section.

Here I had to ensure the plants stayed healthy. No one knew then how lethal I was anywhere near a plant, and in my boredom at hanging around a few green shelves for a whole day, I'd soon overwatered them all and to my horror they began to die.

Many of the other Saturday staff that had started on six-week contracts went on to 'permanent' Saturday employment, so when I was called to see the personnel officer I hoped that my contract was going to be extended. I was so disappointed when she told me I'd have to leave. I felt so ashamed when I told Mum. Over the next couple of years I had more job opportunities, but on each occasion the same thing happened. My vision was too poor, or my lack of hearing led to me making silly mistakes. Soon I would be asked to leave. Each time it 'proved' what Bert was constantly shouting over me: I was rubbish, a failure, mental. I heard these words echoing in my head even when he was being pleasant.

But I loved being with my nan, or going on shopping trips to Wood Green with Mum, who enjoyed browsing round shops; it was fun to go together and often she would treat Lorraine or me to something pretty.

When I was 17 my sister left home to live with her boyfriend and his mum in Poplar. I was happy for her and pleased to have more space in our bedroom. Paul, her boyfriend, was great and Lorraine was doing well at work and now had her own car. Things were looking up for her, but I was still struggling. Bert started coming into my bedroom in the early mornings when I was getting dressed. I wouldn't hear anything and would be completely unaware of anyone being in the room. Then I'd turn round and see him staring at me. Penny was suffering too because, unknown to us, she was developing cancer in her back passage and often screamed when she tried to do a poo. Bert once ran out of the kitchen door and kicked her hard as she squatted on the grass. I was so upset.

At school, life seemed a bit easier now I was in the upper sixth. I had a good circle of friends, and five of us booked a youth hostelling trip. Mum bought me a proper camping rucksack, and with our sleeping bags, cagoules and walking shoes we felt like expert travellers. For the first time I felt fully accepted in a group and my deafness didn't seem to matter as much. The trip did have its moments, though; one day the others wanted to cycle to see the local sights. I'd had bikes but had never cycled along the road as my balance wasn't great. But I didn't want to be left out, so we all chose our bikes and set off. I was at the back when we turned onto a busy A road and suddenly traffic was speeding past. One lorry went by with a roar, peppering me with gravel. I was terrified I would fall under its wheels. When I saw an even bigger lorry approaching, I jerked my handlebars to the left and fell off, subconsciously thinking that if I didn't, I would soon be mincemeat! The next day I tripped over twice when we were walking between hostels, so I ended up somewhat bruised.

Somehow, I managed to hold my own as I continued through the sixth form. I had two teachers who were especially caring and understood something wasn't right in my life, and that gave me a deeper sense of assurance. I even had a boyfriend, Ian, who I'd met on a blind date. I would go round to his family's flat and we'd hang out. At 21, he seemed a lot more mature than me. Yet every time he wanted to kiss or cuddle, I froze up and was overwhelmed with fear.

Over the years I'd buried all my feelings, believing that one day I'd be strong enough to get my revenge on Bert, but for now I had to concentrate on my exams. I wanted to go to the University of Manchester to study to become a teacher of the deaf. The course was the best in the country, so with great hope I sat my exams in June 1982, but was hugely disappointed. Where I'd needed at least three Bs, I'd only passed two and that was with a scrape through in Latin. One grade B in English wasn't enough to achieve my goal. I was devastated. Would I always be a failure? I thought all hope had gone, but one day my form teacher gave me a brochure for a college of higher education in Hertfordshire, known as Wall Hall. My interest was piqued as I saw that apart from the two main degrees, it also offered a one-year Postgraduate Certificate in Education (PGCE) course for teaching deaf children. I'd failed to get into Manchester university, but maybe I could still achieve my goal. 'You only need two A level passes, so you are already set up for it,' my teacher said encouragingly.

In a matter of weeks, I'd been accepted for the BEd degree, studying English as my main subject. I would train with junior children and then do the PGCE for the teaching of the deaf course. Although some of the college board were doubtful I could manage, I was determined. The grant came through, and my accommodation details. For my first year I would be out in lodgings sharing with another student, Helen Rutt. Hopefully we would soon be friends.

10

A Huge Life Change

Did you know there's someone who can hear your faintest sigh?
Someone who can hear your heart's deepest cry?

Marilyn Baker[1]

As I started college in September 1982, I was full of hope. I wanted to make others laugh, to be loving and full of fun, to become a great teacher. I thought that, by leaving home, I'd be able to leave all the nightmare parts of my life behind too. I'd become closer to Mum over this last year and knew that she did care deeply about me and my future, and was doing her utmost to ensure I had every opportunity in life. I felt sad for her that life at home often seemed so fraught, and I felt deep down that much of it was my fault. Mum had been through so much with my illness, losing Dad and coping at the same time with my grandad's demands and death. When she met Bert, she must have hoped for the same kind of loving relationship she'd enjoyed with Dad. I knew she loved him deeply and I couldn't take that from her by opening up about what was happening. I hadn't told anyone, as I didn't know how to. It was all buried inside.

Mum came with me the day I started college, first going to my lodgings where we met my landlady, Mrs Watson, who lived with her elderly father. I was delighted when I saw our accommodation. Helen and I would share two rooms, the twin bedroom upstairs and a converted dining room, which would be our lounge and study. Helen and her parents arrived while we were there and Mrs Watson immediately told her that I was deaf. Unsurprisingly, she looked a bit taken aback, but she seemed kind and I hoped we would become good friends.

Mum then came with me to the college, where we met some of the other first-year students. Ruth Twynham came to say hello. She had wild, curly brown hair and seemed a larger-than-life character. At 20, she was a little older than the rest of us, and explained she had started another course first but had changed her mind and decided to go for teaching instead. I could hear some of this but there was a great deal of noise around with the crowds of new students. I felt the usual shyness sweeping over me as I looked around. Would I ever become a part of college life and make friends, or would I always be on the fringe?

Over the next few days, I gradually settled in. Somehow, I managed to be at the right places at the right times and probably didn't show outwardly how little I was hearing. I loved sharing with Helen, who was fun and who made friends easily, so they became mine too by default. Karen and Janet were also lodging nearby, and on the first Saturday we all went into Watford. I tried hard to fit in despite not having much idea what they were all talking about. I laughed when they laughed and looked at the things they pointed out without having any idea what they were. It was just good to feel like a normal student.

My first teaching practice was at a primary school in Stevenage. My class was first-year juniors, and Mrs Adams introduced me to the children. After the register she set them the task of writing an illustrated story about their Halloween experiences. A little girl came up to me: 'How do you spell "withered"?' she asked, excitedly.

Congratulating myself on having heard her and impressed that such a young child knew a descriptive word like 'withered', I gave her the spelling. A little later Mrs Adams asked me to check some of the stories and this little girl's was among them. As soon as I read the first line I started to laugh: 'As I walked up the road I saw a withered.' I'd been so confident I'd heard her, it'd never occurred to me that she wanted to know how to spell wizard, not withered.

Although I loved the children, my inability to hear and lack of confidence continued to cause huge problems. On my next practice, I spent so long trying to hear the children's names that I did virtually no teaching. When it came to the three-week teaching practice, I was supposed to be handling the class on my own one day, but from the time the teacher left, the thirty 10- to 11-year-olds erupted and, taking no notice of my weak calls for order, they flew paper aeroplanes, raced around the room and shouted. I was overwhelmed. Even as I stood in the middle of the racket, I could hear the constant refrain of my childhood in my head: 'She's useless, look at her, she's pathetic, she's mental, lazy, stupid . . .'

It was early in the winter term of 1983, during yet another long teaching practice, that I finally acknowledged the truth that had been staring me in the face all along. I couldn't teach, at least not in the classroom. My hearing was too poor and I was too weak. How could I teach these children when I was essentially scared of them? I felt devastated. I'd been so determined to become a teacher of the deaf that I'd tried to ignore the difficulties. But now I realised it wasn't going to work. I had failed yet again.

Later I spoke to my tutor and the decision was made that I would finish my year academically and would go on teaching practices as an observer of the children's development rather than as a teacher. If I passed my exams, I would then go straight into the second year of the BA degree, keeping English Literature as my main course and also studying Education as my minor. It was a neat solution and I was thankful to the tutors, but in my heart I felt crushed. Would this pattern of failure always define my life? How would I ever become part of the second-year BA group when all my friends were on the BEd? I withdrew into my shell again and started to drop down in weight.

I'd known from early on that Helen was 'religious', as she kept mentioning church when we were getting to know each other. She started going to the college Christian Fellowship, and to my surprise I discovered that Karen and Ruth were also part of it, together with an extrovert guy called Tim. What was it about religion that was drawing them all? Helen invited me to church with her but I said no, mainly because she said I'd have to wear a hat! But on one particular Sunday I felt really low and couldn't face sitting at home studying, so I agreed to wear the hated hat, and we went off together.

I found it a strange experience. Looking back, I know that Helen was praying hard for me to become a Christian. But, of course, I couldn't hear what was going on. We stood up to sing hymns I'd never heard of and sat down again for the prayers and sermon, both of which seemed to go on forever. I passed the time by counting the marks on the ceiling and was thankful when it ended. But then a sweet thing happened. An elderly couple invited us home for tea. It was lovely to sit in their cosy lounge eating delicious cakes. They asked me some questions, but after I answered in a muddled way, not having heard properly, they let me be and chatted to Helen. To my own surprise, I decided that I would return.

The following weekend, Helen went home, but enticed by the thought of cakes, I found her hat and put it in my bag until needed. I got the bus into Watford and tried to remember my way to the church. But it had been down a side road, and however hard I searched, I couldn't find it. It was only a little chapel, and on the few occasions I asked for directions, no one had heard of it. In the end, I returned to Mrs Watson's and arrived just as Helen got back. She looked most surprised to see me stuffing her by now crumpled hat back into her drawer. When she heard that I'd tried to go to her church she became quite emotional and gave me a hug. I didn't realise that this was because she'd been praying for me!

Despite these happy moments, my depression was taking deep hold. I felt so empty inside, I didn't know how to cope. Often, I cried myself to sleep, weeping as silently as I could so as not to wake Helen. It never occurred to me to try to talk to her about my struggles. What could I say?

One wet evening I felt really low and went for a walk. I wandered along, only conscious of the heaviness within. It was like a rock-hard weight. I suddenly found myself standing by a small lake on the local common. No one else was around and I stood staring at the glistening water. I felt what a relief it would be to sink beneath the surface and not to have to struggle any more. I could hear the lake calling me to enter its peace. I put my bag down and walked to the very edge. I felt totally alone. I took a step forward and my feet sank into the mud. I took another and almost fell as it closed round my feet. The freezing water lapped round my ankles. I heard that voice whispering in my head, 'Go on, Tracy, end it all. You'll never be anything but a disappointment.'

I wept as I edged further in. If I had any hope of becoming the kind of person I longed to be, I wouldn't go through with this. But I'd gone to college full of dreams, and I knew now that I could not fulfil them. Discovering that I was too weak to teach was the last straw.

I turned my head and gazed in the direction of my lodgings. 'Goodbye,' I whispered and stepped forward. But in that instant, I just knew it wasn't going to happen. I did end up fully in the water but only in the process of turning around and scrambling back to the path. My heart was dead and cold. I emptied my shoes, picked up my bag and crept home.

I didn't tell anyone about that night, so a week later, when Ruth invited me to her lodgings and over tea said that while praying God had put an urgency within her to tell me that he loved me and wanted me to know him as Father, I was stunned. Ruth was saying that God not only existed but had communicated with her about me. I can still remember the quietness of that room, sitting on floor cushions as Ruth talked about the miracle of his love. As she spoke about God's desire for us to know him, I found something loosening deep inside of me. I was drawn by the certainty shining from her eyes. This wasn't just something she had studied, this was someone she knew and whose love she was convinced of. How could that be? I didn't understand and yet I felt myself pulled in by Ruth's joyful certainty. The peace in the room wrapped around me and the tiniest crack opened in my heart. Maybe there was hope, even for someone like me?

One day, shortly after that conversation, I was reading a little pamphlet called 'Journey into Life',[2] which explained how to become a Christian. I suddenly knew I needed to talk to God myself. I couldn't just continue to listen to other people's experiences. I needed what Ruth had.

I came to the end, which listed the steps to faith, and found a prayer. It was a typical 'sinner's prayer', although at that time I had no idea what that was. I read it slowly, trying to understand what it meant. Then, for the first time in my life, I started to pray, talking to God from my heart. I told him that I wanted to know him like Ruth did. It was a muddled prayer, but I knew I meant it, and for the first time I was deliberately reaching out beyond myself in the hope of being changed.

I suddenly knew that God was with me. I couldn't see him or feel him physically, but in that moment he became real to me; giving me certainty that he was there and that he loved me.

And so began my Christian journey, which to start with was very exciting. The Christian Fellowship members drew me into their midst, and I started going to church, reading my Bible, praying and acting like all the others.

A few weeks later I was in Garston Church one Sunday morning. This was Ruth's church as well as Sian's and Claire's (Christian friends in the year above me at college). I'd never been in such an informal church before and where there was such a sense of excitement. I felt uncomfortable, and had just decided I wouldn't come back when I heard a voice deep inside me say: 'I want you to be baptised here.' Baptised? What did that mean? Could it be God?

At the end of the service I went to speak to the pastor, David Barker.

'I think God just told me I should be baptised here,' I told him, nervously.

'Great!' David said. 'We're having a baptism service next week. You could join the others and be baptised then.' He smiled warmly and invited me to a midweek meeting so I'd understand properly what I was doing. He then introduced me to a couple called John and Amanda Duncan, who seemed lovely. This church was a friendly place.

The following Sunday evening I was as ready as I could be for my baptism. Mum and Nan and one of my school friends came to support me, and I was amazed as I knew they didn't really understand what I was doing. Twenty-two of us were baptised that evening, including Claire. When it was my turn I stepped down into the water. David, who now knew I was deaf, looked directly at me as he said in loud, clear tones, 'Tracy, in the name of the Father, Son and Holy Spirit, I baptise you . . .' My heart pounded as he tipped me underwater and up again all in one swift movement. I stood dripping, feeling a bubble of joy inside. Everyone burst into song and I joined in, but as I went to climb out, David held me back and indicated they wanted to pray for me.

The church went quiet as he prayed that Jesus would heal my deafness and then asked me if I could hear the name he was whispering into my ear. It was so quiet that I heard him clearly say 'Jesus!' I repeated it and the church erupted into praise. They thought I'd been healed, and momentarily I let myself be carried along, but knew that really nothing had changed.

The next moment a man began to speak out in a way which I later learned was prophecy. I couldn't hear it, but afterwards Ruth transcribed it for me and it went something like this: 'Not only have I caused you to hear with your natural ears, my daughter, but I will also cause you to hear with your spiritual ears. I will give you words for others that show them how much I love them and will draw them close to my heart. For I am the Lord who delights in revealing the secrets of my heart . . .'

It was an amazing word, but for many years I shut it away, believing that because the first part had been wrong, as I hadn't been healed, all of it must be wrong. It wasn't until I started prophesying myself that I realised that nearly every prophetic word has elements of our own understanding mixed in with what has truly come from God's heart. The first part may have been a mistake, but the second part was from God and was to become the centre of my calling – to hear God's heart for those around me.

I finished college that year and went home for the summer holidays knowing I was a different person. While at home I attended the church led by the father of my friend Chris from college. I felt a new sense of purpose and was determined to succeed in the new course I'd be starting in September.

At the end of the first year, Helen and Karen asked me to share a room with them in a college hostel called Otterspool, a beautiful seventeenth-century converted coaching inn. I'd felt anxious about where I'd live so was overjoyed to be included in their plans, despite no longer being on the same course. There were several Christian students in this hostel including Sian, Lynne and Claire, who were to become wonderful friends and spiritual mentors and would even share various homes with me after college.

Yet despite all these hopeful signs that God was changing and healing my life, I was still struggling with overwhelming, negative feelings. Nothing seemed powerful enough to change me, not even God, despite all my hopes that I would now become a different person. One day another student made a mildly negative remark, and it was the trigger that blew away the carefully constructed walls for the wounded me to hide behind. An explosion of years of buried raw emotions surged through me, and shaking with red-hot anger, I jumped up and ran from the room. I couldn't stay any longer in this place that had led me to falsely believe there was hope. In my turmoil I didn't even go back to my room to pack. I was determined I was leaving forever, but I ran from the campus with just my bag of college files and a small-change purse. I walked blindly, only aware of the great pain in my heart.

'You deceived me, God,' I shouted, as I ran down a country road in the pouring rain. Tears ran down my face as I remembered the pain of my stepfather's abuse and the fear of his manic rages.

Eventually I was exhausted. A dark shape loomed up in front of me and I realised it was a bus shelter. I collapsed on the seat, shaking and crying.

The words came with a startling clarity: 'I love you and want to be a father to you.'

'Who's there?' I shouted, leaping to my feet. I was ready to run, when the voice came again. Clear, warm and strong, it pierced through to my heart. 'I love you and want to be a father to you. You may turn your back on me, but I'll never turn my back on you. I love you.'

Stunned, I sank down again on the bench. I knew that this was no person. I wouldn't have heard them anyway! This was God. I'd been running from him, cursing and telling him I wanted nothing more to do with him, yet he was here with me in the shelter, saying he loved me and would never turn his back on me. How could that be? As I sat back, God spoke again in my heart. The first voice had seemed almost physically audible, but now I became aware of little whispers passing through my mind. I could have dismissed them as imagination except that my thoughts were too fragmented to be able to express anything, especially whispers of loving understanding.

I want to be a father to you. You haven't yet come to me as a child comes to her father. I don't want you to pray because that's what Christians do, I want you to pray because that's our language of love and sharing together. I want to hear what brings you joy. I want to put my arms around you and share your tears when you are sad. I want to affirm you, to comfort you and lift you up in my love. Come to me in simple trust as a little child will come to her daddy. You are that child to me and I will never leave you or forsake you.

As these words drifted across my heart I became full of peace, as if all the turmoil was draining away. I was so tired, yet knew that something fundamental had happened. God my Father was there with me and that was all that mattered.

In my book *The Father's Kiss*, I tell the miracle of what happened next, as God led me from that bus shelter to John and Amanda, the couple I'd met at Garston Church. They welcomed me so lovingly when I eventually rang their doorbell at gone midnight, and their love and prayers over the next couple of years opened the door to me starting the journey of becoming truly healed on the inside, learning to let go of the negatives, to take steps to forgive my stepfather and others who had hurt me, and to live as God's beloved daughter.

Part 3

Woven Threads

11

A Divine Encounter

Don't be afraid, trust in my love, for I will never ever fail you . . .

Marilyn Baker[1]

Tracy

Having given up my career plans at the end of my first year of university, I'd had no further idea what to do. I was thrilled that with God's help I had managed to complete my degree, but what about now? All my college friends were making plans, but I felt at a complete loss. One day I shared with my housemate Sian that I was scared I would just end up drifting.

'Have you asked the Lord to guide you?' she asked. 'He really cares about your future, and has a plan for you that will be just right.'

I began to specifically ask the Lord to guide me. I had no idea how that would happen and weeks went by without any insights. I started to look into temporary jobs, but from previous experience I knew that even getting a shop job would be hard. One day a verse jumped out at me from Isaiah 43:8: 'Lead out those who have eyes but are blind, who have ears but are deaf.' It seemed as if God was saying, 'Tracy, lead out those who have eyes but are blind, ears but deaf.' But why? And what on earth could it actually mean?

Over the next few weeks I continued praying, but nothing else touched me as clearly as that verse had. I shared it with Sian, Debs and my other friends, and all felt that God was indeed calling me to focus in some way on the blind and deaf. I didn't know what the 'lead out' bit signified, but the idea of the blind and deaf did make sense as, after all, I'd originally been planning to become a teacher of the deaf.

As this verse was my only clue to my future, I began looking into anything to do with blindness and deafness. This was before the internet, so researching meant spending hours in the library and careers office. One day a particular job description caught my attention – technical officer for the blind. As I read, I felt a 'yes' inside me. The technical officer was someone employed as part of social services to help newly blind people adapt to their sight loss and learn mobility and life skills. This work would be one-to-one, which would be easier for me to manage. It did say that driving was a requirement, but I decided I could cross that bridge when I came to it. Training would be a six-month course and I would have to apply for funding. It seemed perfect and I felt this was the moment my friends had been describing, when you know the Lord has opened the door to something and have a sense of supernatural certainty inside. I applied for the course, due to start the following April, and a fortnight later I had an interview and was accepted; then two weeks after that I received confirmation of funding. Everything was coming together!

One thing required was some experience with blind people prior to the course, so I began to look into any voluntary work I could do. Again, everything fell into place, almost without me trying. There was a boarding school for blind and partially sighted girls in a town called Chorleywood, just a few miles from where I lived in Watford. So now I was very excited. I wrote to the college to ask if they used Community Service Volunteers and explained my need to get experience for the course. In ten days I had a reply to say they did use volunteers, and would be happy to take me on. I could start the following week to get the feel of things at the end of their summer term and then return in September for two terms before my course began. With great excitement, I replied to confirm. In the space of six weeks, God had shown me what career I was to follow and opened every door. This was so unlike all my previous experiences that I was full of awe and thanksgiving.

In June 1985, Debs drove me and my luggage to Chorleywood College and dropped me off outside the main door. I struggled inside with my two cases and smaller bags, left them in the hall and looked to see where the office might be. I felt nervous, as my deafness always made interactions difficult and if I felt stressed it became worse. A girl of about 14 was coming down the grand staircase, and I noticed her gripping the handrail yet looking straight ahead. I moved towards her, hoping to ask for directions, but when she reached the bottom, instead of making eye contact, she seemed to look straight through me and then, arms slightly outstretched, turned abruptly left and started crossing the large open space. I was shocked as I realised she was blind and hadn't even been aware I was standing there. (Later, I realised that she probably *was* aware, but as I didn't say anything, I had not made myself known to her.) I felt shaken, as she was one of the first blind people I'd ever met. It was crazy but somehow I hadn't made the mental connection that I'd be mixing with people who couldn't see *me*.

I was just turning down the corridor to the office when I heard a crash and was horrified to see a young girl sprawled on the floor amidst my luggage. I started to hurry back, but a stern-looking woman beat me to it. She hauled the young girl to her feet, saying something which I couldn't hear. She seemed quite brusque, and I felt sad for the girl, who looked rather dazed.

'I'm sorry I left my bags here,' I said. 'I didn't think. Are . . .'

'No, you didn't think,' she interrupted. 'You're lucky someone didn't break their leg! One rule here, never leave personal things lying around where others can fall over them. What are you doing here, anyway?'

Trying to hide my upset at her manner, I explained who I was, and a moment later found myself in the office being interviewed by a sergeant major-type headmistress.

She quickly fired off lots of info. I was struggling to hear and didn't want my deafness to be too obvious straight away. She then smiled and said that the teacher who would be showing me my duties would take me to my room to settle in. I was horrified when the same teacher who'd spoken to me earlier strode impatiently through the door. Miss Furroughs was in charge of all volunteers and also all leisure aspects of the girls' lives. Without a word, she marched ahead of me carrying my big case, while I ran behind with the smaller case and bags feeling like a naughty child.

That occasion was my introduction to many situations over the next few weeks where, despite all my efforts to do well, I found I had misunderstood things or failed to engage effectively with the girls under my care. Together with about two other volunteers, I was responsible for the younger girls' bath and bedtimes, for overseeing their leisure times and for accompanying them on trips outside the school grounds. There were many lovely times, however, and I soon had a small circle of girls who seemed to enjoy being with me. But overall, things were proving stressful because Miss Furroughs always seemed to be waiting for me to make a mistake. I felt very nervous, but one thing I loved was the opportunity to be involved in the Christian Union, which was led by a friendly teacher called Miss Short.

One day when I entered the chapel, I saw a lady I'd never met before sitting with Miss Short; she was blind.

'Tracy, this is Penny Cooze,' Miss Short introduced us. 'Penny used to attend this school and she's speaking to us today.' Penny smiled at me, and I thought how lovely she looked. She was small with glossy brown hair. I couldn't hear her, but her words were obviously having an effect, as some of the girls were in tears. Afterwards she moved to each of the girls in turn, putting her arms around them and praying for them. I thought she was amazing, and at the end I went up to chat.

'I have to go in a moment,' she said. 'Would you like to come to dinner one day when you're free? I live in Watford.'

I was surprised and pleased, and we made a date before she left. As I watched her go, I had little idea that the meeting was about to open a brand-new door to me.

I did go to dinner with Penny, but was very late as I got lost in Chorleywood trying to find the station. I eventually arrived at a sweet little endterrace house and found Penny had cooked me a lovely but by now rather dried out turkey leg for dinner. By this time, I'd become more at ease with blindness but had never imagined anyone being able to cook without sight before. But Penny had everything organised and the dinner was delicious.

Afterwards, as I was getting ready to leave, Penny suddenly announced: 'I live with Marilyn Baker. Do you know her, the singer? She's away at the moment but will be back in about three weeks. Would you like to come again and meet Marilyn too?'

As I was so shy at that time, I still wonder today what made me say yes. Maybe it was just because I was always up for a free meal! But as it turned out, God was certainly working behind the scenes in Penny's simple offer and my equally simple acceptance.

By the time the visit rolled around, I was regretting my decision to go to dinner with Marilyn.

I had developed tonsillitis and gone home to recover. I'd still been expecting to return to Chorleywood College in September so I'd popped in before term ended to finalise the details and to say goodbye to some who would be leaving. I was telling the headmistress my impressions from my short stay and was totally shocked when she leaned forward and said, 'Miss Williamson, we cannot have you come back to us in September. You are too deaf for us to entrust you with our blind girls.'

I'd stared at her, speechless. I'd been so looking forward to returning. I knew I'd made some mistakes but I didn't think I'd done that badly.

'I don't understand,' I said. 'I was just finding my feet and I am ready to do the job well now, the girls like me and . . .'

'Miss Williamson, I am sorry, but we can't trust you with our girls,' she'd interrupted, getting to her feet. 'Suppose you were guiding a blind girl across a road and a car came but you hadn't heard it? It is too dangerous, and to be honest, we think you are going for the wrong career.'

She'd opened the door and held her hand out for me to shake as I passed through. I did so automatically, but my heart was in turmoil. How could it have ended like this after such wonderful signs that everything was coming together? Had I misheard God? Was I kidding myself that he had a plan for me?

Now, as I made my way to Penny and Marilyn's home, I was still struggling. Who was I to think I could go to dinner with Marilyn Baker? She was famous – a gospel singer! What would we talk about? I didn't know much about Marilyn, and at first when Penny had said she lived with her, I didn't recognise the name, but later remembered the previous year when my housemates Daniella and Sarah had invited me to go with them to a Marilyn Baker concert. With my deafness, I didn't bother listening to music much, and certainly didn't know that Marilyn lived just a quarter of a mile away. I had actually enjoyed going to her concert and could tell that her songs were full of depth and gentleness, even though I couldn't hear the words. At the end people began to go up to say hello and Daniella, being extrovert, immediately rushed up and chatted with her, while Sarah and I hung shyly in the background. Now I was going to have dinner with her! I was a newish Christian, and as she was a gospel singer, she was used to talking about God and had probably been a Christian all her life.

I frantically began to rehearse all the things I could say about God, and I still had Bible verses going round in my head as I rang the bell. I had my smile all ready, but then remembered she wouldn't see it anyway!

Penny answered the door. 'Hello, Tracy,' she said, warmly.

'Hello,' I said. 'I didn't get lost today so I'm on time.'

'Yes, you are,' she said, laughing slightly. I wasn't sure what was funny but laughed with her as she turned and called over her shoulder, presumably to Marilyn, that I was there.

As I stepped inside, Penny turned back to me. 'Marilyn's not quite ready at the moment,' she said, 'so do come in and make yourself at home, and she'll be down soon.'

'I expect she's writing a song,' I thought as I began to slide my jacket off. I was just walking into the lounge when I heard something. I glanced up the stairs and there was Marilyn coming down. I had expected her to look posh like at the concert, but she was wearing her dressing gown and, to my horror, was covered in blood. Her head was bleeding and her dressing gown was red too. My heart began to race; she'd obviously had a terrible accident and I was useless at first aid. She reached the bottom of the stairs and was moving towards me, hand outstretched and smiling. How could she smile? She must be in a lot of pain. I shook her hand and it was only then that I noticed she had a plastic bag on her head. What on earth? And then the penny dropped: this was not blood, it was dye – Marilyn had dyed her hair!

'Oh, my goodness, you've dyed your hair, I thought it was blood!' I exclaimed as a wave of relief swept over me.

Marilyn looked puzzled. 'Blood? Why would dye look like blood?' She threw back her head and laughed. She looked so funny with the streaks of dye running down her face that I began to laugh too and soon we were both helpless. The whole situation was just so different to what I'd expected that I was totally thrown. We went into the lounge and Marilyn launched immediately into an explanation. She was still laughing as she shared how Penny had told her how late I'd been before, so Marilyn didn't think I'd arrive for another hour. Her assistant, Morfudd, had told her never to dye her own hair.

'But that made me all the more keen to try,' Marilyn said, emphatically. 'I didn't think it would take so long, though. It took ages! I'd wanted to try henna because I'd heard it was good for hair and I'd read that people used it in Bible times.'

As I watched this laughing, blind woman, covered in red goo yet completely unabashed, I felt a surprising rush of affection for her. This wasn't a famous singer up on a spiritual pedestal; this was Marilyn, just an ordinary, fun-loving lady having an adventure with dying her hair.

Penny was trying to get our attention to come and have dinner but I suddenly thought of something. 'What time do you have to get this stuff off?' I asked.

Marilyn screamed as she checked her watch. 'Oh no, I completely forgot! It's meant to come off after twenty minutes!'

She jumped up and ran for the door. 'Do you want some help?' I called and then followed her upstairs.

I stopped at the bathroom door. I could tell it was usually blue but now . . . Every surface was covered in blobs of red dye. I began to laugh again as I helped her slide her dressing gown off. The dye was all down her back and even on her bra . . . Eventually both Marilyn and the bathroom were clean of dye. Happy at the transformation, I suddenly noticed her toothbrush, which was standing in a cup on the sink. A big dollop of dye was caught in it so I quickly rinsed it off.

Marilyn was just coming out of her bedroom as I left the bathroom. She had dried her hair; and I was relieved to see that, while definitely much more auburn, it wasn't anywhere near the red of the globs that had covered everything. Now that she was cleaned up and dressed properly, she looked much more the Marilyn Baker I'd expected to meet.

'You nearly ended up looking like Dracula,' I said. 'Your toothbrush was dyed too – but all OK now!'

Soon we were both laughing again. Penny got the dinner out which, like before, had been waiting a long time. The rest of the evening went quickly as we giggled about the dye catastrophe. It was a happy time and I didn't need to use any of those spiritual topics I'd rehearsed earlier. In fact, we didn't mention God once, but I've never been in a social situation in which God has been more present.

When I got home, Debs and Sian were eager to hear how my evening with Marilyn had been.

'It was fantastic,' I said. 'I spent the entire evening cleaning dye off her!' Their mouths dropped open and it hit me afresh how differently this evening had turned out. I'd put Marilyn on a pedestal, feeling I'd never reach her level of spirituality, but I'd made a lovely new friend. I'd thought she would only want to talk about God but she'd hardly mentioned him, yet he was shining out from her in all the fun, laughter and love that I saw in her that night.

I didn't realise then just how much God was in every detail of what took place that evening. Even me being so late when I'd first visited Penny was part of his plan, because it made Marilyn think she had time to dye her hair before I arrived. If the dye catastrophe hadn't happened, our meeting would have been much more conventional and our friendship may not have happened at all. As I went to bed, all I knew was that I'd loved meeting Marilyn and the whole encounter had lifted me out of my depression about Chorleywood College. But it was only later that I discovered just how significant that evening had truly been.

Marilyn

When Penny told me she'd asked Tracy if she'd like to come for a meal, I was excited because a couple of years before I'd lost a very dear friend, Maureen, who was nearly blind and deaf. She was like a sister to me. She'd been living in an old people's home though she was only 28, and Torch Trust put me in touch with her. She would come to my house to do my cleaning and loved that I was giving her responsibility, as she felt no one trusted her. She'd died suddenly after a severe epileptic fit, and now I loved the idea of meeting someone else who was deaf, as I had loved communicating with Maureen. Would I be able to do so successfully with Tracy?

To my consternation, she arrived earlier than I expected. I had read references in the Song of Solomon about henna and knew it was meant to be good for your hair so I decided to put some on mine. Morfudd had warned me it would make a mess, but I thought I could manage it. Then the doorbell rang. What should I do, come down or stay hidden upstairs? I wanted to meet Tracy so much and decided I would come down in my dressing gown and be done with it.

I loved Tracy from the moment I met her. She was such fun, and we laughed so much about my hair – in fact we laughed most of the evening! After her visit I couldn't wait for her to come over again. I could tell we were going to be great friends.

Testimonies

I had them to stay with us and found them such easy guests – and such fun! Marilyn sang and Tracy talked. They came to the Methodist boarding school and had us all singing to each other: 'God Has a Plan for You'; they came to the ladies' group and they came to our church. Marilyn has a gift of presenting God's love in everyday language – and putting it to music. Tracy's testimonies reached people too. Lives were changed. Since then I have heard and spoken with Marilyn and Tracy many times . . . but I will never forget that wonderful weekend.

Valerie

12

A Growing Friendship

I'm constantly amazed at what Jesus has done

Marilyn Baker[1]

After that momentous first meeting with Marilyn, I felt much lighter. I was still disappointed about Chorleywood College, but my course was still happening the following April. God had given me that verse from Isaiah: 'Lead out those who have eyes but are blind, who have ears but are deaf' so every time the doubts came in, I declared it. I asked him to show me what I could do now it was not possible to return to the college, and for him to keep confirming his call on my life.

On further visits to Penny and Marilyn, Penny told me about Torch Trust, a lovely community of visually impaired and sighted people living in a beautiful old manor house near Market Harborough, working together with the aim of providing Christian literature in formats that blind people could read, like audio, Braille and large print. I contacted Torch and just a couple of weeks later was invited to go to visit them for a few days.

When I arrived it was almost teatime, so I made my way to the dining room. Tea was lovely and there was much chatting and laughter around the tables. I could tell that many had visual impairments, but they seemed to be playing just as big a part in setting and clearing the tables as those who could see. One lady in particular, a sighted lady, was quietly helpful to everyone and seemed very friendly. Her name was Carol Franklin. The next morning, she showed me to the big conservatory where the Braille library was housed and where I would be getting some work experience. How wonderful that books which were such an inspiration were being made available to those who couldn't read normal print. I threw myself into the work with great enthusiasm. Little did I know then that one day my own books would become part of Torch's library.

I loved my time at Torch, with its prevailing sense of acceptance and community. Everyone was significant and had a role to play. There were daily chapel times and Mum and Dad Heath, the founders of the work, were pivotal in drawing everyone together as family. To my amazement I discovered that Carol was a very close friend of Marilyn's, having lived with her prior to sensing a call from God to join Torch.

In the end, I didn't feel it was right to actually become part of the community. I went for several visits and each time found it a very enriching experience, its ethos being especially healing after all the instances of being made to feel I didn't match up.

I continued to visit Marilyn and Penny, and it was interesting to see how different they were. Penny was a very precise person and knew exactly where all her possessions were, and where a good deal of Marilyn's were too! When cooking she would place the various dishes and utensils on the work surfaces in exact places and could always locate them quickly. She knew what seasoning she wanted and added it in exact amounts. Marilyn was the opposite, and was like a whirlwind in the tiny kitchen. She frequently lost things – something she still does regularly!

At that time in the mid-eighties, personal computers were only just coming on the scene, so Marilyn's contacts and schedules were all kept on small pieces of Braille card in index file boxes. This meant that tiny bits of card were often flying all over the place as Marilyn would use one, put it down and then forget where it was! With cooking, she loved throwing different herbs and spices into the pot to get the taste she was looking for. There was no precision but there was a lot of fun, and despite their differences, Marilyn and Penny both produced really tasty meals. I found this an eye-opener, as I was a very poor cook and had no confidence at all. Living with four other friends, I did have to do my share of cooking, but it was always with a deep-down sense that others would be laughing at my efforts. My mum had been reluctant to let me help her in the kitchen, maybe because I was quite clumsy. My sister was always helping her and I would sit with my nose in a book pretending not to care.

One day I happened to say to Marilyn that I couldn't cook.

'Oh, I'm sure you can, you probably just need your confidence boosting,' she said, cheerfully.

I was doubtful, but Marilyn encouraged me to watch her and then try myself. As I watched her making a tasty sauce, she told me how she'd been a dreadful cook at school, making silly mistakes, like forgetting to put the cauliflower in the cauliflower cheese.

'I had no confidence and felt I was the world's worst cook. But one day, after leaving school, I went as a helper to a summer camp for blind and sighted children and was asked by Muriel, the lady in charge of catering, to help her in the kitchen. She was amazing,' Marilyn enthused as she added some garlic and seasoning to the sauce. 'I told her I couldn't cook, but she was just so sure I could and gave me lots of tips for how to do things without sight. After that I went to stay with her and we spent a whole day cooking up cordon bleu dishes and then invited a lot of friends to come and sample them. It was such fun! So I am sure you can do it too.'

The funny thing was that although Marilyn and Penny encouraged me to have a go, they couldn't actually see what I was doing! That made a real difference, as it lifted off all my anxiety about being watched and judged.

I wondered how they managed to do the shopping with both being blind. Penny had a lovely guide dog called Isla, a chocolate brown Labrador, and so she would go with Isla to Sainsbury's or to a small strip of local shops. Marilyn didn't have a guide dog. She would go out with her assistant Morfudd or with other friends, but not on her own, as she found the long cane difficult to use. Marilyn also had a very bad back and I felt concerned as I saw how much pain she was in. It was hard for her to walk, so although she loved shopping, she hardly ever went into town.

One day she needed a haircut, and as Morfudd wasn't free, she asked if I could go with her. We needed to go by bus and it was actually the first time I had walked for any distance with Marilyn, or with any blind person for that matter. I felt nervous, but from my experience at Chorleywood knew that Marilyn needed to hold my arm and that I would walk slightly ahead. We got into town OK but it was very busy. In crowded situations, my uneven way of walking can be problematic, and I found I was weaving around rather as I tried to allow for Marilyn as well as me when passing people. Suddenly going off balance, I veered to the side, and of course Marilyn did too, right into the path of a tough-looking girl with a shaved head. They bumped hard into each other and the girl swore and exclaimed disgustedly: 'Blind as a bat!'

Mortified, I looked at Marilyn. 'I'm so sorry about that,' I said, but to my surprise, she was laughing. 'How can you laugh?' I exclaimed. 'Doesn't it hurt you when people say horrid things like that?'

'Well, she had no idea that I was really blind, did she?' Marilyn laughed. 'She'd have been jolly shocked if she'd looked properly.'

Seeing Marilyn react with humour to something that would have upset me had a profound effect. I spent so much time agonising over what people might think of me that her reaction was like a beam of light. I wanted to be able to laugh at things rather than be crushed by them, and be able to see the bigger picture. It was amazing how something as mundane as bumping into someone could become such a channel of illumination.

As I was now unemployed, I was delighted when I saw an advert in the local paper for Christmas workers at the Watford post office depot. It was for evening shift work, and I would travel there and back on the bus. I had recently moved to Garston, a suburb of Watford and was sharing with Sian, Debs and Sarah. The house was about four miles away from the depot, and on the first day I was amazed to realise that the bus stop home was near Marilyn's. The next day Marilyn invited me for tea before work. We had a great time with lots of laughs and the work went well too.

I felt happy as I arrived at the bus stop to return home. Traffic was still busy and people were walking past. At 10.30 p.m. I checked my watch. The bus was due to arrive any second. Five minutes later still no bus, and the street had grown strangely quiet. Suddenly I felt a touch on my arm and jumped as I hadn't heard anyone approach. I turned round, squinting in the darkness. A man stood behind me, his face obscured by a cap. Just for a moment I thought he was also waiting for the bus, but then I felt his hands on my arms. Breathing fast, I tried to move away, but his grip was strong and my arms were beginning to hurt. There was still no one around. He said something unintelligible, jerking his head downwards and instinctively I followed his gaze and froze . . . It was happening again and I was paralysed by the old childhood fears.

I could hear him mumbling and his grip on my arms tightened even more. 'Lord, help me,' I prayed. He leaned in and then with an abrupt jerk, turned and walked away, rapidly disappearing into the shadows. I crashed backwards into the bus stop and caught hold of it, trying to stay upright. I felt dizzy and weak. I had to get to Marilyn's.

When I reached her road I half-ran to her house. I hung frantically on the doorbell, praying she wasn't asleep. She opened straight away as she'd been sitting on the stairs chatting on the phone. I fell inside crying as I told her I'd been attacked. I was in a state of shock, but Marilyn was great. She wrapped a blanket round me and brought me a cup of tea. Eventually I was able to tell her what had happened and we realised what a miracle it was that he'd not succeeded in hurting me. I was so thankful for Marilyn and the wonderful care she gave me. I couldn't bear to think what I would have done if I hadn't been able to go to her. I had no idea why he'd walked away so suddenly, but I was OK, shaken but not harmed and that was what I needed to focus on.

The next day I felt much better. I'd reported the incident to the police but was told there was little they could do as I couldn't describe the man, other than his height and build.

Later that day I heard two things that really gave me a new understanding of the power of prayer. I popped into Amanda's and she immediately asked if I was OK. I was confused, as I didn't think the story would have spread yet. I soon realised that she knew nothing about the attack, but God had put an urgency on her heart to pray for me last night. 'I was dozing but suddenly woke with a start knowing I should pray for your protection. So I prayed there and then until I felt it lift from me.'

'What time was that?' I asked.

'I guess it was around 10.45 and I prayed for about fifteen minutes. What was happening?'

I told Amanda about the attack and she was overwhelmed, realising that when she'd prayed would have been around the point he'd suddenly turned and walked away.

When I got home there was more amazing news. Marilyn had called to say she'd told Morfudd what had happened and she had exclaimed how she, too, had felt a conviction to pray for me from about 10.30. This was astonishing, as Morfudd and I hardly knew each other.

I was deeply challenged by these two accounts. I was growing in my faith, but until then had had no real expectation in the power of prayer. It made me realise how important it is to hear from God and obey any promptings he may give us.

A little word for someone

As I recalled that occasion for this book, I began to have a deep sense that someone reading this feels deep pain because you, too, once experienced an assault in a public place. You've been fearful ever since and doubt God's love for you. I felt his deep compassion and desire to bring healing into that memory. He loves you with an everlasting love and is always there for you, as it says in Hebrews 13:5 (AMP):

> for He [God] has said, 'I WILL NEVER [under any circumstances] DESERT YOU [nor give you up nor leave you without support, nor will I in any degree leave you helpless], NOR WILL I FORSAKE *or* LET YOU DOWN *or* RELAX MY HOLD ON YOU [assuredly not]!

It was around this time that Marilyn told me Morfudd would be leaving after Christmas. Morfudd played guitar and harmonised with

Marilyn, so Marilyn was looking for someone similar, but despite advertising in all the local churches, no one suitable had been found. I saw the advert in my own church newsletter, and a lady from my church called Stephanie applied. She was a lovely singer and I thought she would definitely get the job, but the fit wasn't right. Marilyn said she was beginning to despair they'd ever find the right person, and it was now nearly Christmas. I asked Marilyn when her first booking was in the New Year, just so that I could be praying. She replied that it was a church service and evening concert on 5 January at the Sutton Christian Centre. She paused and then said, 'Do you think you could come with me?'

Shocked, I replied, 'What me? But I'm not musical!'

'That doesn't matter,' Marilyn said, 'but what does matter is having another lady with me. This will be the first one without Morfudd, and I'll be so grateful if you can come to help me with my clothes and just be there with me.'

I was thrown by Marilyn's request, as I'd always avoided doing public things because of my deafness and shyness. I felt even more nervous when Marilyn said I could stay with her the night before and added that she'd be having a party on the Saturday evening so I could help her with that, stay the night and travel with her to Sutton the next day. The whole idea gave me butterflies. But I did want to help Marilyn, as I could see how difficult it would be without another lady travelling with her.

Marilyn

When I was looking for a new assistant, I asked Tracy to help me interview people. One lady came from her church. We saw several people, but none seemed right. January was fast approaching, and there was no one to travel with me. So I asked if she would mind coming occasionally. She was shocked, as she'd always wanted to avoid public occasions, but I felt we would manage fine together.

13

Our First Concert

He will give you the resources of Heaven

Marilyn Baker[1]

Early in the morning on 5 January 1986, Marilyn, Ian (her sound engineer) and I set off for Sutton. Ian was driving and I sat next to him to navigate. At that point, although I'd told them that I was very short-sighted and couldn't drive, they didn't know how poor my sight really was. I'd felt embarrassed, as my lack of hearing seemed a big enough problem for people to cope with. At that time I could still read normal print and generally see, so it didn't seem a major problem – and after all, I was there to help Marilyn!

So now I sat with the map, trying my best to follow it. Marilyn was in the back with her Braille Bibles spread on the seat. It had been a chaotic departure, as first of all we'd lost a brown briefcase that held various Bible translations (called The Bible Case) and after Ian found that and we were putting our coats on ready to go, I suddenly noticed that Marilyn's dress was missing its belt. I ran upstairs but couldn't see it anywhere, so once again Ian came to the rescue, found the belt then told us firmly that if we didn't leave now, we wouldn't make it to the service!

Now I was panicking that I would get us lost. I did give a few misdirections and I think Ian soon realised that I wasn't like Morfudd, with her gift of navigation, and began to work the route out for himself. In the rush we'd had no time to put our make-up on, so we'd still need to do that when we arrived. That was challenging enough as I'd hardly ever worn make-up, let alone put it on a blind person.

I'd been shocked when Marilyn asked me just before Christmas if I could contribute to the morning service with a little thought and then give my testimony in the evening: 'I'll have over an hour's programme in the evening,' she said, 'so it'll be lovely if they can hear your testimony.'

She had smiled encouragingly, not realising the panic her query had induced. How could *I* speak? How could *I* share 'a thought'? I didn't know what kind of 'thought' she meant, or how I would do it. And how could I tell a vast group of people my story, when I'd hardly divulged it to anyone? It seemed impossible. But despite my misgivings, something made me say yes. I hadn't even been sure what the word 'testimony' meant. One of the problems of being deaf is that so many everyday terms just go over my head, so I thought a testimony was just a law term. At first I felt too embarrassed to ask, but realised how silly I was being. But even though I now understood, I still had no idea how to share one.

When we arrived at the church, the minister told us there would be a pre-service prayer meeting in the main sanctuary in fifteen minutes, so we had time to pop into the ladies to smarten up. Rather tentatively, I helped Marilyn put some foundation and blusher on, but balked at trying to do her eyes. I did my own make-up and we both brushed our hair. Marilyn came out of the loo and I checked her over before we went into the prayer meeting. She looked nice and I began to relax.

I opened the glass door into the sanctuary, and we were just about to go through when an old man came up behind Marilyn. He reached out, saying something that I couldn't hear. Marilyn went bright red and began to laugh. 'What did he say?' I asked, puzzled by her reaction. Marilyn just shook her head, still laughing. Later she told me he'd said, 'My dear, we can't have you going in like that!' Her dress was caught up in her knickers! I'd checked her from the front, but it never occurred to me to check her from behind too. No wonder she was laughing. And when I asked what he'd said, she'd thought, 'I can hardly tell Trace in a loud voice that he'd said, "Your dress is all caught up!"'

The service went well after all the hiccups. We sat at the front and I was delighted that they used worship songs that I knew, as being a fairly new Christian I wasn't familiar with many. When the pastor invited us to share, I took Marilyn to the piano, which was situated down one side of the church. It was an unusual position as it was hard for people to see her there. All that morning I'd been trying to think of a 'thought' I could bring. Suddenly an idea popped into my head to do with it being New Year. How we make resolutions, which for most of us don't last. I felt God wanted to release people from condemnation about their lives and I read some verses from Colossians 3:17: 'And whatever you do, whether in word or deed, do it all in the name of the Lord Jesus, giving thanks to God the Father through him.'

I shared how I always failed in trying to give up eating chocolate but that 'doing it in the name of the Lord and giving thanks to *him'* was a key to living our lives out of that place of closeness and intimacy with him, and then he would help us to do the best things. But when we try to change ourselves just because we feel we should, we set ourselves up for failure . . . Marilyn then sang a lovely song called 'Turn to Jesus', about letting him be the centre when we are struggling. I could see people were really being encouraged. I was delighted with how the Lord had helped us, but I still had the biggest hurdle to overcome – the concert that evening and my testimony. Even as we enjoyed lunch with our hosts, I could feel my stomach churning within me.

Then, at last, the concert was beginning. I helped Marilyn to the piano, which was now on the stage. I sat heavily in my own chair, a short way from her. The congregation stared up at us and I breathed deeply, trying to stop my legs shaking. For the first time, I was sitting in full view of a big group of people. How could I have agreed to this?

My heart hammering, I gazed out over the sea of faces. Marilyn was singing and the audience listened raptly. A deep quietness stole over the church and I felt my heart loosening. I'd not been able to hear music properly for ages, but amazingly, from here I could hear more than I'd expected. Her voice was beautiful and full of warmth, conveying God's love so powerfully that I felt close to tears.

The song ended and I clapped along with the audience. I was beginning to relax until I heard Marilyn's next words.

'Tracy will now share her testimony with us,' she said, turning round and giving a little nod, which was our prearranged sign in case I didn't hear her. The audience stared as I rose and walked towards the microphone. All I wanted was to run from the stage and never get on one again.

'Lord, please help me,' I prayed. 'I can't do this.'

As I began to speak, I tangibly felt his presence as if he was standing right next to me. A deep peace filled me, and without any plan, I found myself describing my childhood; how I'd become a prisoner of self-hatred, unable to love. I'd hardly ever admitted these things even to myself, but now the words came with real fluency. The church was still, faces turned up to me, and some were wiping their eyes. I felt a warm wave of their empathy flowing towards me. They believed me and were listening. I began to make eye contact, and was suddenly filled with a longing to tell them that God loved them and could truly heal their broken hearts. I shared the miracle of my salvation, the deep healing that was still unfolding in my life, how he was freeing me to become someone who could reach out with his love instead of hiding away; that this is what he longs to do for each one of us.

I finished and glanced at Marilyn. She began to applaud, and soon the whole church was clapping. I stood stunned as they continued, many still crying. Marilyn started singing, choosing songs full of joy and celebration. I felt like dancing: there was such a bubble of joy in my heart.

At the end the pastor came up on the stage, gesturing warmly in our direction as he spoke fervently. Although I couldn't hear him, I guessed that he was making an evangelistic appeal. 'Lord, please may they respond,' I prayed, silently. People began to rise to their feet and the hairs on my neck prickled as, one by one, they made their way to the front. The band started to play 'Amazing Grace' and tears came to my eyes as I stood and sang. I felt overwhelmed that the Lord was touching these dear people so deeply.

We later found out that more than twenty had made commitments or rededicated themselves to the Lord, and many more had responded wanting prayer or blessing.

I little knew then that what I'd considered to be a one-off was the beginning of an amazing ministry partnership that would see me taking steps I would never have dreamt possible. I'd believed I was doomed to failure, but through the power of God's love, even my darkest memories would be turned into the ability to touch others' lives with God's love.

14

The Isle of Sheppey

The people that know their God, shall be strong and do great things
Marilyn Baker[1]

In the second week of January, Marilyn asked me if I could accompany her for a week of events on the Isle of Sheppey. I was still unemployed, so I rather nervously agreed. This would be very different to the one-off event I'd done before. What would it be like staying with people I didn't know, and going into schools and prisons as well as churches?

A couple would also be travelling with us, whom Marilyn's minister John Boyers had suggested could accompany Marilyn musically from time to time. Paul Donnelly had been a session rock musician, touring with groups such as the Nolans, but had to give up after developing diabetes and tinnitus. His wife Alison, a trained singer, had become a Christian, and soon Paul did too. Although their musical style was different to Marilyn's, the combination was lovely. The Isle of Sheppey would be their first tour with Marilyn. Sometime before this, the trustees had decided that MBM now needed a van. MBM didn't have enough money, but after prayer, an amazing thing happened: Jean and Elmer Darnall offered their Toyota HiAce at a very reasonable price. They'd had it specifically converted to be a ministry vehicle and it was perfect for MBM, with a big space at the back for equipment and a middle section for the 'crew'. This was before backseat seatbelts were compulsory, and there was nothing but the wide bench-type seat to separate the passenger section from the back, so it was a very noisy and bouncy van indeed.

The day arrived for our trip and we all climbed aboard. It was the first of many fun journeys. The equipment rattled and banged as we went round corners, and the van resounded with laughter as Paul cracked jokes. Our hosts, Carol and John, were lovely. They had a big house and were able to accommodate us all. They welcomed us enthusiastically and were soon laying out what looked like a banquet. Carol asked me with a big smile what Marilyn would like to eat, but I couldn't hear her so suggested she asked Marilyn. When I discovered what she'd been saying I was surprised she'd not asked Marilyn herself, but came to re-alise that people sometimes felt nervous about approaching a blind person. I was so glad that I hadn't been able to hear Carol, as it broke the ice and enabled her to relate to Marilyn from the beginning. It was also much better for Marilyn to choose for herself, as I would have given her a somewhat smaller portion!

I was discovering the tricky side of working with Marilyn: the or-ganisers would expect me to be the one to liaise with them about the tour's details, but of course I couldn't do that and had to keep directing them to Marilyn, which was a new experience for her too.

Marilyn

Having Tracy as my helper was very different from any other assistant I'd had. I'd always been used to them knowing our itinerary and details of our accommodation. It was a great shock when I realised that or-ganisers were relaying information to Tracy that she couldn't hear. She was good at trying to guess, but not having enough sight to lip-read (everyone presumed she could) meant that she was always asking me what they'd said. I had to learn to take note of everything and then tell Tracy. It was time-consuming and tiring for both of us. Trace was out of her comfort zone, and so was I. But her ability to sense what the Lord wanted to do in our concerts and for people seemed so important.

Her testimony never failed to move people. She would read out Bible verses for me, too, and occasionally read the wrong verse! I remember one time especially, when I was giving a gentle evangelistic message to a group of people who were not regular churchgoers. Instead of the encouraging verse I had chosen, Trace started to read 'you brood of vipers . . .'[2] at which point I laughed and we quickly moved on to something else, explaining we'd got the wrong verse!

In the end I got used to assimilating information, and it has become part our lives together: I always want to explain as much as I can because her contribution to the conversations is always so relevant. I love hearing what she has to say and hate it when she can't enter in.

Tracy

In the afternoon, the event's organiser, Jeff, came to pray with us about the week's programme. He was friendly, but as he talked I became aware of a feeling of deep heaviness. I prayed quietly, asking the Lord about these strange feelings. To my surprise I sensed that it was to do with Jeff. That seemed odd, but I remembered how the day before I'd felt compelled to read some verses from Isaiah 45:2,3:

> I will go before you and will level the mountains. I will break down gates of bronze and cut through bars of iron. I will give you the treasures of darkness, riches stored in secret places, so that you may know that I am the LORD, the God of Israel, who summons you by name.

Now in the lounge as we all prayed together, I felt that God would be using the events to break through barriers of fear and darkness in people's lives and bring out 'treasures' of lives restored and set free. I shared this, and Marilyn became very excited as we all began to sense a new purpose for the week.

The timetable looked very busy. There would be concerts most evenings, three separate church services on the Sunday and various school, care home and prison visits.

On the first morning we were up very early to take a primary school assembly. Ian set up microphones and speakers and connected Paul's electric guitar too.

I felt full of butterflies as I watched the children filing in. The smallest sat on the floor just a couple of feet away, with the eldest on chairs at the back. Jeff introduced us all and then Marilyn sang a couple of her songs that she invited all the children to clap along with. She demonstrated how she wanted them to clap on the offbeat. But despite both Alison and I making a big show as to when to clap, the children did it whenever they fancied with a resulting cacophony of noise. But they enjoyed themselves and Marilyn sang as loudly as possible, trying to be heard. Paul and Alison also played some of their own jazzy songs, which the children loved.

Then Marilyn demonstrated how blindness can affect a person. She asked me to guide her around the room telling the children how a blind person needs to hold someone's arm to follow their movements. She then asked who would like to guide her. Hands shot up all over the hall, and the head teacher called out a girl of about 7. She looked so small as Marilyn took her arm, and my heart was in my mouth when, rather than taking her along the front, she tried to cut through the middle. But the children moved aside and she did really well. Everyone gave her a clap and she sat down with a huge smile.

After another song, a quieter one, which amazingly the children sat still for, Marilyn shared about the difficulty of identifying objects when you can't see. She had tins of food such as baked beans and asked how she could know what was inside. Suggestions were shouted out like, 'Look at the label!' or, 'Open and try it.' Marilyn laughed, then showed them a little magnetic label she could write Braille onto and then stick on the lid. She passed it round and soon the youngest children were having great fun trying to stick the label on each other's glasses! She described how she would feel the edge of a coin to tell what it was. A boy of about 8 came out, and we made sure his eyes were tight shut and then put a 20p piece in his hand. I was surprised at how long it took him to recognise it, but when I tried myself later on, I discovered it's much easier to see the hexagonal edges than it is to feel them.

The next demo proved the most popular and has remained so ever since. Marilyn talked about the difficulty of finding small things that fall on the floor and get buried in the carpet. She gave an example of when the two parts of her earring had flown in different directions before landing. She'd searched around but couldn't find them and was sad. So she prayed and then got on her knees and felt around again and this time found both parts straight away. She told the children they could always pray about the things that mattered to them, and God would be listening and ready to help them. She then got out the 20p piece and asked for another volunteer. A boy of about 9 came up, and Marilyn told him to shut his eyes tightly and listen hard while we threw the coin onto the floor. He would then have to search on his hands and knees to find the coin without opening his eyes.

'He will need all of your help,' Marilyn told the excited children. 'So when you see he's getting close to the coin, clap, but when he's moving away you must all hiss!'

I was amazed how Marilyn had managed to engage with this huge group of children – there was such a buzz of excitement in the room. Alison and I tied a scarf round the boy's eyes and checked he couldn't see.

'Silence now!' I called out.

I threw the coin, which went a short distance, and Alison and I helped Steven onto his hands and knees so he could feel for the coin. 'Clap or hiss to help him,' I called. In an instant they were clapping wildly as Steven's fingers drew near the coin but then hissing like a pit of snakes as he missed and turned the wrong way! I had to laugh as they were so excited by something so simple. But they got the message, and we did it three times with different children. There was a real buzz as we finished with a couple more songs. I felt excited. I found it a really positive experience and was looking forward to the rest of the week.

After lunch we were singing at an old people's home before preparing for the concert that evening. The residents were very old and hardly seemed to notice us. How could we talk meaningfully about our faith when most of them seemed to be in a different world? As the home manager introduced us, people were mumbling and moving around. Several were obviously falling asleep as Marilyn started to sing. I felt despairing and prayed that the Lord would break through all the barriers of age and sickness. It was during the second song that something began to change. Marilyn was singing 'He Gives Joy', with Alison harmonising, and some of the residents began to join in! From that moment there was a real connection, where before there'd been none. Paul and Alison sang and even I shared a little story. At the end, people were happy to shake hands and some had obviously grasped that it was all about God's love for them. The whole experience made me realise the power of prayer to bring the kingdom of heaven through every earthly barrier.

The first of the evening concerts was in a very formal church. People filed in silently and sat in the back rows first. The church building was cold and the atmosphere was grim. We'd arrived in high spirits, but it felt really weird walking into the silent church.

Everyone watched while Ian took Marilyn, Paul and Alison through their sound checks. The quiet was even more unnerving once the concert began. Marilyn tried to engage with the audience, saying how much we loved being there and how excited the schoolchildren had been. Some of the audience smiled, but there was no sense of feedback. Marilyn sang 'He's My Saviour', which would usually melt the ice, but this time, despite Marilyn demonstrating how she wanted them to clap on the offbeat, and Alison and I leading into that from the stage, only a couple of people near the back attempted to join in, and they soon petered out. At the end of the song there was dead silence, no applause, no murmurs, nothing for it but for Marilyn to plough on. What on earth was wrong?

During the interval we disconsolately grouped together in the cold vestry. No one brought us drinks, so Paul went in search of tea and coffee. At least the drinks were hot! We decided to pray, as we just didn't know how to proceed. I couldn't hear the others, but I remembered that verse about breaking 'bars of iron' and prayed that the Holy Spirit would smash through every such bar that was stopping the people from receiving God's love. Marilyn had a word about witchcraft, so we

Marilyn playing a harmonica as a child.

A prophetic picture. Marilyn singing to her teddy.

Marilyn and Tracy with Jennifer and Tony Larcombe and background guests at Hothorpe Hall, 1992.

Marilyn singing with
Carol Franklin.

Marilyn with
Paul and Alison
Donnelly at the
Isle of Sheppey,
1986.

Carol Joyce,
Marilyn and Ian
Valkeith.

Marilyn, Sharron
Pearcy (Lovelight),
Penny Misselbrook,
Carol Franklin and
Peter Emberley
(Lovelight) at
Marilyn's silver
jubilee, 2007.

Marilyn singing with
Morfudd Bowen.

Marilyn with Lovelight,
left to right: Ian,
Sharron, Pete and
Marilyn.

Marilyn singing in
Cromer Parish Church.

Marilyn with Jen
Larcombe at the
launch of the *Joy of
My Heart* album,
2019.

A kaleidescope of Marilyn's album covers and photos,
from a display.

A glimpse of some of the many articles
about Marilyn, from a display.

Marilyn presented
with her Gold Disc in
1992 for 50,000+
albums sold.

Lorraine, Tracy and Dad.

Tracy with Lorraine, Mum and Penny dog.

Tracy, Marilyn and Penny Cooze on
Marilyn's 40th birthday.

Tracy with Goldie, from Hearing Dogs for Deaf People, 2011.

Tracy, Marilyn and Giles at a Christmas houseparty.

Tracy and Marilyn rowing a boat together on Loch Lomond.

Tracy dancing as Marilyn sings, in India.

MBM Team, 1989. Back row, from left, Tracy, Chris Matthews, Trevor Houiellebecq. Front: Marilyn, and Trudy Wheeler.

Rachel Barr, our longest-standing administrator.

Tracy at *The Father's Kiss* launch with Julie Hillary.

Paul Wood, Marilyn, Tracy and Giles.

Fun at conferences: Lilian Wild with Tracy, Marilyn and Pennie dog.

Marilyn and Tracy in 2014 – Tracy's 50th birthday makeover pictures.

prayed against that. Paul began to play his guitar and suddenly our feelings of defeat lifted and we knew the Lord was with us. Marilyn asked if I could share my testimony and if Paul could end with an evangelistic message.

After that it was time for the second half, and the first thing we noticed was the warmth. The heating had been turned on and it made such a difference. The minister smilingly announced that we were starting again and told people to take their seats. I could see them leaning forward, ready to listen. That was so different! Marilyn had planned to start with a quiet song, but she changed her mind and announced her one and only rock and roll song called 'Build Up Treasures'. With Marilyn hammering on the keyboard accompanied by the drum backing track and Paul playing guitar, the sound was authentically loud! People visibly relaxed, tapping their feet and jigging around. At the end they applauded for the first time. An iron bar had been broken down. The Lord was at work.

After a much quieter song, Marilyn asked me to share my testimony, so I shared how God had started healing me after I asked him into my life. I could sense people's responsiveness and then Marilyn sang 'Arms of Love'. Suddenly I had an amazing picture of Jesus walking through the rows of people, gently touching their hearts and releasing them to feel again. I was astonished how different the atmosphere was now. The first half had felt as if we were trying to communicate through a wall of ice. But now people clapped at the end of each item, and I even saw some wiping their eyes. Could our little time of prayer have really made so much difference?

At the end of the concert, Paul gave a powerful evangelistic message and invited people to raise their hands if they wanted to become Christians. To my great delight, I saw about three hands go up. Paul prayed and asked people to come and tell us if they had asked Jesus into their lives, and then the concert was over. I felt a buzz of joy as we returned to Carol and John's. We had felt so powerless, yet as we prayed and shared the truths of God's love, something significant had taken place. I understood, as never before, that it's all to do with God's power, not ours. It was a lesson I am still learning today.

The week in the Isle of Sheppey passed quickly, each day full with different events and experiences. John and Carol were such loving hosts, cooking amazing meals and doing all they could to ensure we were comfortable. As well as the events, there were many fun times together, like when I said to Alison that I loved to see her and Marilyn singing and wished I could hear enough to sing myself. She told me about her music college training, and how they were taught to place something large like a plate behind an ear in order to get a true perspective of how their voices sounded. She wondered if that method would help me hear my own voice. I asked Carol for a dinner plate, saying I wanted it to try singing. She looked most surprised and even more so when I held it behind my ear. Then sitting at the table, Alison and I began to sing together. I was full of excitement, thinking that my voice must now sound as beautiful as hers. Alison was very diplomatic, saying it could be good if I spent time practising!

It was on the Isle of Sheppey that I had my first of what would be many prison visits. We were asked to sing at a men's prison and had to say beforehand exactly what we'd take in with us. When we first arrived at the security gate, we had to give all our details, which were then entered into a database. We were given passes and the security guard came to escort us through to the chapel. It was quite scary. Two burly officers were standing by the first door and they had to go through our identification again, even though they must have seen us giving it just minutes before. Once they'd checked it, they then frisked us. I found it unnerving, as I'd never even travelled abroad before, so had never been body-searched.

At last they opened the door, using a huge bunch of jangling keys. I was shocked to find we were just in a tiny area about the size of a lift. We all crowded in, and it wasn't until the first door had been locked that the officer took out his keys to the next door. It brought home to me that we were entering a different existence, one that was so foreign to me but for so many was their daily experience.

It was a relief when we eventually reached the chapel. That at least looked like a typical place of worship, and I began to relax. We used the chapel piano and Ian soon connected a small system of amplifier, speakers and mics. We prayed together and then the inmates arrived.

The first thing I noticed was that they were all wearing a kind of prison uniform: blue dungarees and blue sweatshirt. I don't know why, but that really impacted me as I realised that, once in prison, they all had to fit into the prison system. They couldn't be individuals even in their dress, and certainly not in their life choices.

The men sat in the chairs, quietly waiting. With my background, I was always a bit nervous around men. I was expecting these particular men to be derisive, and felt very vulnerable. But after the chaplain introduced us, the men clapped and focused on Marilyn as she began to speak. I felt amazed at their attentiveness. She asked them to clap on the offbeat in her first song and they all did. I could tell they were clearly enjoying themselves, and at the end they applauded loudly. I realised that these were just ordinary men whom God loved.

Suddenly I sensed him whispering, 'Share how I empowered you to forgive.' Forgiveness? I hadn't expected to share about something so emotive in front of male prisoners, yet I knew God had spoken to me. My heart was in my mouth as I spoke about my past, and how God had drawn me to know his love and had begun to take away my shame. Looking at their attentive faces, I told how he'd asked me to forgive my stepfather and not to hold onto my hatred any more, as it would destroy me. I shared how one day when I'd gone home after becoming a Christian, my stepfather had shouted at me, slamming out of the room and catching his hand in the door, badly cutting his fingers. Then, even as I'd stood gloating, I'd felt the Lord whispering, 'Now's your chance to show your forgiveness is real – love him!' I told them how, with God's strength, I was able to sit him down, bandage his hand and make him a cup of tea.

As I spoke, I could tell the men were listening. I had forgotten this incident and felt amazed that it had just popped into my mind as I talked. I looked around the chapel, trying to make eye contact. Could it be that some of these had turned to crime out of life traumas? As Marilyn started to sing, I was shocked to see that some of the men were crying. God was at work, and I prayed that they would find his love and be empowered to live differently.

Over the years since, we have been to many prisons, from high security ones like the notorious West Wing at Durham prison to young people's correctional centres. We have shared God's love with seasoned criminals, young offenders, and men and women who have got trapped in addictions. Everyone's story is different. Once, at a high security prison, a man gloated as he shared the adrenalin rush of ram-raiding a shop, saying that there was nothing like it, and that it was better than any drug. I felt shaken when he told us how it made you feel powerful like God and that you could do anything you wanted. How could we answer him? He was so full of it, but he was silenced when Marilyn told him that the power of God in his life would be even more fulfilling, and would turn his life around rather than imprisoning him.

At this same prison, another man cried as he told us how he'd lost his job and was desperately trying to pay his bills. I felt moved as he shared how he'd started stealing in order to buy his children Christmas presents and then realised how his actions had made things so hard for his family. He was full of regret. We talked to him about God's love and forgiveness. He was receptive and we could only pray that God would reach him.

Back in 1986, as the week at Sheppey drew to a close, we saw more and more how the Lord could use the combination of music, testimony and prayer ministry to bring deep release and healing to hurting people. In one concert where I'd shared my testimony of inner healing, a lady came up at the end. She seemed to be struggling to get to us, as if her body was in conflict with her desire. When we asked her if she wanted prayer, she couldn't speak but folded over onto herself as if trying to hide. Marilyn and I had started to learn finger spelling for the deafblind, so I wrote on Marilyn's hand that the lady couldn't speak. Marilyn wrote back, 'Let's just pray.' We prayed for the Holy Spirit to come in power. The word 'rape' suddenly dropped into my mind, so I gently prayed that the Lord would free her from any sexual trauma. To our shock, she leapt up and started leering and swearing at us and tearing at her clothes, as if to pull them off. People around were staring and we needed to quickly deal with this demonic manifestation.

With God-given authority, Marilyn commanded all violating spirits to leave and declared that the lady was covered by the blood of Jesus. The lady jerked violently and collapsed on the floor. We continued praying and declaring Bible truths that she was clean and pure in God's eyes, and his beloved daughter. A look of great peace came over her face and when she got up a few minutes later, she was a different woman. A very significant deliverance had taken place, and I remembered how, when I first became a Christian, I'd received such prayer myself, which had been greatly instrumental to me becoming more whole. I'd never thought I'd be praying for others in that way, but the Lord had led so clearly that we'd just had to lift up the power of Jesus' precious blood and he did the work.

The next day a lady called Jean came to us wanting prayer about problems in her marriage. She was chatty and thankful for our time, and we prayed about the issues she shared. I was just thinking that the prayer time was over when Marilyn said, 'I keep getting the feeling that the Lord wants to release you from conflict.' Jean's head whipped up and her hands were in fists as she leapt up and screamed, 'Conflict?' Our mouths dropped open, but Marilyn realised instantly that this was another satanic stronghold and prayed in tongues before commanding the spirit of conflict to go. Alison worshipped out loud and the Lord gave me names of other areas that Jean needed release from. As we spoke against rage and control, her reactions were beyond aggressive, but as soon as we spoke out the name of Jesus, the evil power would be broken. It was awesome and made me realise how powerful the name of Jesus is and how great is the privilege he has given us to work in partnership with him to set the captives free.[3]

On the final evening, Jeff came round to thank us and we had a prayer time together. I said how beautiful it had been to see the Lord fulfilling that verse about breaking 'bars of iron'. Suddenly Jeff began to cry as he shared how depressed he'd become prior to our visit. He said all the churches in the area were locked into conflict, and he hadn't felt he could continue. 'I was going to get through this week and then resign,' he said, 'but that's changed now; your coming has softened people's hearts. The churches are discovering "the joy of the Lord"[4] again, and so am I.'

We were humbled and overwhelmed. We'd felt so weak, and doing a tour together was new for us all, but God was in charge. He truly had smashed down the 'bars of iron' and brought out the 'treasures of darkness'.

15

Off to Yorkshire

Seek and you will find Me

Marilyn Baker[1]

A few weeks after our return from the Isle of Sheppey, Marilyn asked if I could travel with her and Ian to Yorkshire. I was excited as I'd never been there before. I loved the James Herriot stories and couldn't wait to see the Dales that he'd made so famous.[2]

I needed to find us suitable outfits for the concerts and church services. It was mid-winter and a particularly cold one, too. As I rifled through Marilyn's wardrobe, my heart sank. All her 'posher' clothes seemed to be thin, and unsuitable for freezing weather. Well, I guessed she was used to it, as she'd been travelling for several years. I shrugged as I chose the warmest options. My own wardrobe wasn't much better. I was only just out of college, so most of my clothes were cheap and cheerful.

It began to snow soon after leaving Watford, and the further north we drove, the harder the snow fell. It was hard driving for Ian. The traffic slowed to a crawl and we wondered if we'd need to turn back, but we were stuck, so all we could do was slowly creep on. Eventually we arrived at our first destination, Harrogate. When we got out of the van, our feet sank into thick, crisp snow. I'd hardly experienced deep snow before, but of course it was freezing cold.

I was relieved to see the vicar, Simon, coming out to welcome us into the large traditional Anglican church where we'd be singing that night. I was desperate to get warmed up, but to my dismay the church seemed almost as cold inside as out! Simon seemed oblivious to the cold, but it was all I could think of as he showed Marilyn and me into a dark vestry to get changed. The only heating was via a tiny fan heater in the corner. I'd hoped for a lovely hot meal, but with us being so late we only had time for a quick cuppa and a sandwich.

I really hoped there'd be some heating on when the concert began. Shivering, I pulled on my tights and changed into my skirt and blouse, then laid out Marilyn's outfit. But when I said it was her turn to change, I discovered a rebellious side of Marilyn that I'd not met before.

'What on earth is this you're giving me?' she exclaimed. 'It's the middle of the winter and snowing! You must be mad if you think I'm going to wear that silly, thin blouse.'

'But all your smart clothes are like that, so you haven't got any choice,' I protested. 'Mine are the same, so it's not just you.'

'I don't care what yours are like. It's up to you if you want to freeze, but I'm not changing. Everyone will be wearing thick winter coats, so why should I have to shiver in a blouse?'

I could see Marilyn's point, but then the audience wouldn't be singing in front of everyone. I started to say that being in public meant you needed to look smart whatever the temperature, but one look at her mutinous expression and I knew that Marilyn wouldn't be budging! Sighing, I changed back into my jeans and sweatshirt. There was no point me getting sacrificially dressed up if Marilyn was in her coat! I had to admit it felt wonderful to get 'proper' clothes on again. At least we could put on some make-up and smarten our hair.

Marilyn was right, of course, that the audience were all snugly wrapped up in hats, mittens and thick coats. I was probably the only one concerned that we weren't wearing our glad rags.

The concert began and although the heating was now on, the air was still frigid. Marilyn was playing a grand piano but that seemed to be suffering from the cold too, because the pedal had a terrible squeak which even I could hear.

Marilyn sang some lively songs and encouraged everyone to clap along to get warmed up. I found it amazing how the audience literally did warm up, not just physically but in their responsiveness. By the third song they were laughing at the stories and clapping with enthusiasm. God was melting hearts and as Marilyn began to sing 'Whenever You're Lonely', I could see that many connected with the words: 'life that's just an empty space with memories you can't forget...' It had a catchy chorus:

Whenever you're feeling lonely, whenever you're sad,
Just come to the Saviour and he will make you glad.[3]

Everyone joined in, singing enthusiastically. I felt a deep joy welling up within me as I gazed around. Gone was my concern about what people might think of us being in casual clothes. I realised that our message and the spirit in which it was communicated were so much more important than what we were wearing. God was there, touching people in their hearts. These were tough Yorkshire people who didn't easily show emotion, but now I could see some wiping away tears or gripping their neighbour's hands. God's love was flowing. I'd felt exasperated when Marilyn had refused to change, but seeing the conviction shining in her face as she sang, I was full of wonder, realising that the reality of God's love was so much more important than a posh dress.

We were staying overnight with Simon and his family, and I felt a bit self-conscious about my deafness and the possibility of making silly mistakes while trying to communicate. Jane, Simon's wife, warmed up the meal in readiness for our return, and it was lovely to have hot food. It was late, so she showed us to our rooms straight after dinner. The heating was off, and being a vicarage, the house felt freezing. We got undressed as quickly as possible and dived under our duvets.

In the morning, I was slightly thrown to find a teenage boy in a wheelchair at the dining table. 'This is our son, Harvey,' Jane announced, lovingly touching Harvey's shoulder as she spoke. Harvey grimaced, rolled his head and garbled something unintelligible. He was severely disabled and couldn't do anything for himself. I helped Marilyn to cereal and toast and watched covertly as Jane combined serving us with feeding Harvey and helping him to drink. Having experienced mockery about my own disabilities, I felt moved at the respectful way she worked with her son. After Harvey's carer arrived, Jane and Simon shared how he'd been diagnosed with profound disabilities as a baby. Jane cried, remembering a healing conference where they'd asked for prayer for Harvey and the beautiful way the team had gathered round him.

'We feel sure the Lord is going to heal him,' Simon said. 'We pray for him every day and claim God's promise. It will be so wonderful to see him walk.'

I felt their pain, and was challenged by their faith and commitment to their son, despite his severe disabilities. 'Can I have a photo of Harvey?' I asked. 'I'd like to be praying and keeping in touch.' They gladly gave me one. It felt such a privilege to be part of this caring family for a short while.

We drove back to the church with Simon to collect his car, as he'd travelled in our van the night before. We got out to say goodbye to some church folk. I was guiding Marilyn when suddenly there was a thump. Simon had slipped on some hidden ice and was sitting in the road. I let go of Marilyn and, forgetting she had no idea what had happened, rushed back to help Simon, but then realised that Marilyn was floundering without anyone to guide her. I still had so much to learn. It was obvious to me what had happened and why I'd rushed back, but my first priority had to be Marilyn. Just telling her 'Simon's fallen' would have been enough to put her in the picture. I prayed the Lord would help me become much more aware.

The next concert was also in a large, traditional building but was much warmer than the night before. We arrived in good time and the meal was cooked at the church, so it was a joy to sit around the large table with about fifteen others and get to know each other over a tasty dinner. I was beginning to enjoy being the 'visiting speaker' and the recipient of such lovely meals. The vestry was beautifully heated and

Marilyn changed into her concert clothes without demur. It was nice to feel that we actually looked the part, but I didn't forget the awareness the Lord had given me of what was most important.

Before I travelled with Marilyn, I thought that the concerts would all be similar in style, with Marilyn singing the same songs and sharing the same stories. But even though she did use the same songs, the emphasis was different on each occasion, and what really challenged me was how Marilyn expected the Lord to show her what to bring. Last night it had been the Lord's comfort and the reality of his ever-present help, but tonight she strongly felt that she needed to reach out to non-Christians. I was moved as she told of finding faith as a teenager when she was grieving the loss of her grandmother and her struggle to understand how Jesus could have been God. The atmosphere was electric as she shared about a book called *The Overwhelming Proof of the Divinity of Jesus* coming all the way from the USA to her boarding school with her name on the address label. 'How was it possible?' she asked. 'That book must have been posted before I prayed, when I didn't even know anyone in the USA. Only God could bring about something like that.'

As Marilyn continued, I could tell how engaged the audience were, obviously hanging onto her words. I hadn't heard her share this story before, and it brought home a verse in Isaiah 65:24: 'Before they call, I will answer'. I found it really inspiring to think how well God knows us, and acts to answer our prayers.

After the interval, I shared how God used even the deeply painful things of my life to draw me into a realisation that he loved me. I was getting a bit more relaxed about speaking now, following the Isle of Sheppey tour, but it was still hard to share so personally. I suddenly had a deep sense that someone's dad had left them when they were young, and although a Christian, they found it hard to trust that God would always be there for them. I wasn't quite sure how to bring this thought, so I tacked it onto the end of my testimony. The audience clapped as I sat down and Marilyn started singing a lovely song that she just called 'Jesus', explaining that it had been written by her friend

Lou Lewis (née Hayles) whose life had been in a mess but was turned around when she became a Christian.

I was captivated by the song's pathos, and when Marilyn prayed a simple prayer of commitment at the end, I was sure many had responded. We came down from the stage and people immediately began to crowd around. One lady tapped me on the arm and when I turned to her, she was in tears.

'I was the one whose dad left,' she said.

I couldn't hear her properly but knew she was responding to my word. 'God loves you and wants to be a Father to you and make up for what you didn't have with your dad,' I said to her. She nodded and squeezed my arm before moving away so someone else could come. I was so glad I had shared that God-given insight.

An excitable lady pushed through the crowd. She had a camera in her hands and kept telling people to move back so she could take a picture of Marilyn, Ian and me.

'You're coming back to us next year,' she proclaimed. 'We need a photo of you with your team for the publicity. The picture you sent for this event was with Morfudd!'

'Take one of me and Ian, then,' Marilyn replied. 'There's no point including Tracy, as she's not going to be with me. She's just helping out until she starts her course.'

'Ee, I don't know, Marilyn, you get through your assistants like shelling peas, don't you!' she laughed.

Marilyn laughed too, but she told me later that the words had really made her think. For the first time since starting her ministry, she'd felt the joy of sharing the spiritual burden of the concerts with someone else. I couldn't sing or play guitar, and certainly couldn't drive her to events. But could it be that I was part of the 'something new' that the trustees had felt prophetically? However, Marilyn knew I had my heart set on my course. She'd just have to keep praying that the Lord brought the right person to be her assistant before I moved on.

Unknown to Marilyn, I was also thinking hard. The truth was, I felt a deep joy in knowing God was helping me to hear him and to share about his love. I could hardly believe it was me standing at the front speaking, yet it was. I wished I didn't have to leave. I wished I could have been in that picture too. But I knew Marilyn really needed a musician to take Morfudd's place.

When we got back to our hosts and were getting ready for bed, Marilyn suddenly asked me if I was enjoying the travelling and if I'd ever consider officially joining the team? I was shocked. My mind had been swirling round so much, I could hardly believe she'd expressed what I was thinking. I explained haltingly how happy being part of her ministry for that short time had made me feel, and that I couldn't imagine anything else bringing me that same joy. Suddenly I saw, to my shock, that she had tears in her eyes.

'I can't believe it,' she said, struggling to get her voice. 'I'd been feeling since Sheppey that I wished it could be you, but I knew you had your heart set on the course. Now you say you've been feeling the same thing!' She threw her head back, laughing. 'This is amazing!' she said. 'But are you sure this is what you want to do? Joining a small ministry is very different to starting a career.'

Feeling a roar of wonder growing inside me, I laughed and squeezed her hand. I couldn't believe Marilyn felt the same, but it seemed she did.

'The management group will have to decide if its right,' she said, 'as I'm not sure what they will feel about two of us having disabilities. I will talk to them when we get home and let you know.'

A few days after our return, Marilyn asked me to visit. 'The management group want to meet you officially,' she said, 'but they are happy for you to join us, if we also employ someone else to keep things organised and act as road manager.' I was stunned as I was sure they'd say no! Marilyn also spoke to my church leaders, and John and Amanda. I wasn't sure how the church would feel about me joining a ministry when I was so young a Christian, but to my surprise they totally endorsed it and invited Marilyn to come one Sunday, where they laid hands on us both and commissioned us together.

A few days later, Marilyn, Penny and I went to a lovely local pub to celebrate – our first of many happy visits to come. I felt overwhelmed at all that God had done. Just three years before, in 1983, I'd been so desperate I'd tried to take my life. Now God had not only saved me and set me on a path of restoration, but he'd opened the door to me sharing his love with others. Even as we talked and laughed over our meal, I prayed that I would grow deeper in his love and become a true channel for other broken people to find him.

After I'd been interviewed and officially became Marilyn's personal assistant, they started advertising for someone to be the road manager. Carol Joyce applied and came to meet Marilyn, who gave her a simple lunch. I wasn't there at the time but had to smile afterwards, as apparently all the food was perfect, but when she offered Carol a drink of what she thought was orange, Carol said, 'Er . . . I don't think I can drink that!' The orange turned out to be cooking oil!

Carol was lovely, good fun and stylish and just a couple of years older than I was. It was immediately obvious that she was the right person for the job. She was working in an accountant's office at the time and was an excellent secretary, but also a very committed Christian. Taking quite a drop in salary, she moved from Buckinghamshire to Watford to join MBM and started sharing the church-owned house where Morfudd lived and where the MBM office was also based. Carol helped the office administrator, who was Ian's wife, and also liaised with the event organisers as we travelled around. As my balance was poor, it also became Carol's role to help Ian load and unload the equipment at each event. At that time, this equipment, including a large mixer in an even larger flight case, was all housed in Marilyn's little music room at the back of her lounge. Sometimes we didn't get home until 2 a.m. and poor Ian and Carol would have to try to get everything out of the van and into the house!

Soon after this, our administrator decided to move on from MBM in order to study for a music degree. A lovely lady from Marilyn's church, Trudy Wheeler, was perfect for the job and started working part-time.

At that time, we had several concerts each week. Some were in large halls, others were with small groups or in care homes and prisons. We also did big tours each year with Lovelight and went to Austria and Scotland with WEC International to help with their house parties for retired missionaries. On one occasion in Austria, we got separated from the group when on a trip to Grossglockner and suddenly found ourselves walking across a narrow glacier! No one else was around; the path was covered in ice and there was a sheer drop on our left down into the ravine. It was terrifying, but somehow we got across safely. God must have sent his angels to protect us!

Some amazing letters came to the house with stories of how people's lives were being touched by Marilyn's songs. For example, Gerry told us how he'd become an alcoholic after his wife died. He was self-destructing, but a friend gave him 'He Gives Joy'. Gerry wrote of how he cried and cried as he listened to that track; he suddenly understood that God was there with him, loving him. He said all his craving for drink lifted, and not long after, he gave his heart to the Lord and his life was turned around. Later we heard he'd remarried – a lovely Christian lady. We were amazed and humbled.

Another letter had us in tears. Clare was writing from prison where she was serving a life sentence. She shared her story of terrible childhood abuse and then marrying someone equally abusive. She told how something snapped inside her one day when her husband was in a drunken stupor, and she lit a small fire to give him a shock. She was sure she could put it out, but it took hold so quickly that he died, and tragically so did her 11-year-old daughter. Clare told us how in her despair she was going to kill herself on Christmas Eve but someone sent her one of Marilyn's tapes, and as she listened to a track about God's forgiveness, she heard a voice saying, 'You can begin again,' and suddenly knew she did not want to die any more. Soon after that she became a Christian. We were so moved, and became her pen friends. We visited her in prison on several occasions, and later she wrote to tell us of an amazing dream in which she'd met the Lord and finally come to know that she was totally loved and forgiven.

Testimonies

I first came into contact with Marilyn Baker Ministries in the late 1980s. There was a youth outreach event at the Imperial Rooms in Matlock and I was running the bookstall. On walking into the building, the atmosphere was electric and there was such a sense of excitement as people came in. This atmosphere continued throughout the whole evening, and Marilyn's singing was amazing. Tracy spoke at the meeting as she had recently joined Marilyn in her ministry. Since then I have been on three retreats run by Marilyn and Tracy, with my dear friend, Bernice. We have some wonderful memories of such precious times of learning and worship and have met some lovely people.

Eileen

Part 4

Glimpses of a Growing Picture

In the following chapters, the chronological style will change as we look into different threads of our lives and ministry together. The timeline may suddenly change, team members and dogs will come and go; we may live in Watford at one moment, then Tonbridge the next! Stay with us and be drawn into our moments of weakness, of joy, of connection, tears and laughter, and discover through these glimpses, our wonderful God who is weaving the threads together to create a beautiful tapestry in us all.

16

The Joy of the Bible Festivals

He is the rock on which you can stand

Marilyn Baker[1]

'Do you know of Spring Harvest?' Marilyn asked me one day.

'Oh yes,' I said. I'd been with friends from college in my second year as a Christian. It had been a great time, and I remembered sitting in the big top with thousands of other Christians and my heart had been stirred to truly make God central in my life.

Now we were going as part of the team. Marilyn would sing in the Big Top celebrations and in the After Hours entertainment, and we would be visiting all the sites, from Minehead, to Skegness, to Pwllheli – a tour of huge proportions!

On the first night, I found it overwhelming to sit on the stage of the Big Top with all the 'celebrities'. But many of them came up to greet Marilyn and were so welcoming to Carol and me too. I began to relax.

Graham Kendrick and other singers led worship and there was an intoxicating buzz in the atmosphere. The drums were powerful, the music exhilarating. Marilyn would sing a couple of songs at the end of the worship and I wondered how it would go down, as her style was so much gentler. Carol took Marilyn to the keyboard and the auditorium fell silent as she said how delighted she was to be there. She then began to sing one of her classic songs: 'God Has a Plan for You'. I'd hoped she would do a livelier song to follow on from the previous musicians, but she believed this was the right song, feeling that some people were insecure in their relationship with God and fearful about their futures.

The audience was so still that even I could hear the beauty of the melody and God's heart speaking as she sang the chorus:

> God wants just you, yes no one else will do,
> Listen to Him call you by name . . .[2]

The sense of God's presence was electric. I could see how people in the front rows were being touched deeply and suddenly realised that God really wanted us to be ourselves, not clones of others. I'd been negatively comparing Marilyn's to the worship leaders' style, but God now wanted to minister his love and bring people into his peace. As Marilyn finished, everyone rose to their feet clapping, and many on the stage were also moved. What had counted was listening to God's heart and obeying the promptings of his Spirit. Many were blessed by that one song and later when Marilyn performed in the After Hours, there was again an overwhelming sense of his love present with us.

I've discovered over the years of attending Bible festivals that late evening events were expected to be entertainment more than ministry; they were times for people to relax after a busy day of listening to teaching. We would try to fit that bill and crack jokes and tell happy stories, only to find that God had other plans and wanted people to receive his healing love. I started sharing my testimony and listening to God for any words he might give me, and on one occasion in Skegness, so many people came up in response to words and pictures that we were still praying for them as the sound engineers worked to close the venue for the night.

One year in the late nineties as we travelled again to Spring Harvest, I was praying for inspiration for what to share that evening. Suddenly I had a strong sense that I should read 1 Peter 2:4,5:

As you come to him, the living Stone – rejected by men but chosen by God and precious to him – you also, like living stones, are being built into a spiritual house to be a holy priesthood, offering spiritual sacrifices acceptable to God through Jesus Christ.

As I reflected, a vision came to my mind of a tower that was being built. It was standing in darkness yet seemed to shine with an incandescent light. The very bricks were glowing and each had a unique colour and shape. I was overwhelmed by the tower's beauty and felt the Lord say, 'This is my dwelling place – the lives of those who love me and whom I love and died for. They are being formed into an invincible tower that is called by my name and will reveal my glory in the darkest places.'

I thought, 'These must be very special bricks for the Lord to use them.' The picture changed, and I saw Jesus choosing the bricks he wanted. Far from being perfect, as I'd envisaged, he was burrowing for them in a pile of rubble. With his bare hands he tore the rubble apart for one particular brick at the bottom. This was crushed and misshapen. He said, 'This is someone who has been crushed in life.' Another cut his hands because it was jagged with broken glass. Ignoring the wounds, he cradled it tenderly, saying, 'This is someone who has been very hurt and has become hard and embittered.' Another was covered in mud. This was someone who felt completely worthless because of their sin. He held each brick gently, breathing on them and speaking softly. An amazing thing happened. The dirty and rough edges became smooth and clean and a beautiful colour emerged. He then took each one to the tower and placed it to blend in perfectly. It was incredible to see that while no two bricks were the same, yet as he set them in place they seemed to fuse together and become as one; each brick supporting and uplifting those above and around it, while in its own turn, it was also supported and uplifted.

Then I saw something that was causing Jesus great grief. Some bricks began to jump out of the tower. One said, 'I'm too ugly.' Others said, 'We don't want to be in the tower, we are strong and beautiful and want to be where we can most glorify God.'

Jesus wept as he picked them up. 'Can't you see what I am doing?' he asked. 'The tower is beautiful because it's made up of so many unique bricks, all supporting each other. On your own you are just one, but together you become a tower that the very satanic hosts cannot break through.'

But the bricks still refused to be part of it, saying, 'We don't like being with those around us. Only part of us can be seen. Surely people will get a narrow view of God if they see us like that?'

Jesus wept again as he surveyed the gaps. 'It's in true love and support of one another that the world will see me,' he said. 'When people go their own way, they leave gaps where the enemy can fire his arrows. In going their own way they cause others to be weakened and damaged.'

He turned away with the rebellious bricks still in his hands. 'I will love you until you are softened inside. There's no brick I will not use, however dirty or jagged, because I am the One who creates beauty out of brokenness. But they must be joined together; otherwise, however much I long to use them, I will not be able to.'

I was overwhelmed by this vision. It was so powerful. I had never before seen so clearly into God's heart. It reminded me of some of the Old Testament stories of when heaven was opened to the prophets. I longed that people might understand the greatness of God's love for them and have new revelation of the amazing work he was doing in their lives. So many churches needed to hear this vision.

As I jolted around in the back of the van, I got out my notebook and wrote down all that I could recall of it. Ephesians 2:19–22 came to mind and it seemed such a confirmation of what I had seen:

> Consequently, you are no longer foreigners and aliens but fellow-citizens with God's people and members of God's household, built on the foundation of the apostles and prophets, with Christ Jesus himself as the chief cornerstone. In him the whole building is joined together and rises to become a holy temple in the Lord. And in him you too are being built together to become a dwelling in which God lives by his Spirit.

I knew God was speaking deeply through this vision into my own self-understanding: 'You are one of those bricks jumping from that tower,' he said. 'I love you as my precious daughter and have called you to bring my encouragement to others. As a chosen stone in my tower, I have given you a beautiful colour and shape with which to reflect my beauty. I have set you in a place of influence where you can uplift those around you. But so often you listen to the voice of unworthiness and hide away from the truth of what I have made you to be. Rise up in that truth, beloved one, for if you always hide away there will be gaps in that tower where the enemy can send his arrows.'

As these thoughts came to me, my heart was overcome. I knew they were true, as I did still struggle with all the negatives of my past and often felt inferior to others. God wanted me to have a new foundation of trust in his love for me, and I knew that many others would be the same.

This word is for you too

As I write this story many years on from that experience, I sense God wants you to receive those words too. Take some moments to read that personal prophecy again. Insert the word 'son' instead of 'daughter' if needed. God is speaking to us all and wanting us to take on board that we are part of his plan and beloved to him. Let go of any way that you have been hiding yourself and, as it were, jumping out of that tower. Allow him to tend to any wounded areas in your life. You are precious and chosen in his eyes.

Tell him that you choose to believe you are one of those bricks in that tower: beautiful, unique, yet with that special calling to love and support those around you.

On this occasion I shared the tower vision in our After Hours concert, and there was a tangible sense of God's presence in the room as Marilyn then sang: 'He Called My Name'[3] and 'My Heart is Now His Temple'.[4]

Many asked for prayer that night, including several ministers who were excited by the vision and longed for it to be made real in their own churches.

In MBM, the vision's themes of God's love, care and transforming work in our lives, as well as his amazing plans for us all, became more and more part of our message. We were delighted a couple of years later when an artist friend, Jenny Cooper, felt so inspired by the vision that she painted a beautiful picture of it and then had it printed into posters and cards which we still have today.

In 1987 when I went on that first Spring Harvest tour with Marilyn, I had no idea the blessing, fun and joy we would have through taking part in events like Spring Harvest and New Wine. We've had some amazing connections come into being through these events too.

At that very first Spring Harvest tour in 1987, we were praying about our upcoming sabbatical. God had put on our hearts to go to Bible college for a term, but we had no idea which Bible college. One day while in the resources exhibition we bumped into some very friendly exhibitors, Joe and John. They were representing a small Bible college called Emmanuel Bible College[5] which was located on The Wirral. It proved to be an amazing 'God connection', for this was where God wanted us to go. We were surprised, as we'd been expecting somewhere more charismatic, but the leading was clear and in January 1988 we went to Emmanuel for three months. It proved to be a very thought-provoking time and helped us both grow in our faith. While there we also made connections with the brand-new ministry centre called Ellel Grange in Lancashire, which was to play a significant part in our understanding about the importance of the cross for healing and inner release from the works of the enemy.

Taking part in these big festivals was not just joy and hallelujahs, though. The travelling was immense and our tempers became frayed as we negotiated the pouring rain, traffic jams and endless stop-start journeys. I would frequently get us lost in the huge Butlin's campsites that Spring Harvest used, and sometimes we would arrive only to find that there'd been a miscommunication about our accommodation and someone else would be in our chalet!

On one memorable Spring Harvest tour, the new Scottish site in Ayr had been added to the itinerary. Minehead to Pwllheli to Skegness to Ayr couldn't have been more of a stretch, especially as we were travelling to a new venue each day. The last stage from Skegness to Ayr was the worst, and we felt so sorry for our driver as the hours rolled by. When we arrived, feeling rather jaded, we found that they had double-booked the After Hours slot, and it was meant to be the well-known comedian Roy Castle. As we'd travelled so far, they said we could share it with him, but he was obviously the main draw.

He was very ill with lung cancer and was sure that God was going to heal him, so everyone was eager to hear him. He was playing his trumpet and cracking jokes with the audience. He was great but time was going by, and we started feeling very tense. Eventually Roy 'realised' that he needed to end and came down from the stage to rapturous applause. We had less than ten minutes, and it was tricky to know how to follow on from Roy in such a short time. Should we even do it? But the audience hadn't left as we'd half-expected, so we went ahead. I whispered to Marilyn that I had a little word from the Lord and then she began.

Letting go of her tension, Marilyn started by honouring Roy for all he'd brought to us and prayed a prayer of blessing over him and his wife, Fiona. Then she sang two beautiful short songs expressing God's faithfulness and the peace he gives us. We hadn't conferred so I felt amazed, as her choice of songs tallied so closely with the word I was going to bring. From bouncy laughter, fun and applause, the audience stilled and received the Lord's peace and rest. It was such a short time but became a special divine moment. But, of course, we did feel disappointed that, after all that travelling, we had so little time in which to minister.

Several other incredible connections have come about through our participation in these events. In 1992, our sound engineer Alistair Shenstone was leaving, so we advertised around our local churches for a replacement. We also ran an advert in the resources exhibition at Spring Harvest Minehead. There was only one response to all our adverts, and Karen Walker, who had replaced Trudy as our administrator, read it out to us. The applicant was a man in his twenties called Paul Wood, and he lived in . . . (Karen paused for dramatic effect) 'Watford!' We laughed with surprise as Karen went on to tell us that in fact Paul lived just five minutes away from Marilyn's home. He had not long moved to Watford and had not found a church yet, so would never have seen the local adverts. Paul came to work for us for seven years and was so gifted in many practical ways. Once again, God had wonderfully provided.

There have also been many funny incidents. In 1997, we were at New Wine with Paul. The organisers were supposed to book us a six-berth caravan so that there would be a bit more space for us three singles and Giles, Marilyn's guide dog. But when we arrived we found that the six-berth was now a three-berth old model. There was just room for Marilyn and me to share a small double bed at one end and for Paul to squash into the child's bed at the other. There was a rather tattered awning, so Paul promptly said that the caravan was too small for Giles and he'd have to go in the awning. Giles looked most put out when we tried to make his bed out there, but Paul was adamant and we could see his point. Unfortunately, that first night the heavens opened with torrential rain and huge gusts of wind. At about 2 a.m. there was a crash and Marilyn could hear Giles barking and whining. When I opened the door, poor Giles was standing on a tiny canvas island in the middle of a sea of water and collapsed awning! He threw himself on us and needless to say was soon in with us, room or not!

One thing I discovered about Marilyn early on was how little she likes being put on a pedestal. She is aware that her blindness can be a barrier, making people nervous of approaching her, so she never wants the fact that she's a singer to be yet another cause of isolation. So I was soon to discover how Marilyn loved getting to know everyone. Apparently, when she was first invited to Filey Christian Holiday Week, she announced in the big celebration that she would love to get to know people and be invited for a cuppa. In the end, she got so many invites she had to say she couldn't possibly drink any more tea!

At the more recent Revival Fire Bible weeks, led by Revd Eric Delve at the West Kent Showground in Detling, rather than go into the team lounge between sessions, Marilyn would offer tea and coffee to all (or so it seemed) friends that we knew already and friends we made there. The kettle would go on in our caravan, and soon a big circle would form, with people chatting and laughing. Just occasionally, while trying to correctly hear twelve or so drinks orders and make them simultaneously in a squashed corner of the caravan, I'd nostalgically think of the hot drinks' urns and comfy armchairs of the team lounge. But, in reality, we both loved getting to know and be with people, and this was a great way to do it.

Another amazing Spring Harvest connection was with a lady called Evelyn Smith, who we met at Skegness in the mid-nineties. She was very friendly, and over a cuppa, told us about her work as director of Canaan Christian Centre, a large seaside bungalow that was both her own home and a Christian place of safety for troubled families. I was moved as she shared about the lives that had been changed through Canaan. Children and their mums experiencing devastating abuse coming face to face with God's love and care through Eve and her team. Eve was also involved in many children's' clubs and activities in her church and community, and travelled regularly to countries such as the Ukraine and Hungary to visit their orphanages and bring the children help and hope. I felt humbled. Eve was single, like me, yet hadn't let that be a barrier to her building amazing relationships with children of all ages, and in fact saw them as the babies God had given her. With her love of dogs, the seaside and the snow, Eve was great fun and soon became a wonderful friend. Over the years, it has been such a privilege to share in her ministry, taking part in her annual thanksgivings and Christmas events and holding our own renewal conferences in the prefab conference room at the end of her garden, which was built entirely from prayer and trust in the Lord's provision.

One time when we were ministering at Canaan, I was praying and suddenly a picture came to mind. I could see a bicycle wheel with the central hub holding all the spokes, which were then held in place by the outer rim. I felt the Lord was saying that the central hub was

Canaan's ministry. He himself was the outer rim that held everything together and enabled the ministry to move forward. So, what were the spokes? The most amazing thought came to me that they were the symbols of new works, even new Canaans, that would spring out of the original vision but would be in different countries. How could that be? I shared it with Eve, and at first she was shocked, as she'd been wondering if the work might start winding down! She started to pray into it and, incredibly, within about eighteen months we were in Pápa in Hungary celebrating the opening of Kanaan Haz, which several needy families were already booked into. Later an orphanage house was bought in Nigeria, and Canaan have helped a similar work in Brazil and are currently exploring a vision of one in Spain.

It's awesome to hear Eve's stories, and we were thrilled when in 2009 she received a bronze medal from the orphanage in Hungary.[6] Each year the children and staff voted for who to give it to: someone who had made a difference to their lives. That year they voted over-whelmingly for Eve.

Evelyn shares

Every year I had taken Christmas gifts and also Easter eggs and, in fact, all the things they needed, like bicycles, puncture repair kits, food, clothes, etc. and even had groups of them come to England to visit us. No one outside Hungary had ever received the medal before. It was a huge surprise to me.

It was through Eve that we made a lovely connection with the work of Len and Phyl Holder in their Christian guesthouse in the Black Forest, Germany. When Eve was planning her 60th birthday, she heard about Haus Barnabas and, with her love of snow, decided she wanted to celebrate there. With Eve's birthday being in early January, the snow was deep and beautiful. Even Marilyn tried tobogganing with a few of us running beside her as the toboggan shot down the slope! On Eve's birthday, Len organised a sleigh ride, which was magical. Len and his wife Phyl, and their partners in the work Tim and Debbie Brookes, shared a vision to bring God's love to their local community as well as give holidaymakers a beautiful peace-filled break. We became good friends, and it has been a great joy to go many times since, leading little house parties with Marilyn doing concerts for the locals.

On one memorable day, a group of us visited a tourist resort called Lake Titisee. As it was an exceptionally cold New Year, the whole lake was frozen, an incredible sight. Many people were walking on it, so we decided we'd go onto the ice as a group. Arms linked, Marilyn, Eve, me, and a couple more friends from our group at Haus Barnabas walked out onto the ice. It was exhilarating. But Marilyn heard a creaking sound and, worried the ice was going to crack, made us get off. Unfortunately, I wanted more of the adrenalin rush so went back on my own. It felt amazing, but I'd only taken about six steps when I slammed down hard onto my face. Broken glasses, a cartoon-sized lump on my head, a huge black eye and a sprained wrist soon showed me I hadn't made the wisest choice. The next day, still feeling shaken up, I decided to not go on the arranged trip and Marilyn and another blind friend, Kathy Baldock, stayed too. We caught the bus, and with me guiding both Marilyn and Kathy along the snowy pavements, we visited a café specialising in Black Forest gateau. They sprayed on extra kirsch especially for us, and Marilyn said she'd never seen me perk up so quickly!

17

Hearing the Father's Heart

Can it be you're hearing the whispers of God?

Marilyn Baker[1]

Although Marilyn and I are in the public eye, we have our struggles and weaknesses like everyone else and need to keep leaning on the Lord for his transforming work in our lives.

Marilyn

It's amazing how when we hear negative words about ourselves, they stay far more in our minds than positive ones. When I was in New Zealand on my first major tour with Penny Misselbrook, we had loads of wonderful comments from people who attended the concerts. Pen would read the feedback forms to me – they were incredibly encouraging. But one day there was one that greatly troubled me. Instead of being appreciative, the person seemed markedly unimpressed. They commented on my clothes being old-fashioned, and said in their opinion it had been a wasted opportunity for Jesus Christ: I was shocked! I had ended with my song 'Jesus You are Changing Me' which had gone down well, but they said they hoped I would soon experience that change myself, which was obviously much needed!

That one form really got to me. I kept asking Pen, 'How old d'you think they are? Is it a man or a woman? Are they just a fault-finder?' It didn't matter how beautiful all the other comments were, all I could think of was that one.

Eventually, as I asked more questions, the truth emerged to guffaws of laughter. Pen had decided all the ecstatic comments needed some tempering, so she'd written a comment card herself, pretending to be a comic character I'd invented called Luigi Macaroni! It was extremely funny and Pen knew that once the joke was out, I would love it.

But the story brings over my point about how negative words do stick to us and can cause deep damage to our hearts if we inwardly digest them.

This was the case concerning my dad's words that I would always be a nuisance if I asked people for favours. Though they were spoken when I was a teenager, they had penetrated into my thinking, shaping my attitude to myself, so that although I am an extrovert, I often just could not believe that others would want to be with me. And because I was terrified of being a nuisance, I hardly ever asked for help or lifts, and held back from joining in activities in case people found my blindness a problem. I so needed a breakthrough.

One day, I attended a healing seminar at our church, and we were asked to think of the negative things we believed about ourselves that didn't line up with God's Word. Then we had to undo the wrong belief by replacing it with the truth. They suggested we find Scriptures that confirmed God's truth and write a statement opposite the negative lie. They said that as we rehearsed the new truth, it would become a core part of our mindset and identity.

For me, the lie was that I was a nuisance. I wrote down that God had made me to be a blessing to people, and that because he lived in me, I would bring his love to others. Habits of a lifetime are hard to break though, but I now knew God's words about me and really needed to drink them in.

This healing process was put to the test quicker than I'd anticipated. It was near Christmas, shops were busy, and I needed to go into a supermarket for some Christmas goodies. My heart sank; how could I go in and ask for assistance when all the staff would be so busy? I was bound to be a nuisance, I thought. God pulled me up short and reminded me of all I'd been learning. I said sorry for doubting and vowed to go in with a new attitude that I would be a blessing. I had to wait for help, but eventually a lovely lady took me round. The time flew by as we laughed and joked. To my amazement, at the checkout who should arrive but Tracy, who'd had the same idea to buy things as me. As we left, she said casually, not knowing the battle I'd just had, 'I don't know what you and that lady were talking about, but I could see you really made her day. I think you were a real blessing to her!'

'Wow, Lord, you did it,' I thought, 'and you used Trace to confirm it to me.' I was beginning to walk in a new direction. It took practice and some counselling to really embed the fact that I am a blessing, not a nuisance, into my heart. But after one counselling session, I woke up the next day and could see as never before that the lie I'd lived with for more than forty years had robbed me of so much, and that by believing I was a nuisance, I had grieved my dear heavenly Father who had made me in his awesome image. With tears, I turned around from that attitude in a very real way. If I am ever tempted to revisit it, I remind myself that Jesus would still have died on the cross just for me if I had been the only one needing to be saved. That is the inestimable value he places on my life and, indeed, on all our lives.

Tracy

The tender way the Lord dealt with Marilyn's negative belief reminds me of a time when he was doing a similar healing work in my own life. One day when still a new Christian, I'd been very distressed while at John and Amanda's, and Amanda felt the Lord wanted me to read a phrase from Isaiah 43:4: 'Since you are precious and honoured in my sight, and because I love you . . .'

'Mull those words over with the Lord,' Amanda said. 'Ask him what he wants to say to you.' It was then, as I thought about him honouring me and me being precious to him, that the memory of the childhood

Easter hat disaster came back to me. I'd locked the humiliation deep inside, but it was still hurting me.

Father God then spoke into the memory: 'You'd envisaged in your heart how you wanted your hat to look, beautiful and full of colour, and you were crushed when your teacher treated it as rubbish. I, too, envisaged all the beauty and colour that I would weave into your life, but unlike that teacher, I will never crush you. You are precious and unique and I am proud of you.'

This word from the Lord and the way he spoke through the verse into my hurt was deeply significant and made me realise the importance of hearing from the Father to heal and change us. Another time at college he spoke to me through the beautiful landscape as I walked from Otterspool up to the campus. I'd been rushing along in my usual anxious way but suddenly felt I should look properly at the view before me. As I gazed over the fields and saw the tiny flowers and the majestic trees, he spoke into my heart, saying, 'I made all this so you can know that I am good and loving in all my ways. But none of this is as beautiful to me as you are.'

Again, this was hugely significant to me, as I'd heard for so long that I was rubbish and ugly. It was a real step forward in my healing, my loving Father affirming me.

After my first book *The Voice of the Father*[2] came out in 1995, I began to do workshops on listening to God. We now include this in all of our conferences, as it is so important that people learn to hear God's voice for themselves. I always encourage people to notice things around them and ask God what he wants to say to them, just as Jesus encouraged the disciples to look at the flowers and birds and hear God speaking to them, telling them that they were valuable.

In one workshop, a lady became very excited, realising that God had spoken to her that very morning through something she'd noticed. She'd had to climb a steep hill and had noticed a man and his son with Down's syndrome riding a tandem bicycle. They were both pedalling hard, but after they crested the hill the dad coasted down the other side, but the son didn't understand and was still pedalling furiously. The lady saw all this, but it was only when I said God could speak through things we notice, that she asked him what he was saying. He told her she was like that son and was struggling and striving when sometimes she just needed to rest and let God carry her. She was so excited when she shared. It was life-changing for her, and many others have now experienced the joy of hearing God for themselves.

Marilyn

One of the most amazing things about working with Tracy is that God uses her in bringing what we know in church lingo as 'words of knowledge'[3] to people at our events, helping them understand as never before how much God knows and loves them. In the early days especially, when people came for prayer after an event, it was too difficult for me to tell her what they were saying. There was often a queue, and though we used finger spelling, it was too slow. So I would pray with the person while Trace would quietly listen to God. She would often then tell them something the Lord had shown her that was absolutely on the ball: like a picture from the Holy Spirit which specifically dealt with the person's need. She was tuning into Father God who wanted to communicate his deep care for the person. They were often amazed, as they knew Trace was not able to hear the conversation. It shows me that the Lord will go all out to reach those who are struggling or whose hearts are breaking.

One important thing, people sometimes say the reason Trace can tune into God's words is because she can't hear physically. Trace disagrees and points out that the Bible is clear that *all* Jesus' sheep can hear his voice.[4] The nature of her deafness means that her life is actually full of noise and unintelligible conversation, so she's far from sitting in a cocoon of serenity all the time!

All of us, when spending time in his presence, have the ability to hear him because we have been given 'the mind of Christ'.[5] All his sheep can hear his voice. He has no favourites and he makes himself known to all his beloved children.

Tracy

One day, at the end of a concert a lady came up and asked for prayer. She was crying as she spoke, and I couldn't hear her or easily follow Marilyn's finger spelling because I was tired. I decided I would just pray as Marilyn talked with her and ask God to give Marilyn the right words. But as I was praying, I suddenly 'saw' in my mind's eye a picture of a wedding ring. I was wondering what that meant when a Bible reference also came to mind. I looked it up and found it said: 'as a bridegroom rejoices over his bride, so will your God rejoice over you' (Isa. 62:5).

I continued to pray, as I still had no idea what the picture or verse meant for this lady. She was so distressed, and I longed that she might be comforted. Some thoughts began to form in my mind, almost as if I was thinking them myself, yet they had a real conviction and certainty about them: 'I cherish her. She is the apple of my eye. I want to woo her and show her how beautiful she is to me. I love to spend time with her. I want to be as a husband to her, to adore her as my beloved bride.' I realised that the picture of the wedding ring and the Bible reference were all tying in with the prophetic message. It was so tender and I prayed it would touch her. When I shared it, she looked astonished. Apparently, she'd been telling Marilyn how her husband had left her for another woman and she'd felt so betrayed that she'd lost her faith and was ready to go off with any man who asked. As I shared what the Lord had said, it was as if her anger tangibly fell away. We were able to pray with her to let go of her husband and open her heart afresh to the Lord's love. She looked so at peace as she left us.

As time went by, I began to understand how much God longed to speak into all kinds of situations to bring healing to individuals or a new perspective to a whole church. On one occasion when we led a renewal weekend for a church, the Lord gave me a picture of a crowd of people milling around. They seemed to be struggling to connect with each other, reaching out to make contact but to no avail. I realised that each person was in a plastic bubble. They could see out and others could see in, but they couldn't reach each other. I felt the bubbles were there because of their fear of being too closely involved with each other, and it was only as they each chose to be led by God's love, rather than fear, that the bubbles would burst.

This was a challenging picture; supposing it was wrong? But I shared it gently during the first session and Marilyn backed it up as she sang her beautiful song 'Love'. Afterwards, the minister was in tears and said how apt the picture was for the church. Throughout the rest of the weekend, the whole church specifically sought the Lord, longing to be changed and set free to leave their fears behind and step out of their bubbles. We were amazed at how he'd given us just what was needed to touch this church so deeply.

It was easy, once I'd started getting words and pictures in the concerts, to fall into a set pattern of bringing them, which wasn't necessarily always a good thing. Sometimes Marilyn would say, a tad exasperated, 'Trace, that prophecy took over ten minutes!' Once I started a prophetic word very dramatically with the words, 'Tick, tock, tick, tock . . .' It was all about time running out for someone who needed to respond to the Lord before they died. I've no idea if anyone responded, but they did on another occasion when I noticed a flower display on the stage and saw that some flowers were dying even while the rest were still in bloom. I felt the Lord was saying that the flower display represented someone who'd made it their life goal to achieve, but they'd never acknowledged God. The lavish blooms indicated their success, but the fact that some flowers were already dying showed how fleeting such prestige can be. God longed for their security to be in his love and gift of eternal life rather than in their achievements. I was nervous about giving it, but at the end, one of the church prayer team told us that a wealthy businessman had talked to them and said that the word was for him. He'd asked them to pray for him and they had led him to the Lord.

Marilyn

Nowadays as we lead our events it's wonderful to see how God gives gifts of prophecy, words, Scriptures and visions to all, and when we share them, we can see a beautiful picture emerging of what God is wanting to show us. At a conference some years ago, MBM team members Ron and Val Seale were praying with a very distressed lady whose husband had left her because she couldn't have children. As they prayed, they remembered an old picture they had of Jesus sitting with children on his knee, but it was as if she was superimposed over Jesus. They felt he was saying 'she will have many children', and they prayed God would fulfil that in her life. I was shocked when they told me this, as I felt the false hope would be crushing for this poor lady. But an amazing thing happened. Sometime later, Ron and Val heard that she'd gone on a church mission trip to Romanian orphanages and ended up following God's call to move there permanently to look after the orphaned children. The beautiful end of that story came later still when they heard she'd remarried and was now expecting her own child!

18

In Times of Weakness

Lord in all Your gentleness, in all Your mercy and tenderness
Marilyn Baker[1]

All the way through this journey of ministering together, there have been times for both of us of illness, depression, weariness, lack of love for the Lord, tension with each other and other people, helplessness to know what to do . . . But the Lord shows again and again how he is always there for us, wanting to help us. These are a few glimpses into those times of weakness.

Marilyn

For over a year my back had been giving me a great deal of pain, and in February 1986 I went into hospital to have a dye injected into the lumbar fluid, to see if that would show what was causing the problem. The injections gave me a terrific headache, and I was glad that Tracy was allowed to stay with me. She read me an exciting book, which helped pass the time. The tests didn't show anything, and by this time it was increasingly difficult to walk, sit or stand. Even lying down was painful.

Tracy

Although the concerts were touching people's lives, it was obvious that Marilyn was finding it difficult to cope with the constant pain. Along with many others, I was praying that the Lord would heal her. Often the leaders of churches we were ministering in would pray at the end of the concerts for her. Sometimes there would be a noticeable improvement and Marilyn would excitedly think that the pain and struggle was over, but something would always happen to set it off again, like a trip or a sudden jolt in the van. Every time I saw Marilyn struggling, I prayed, 'Lord, please take this pain away.' But as time went by, Marilyn became more and more depressed, wondering if God was hearing her prayers at all.

One night I had a dream. It made me smile because it was about Marilyn and me shopping together in Watford High Street. We'd hardly ever been shopping together since we'd become friends in 1985, as the walking was too difficult. By now Marilyn was quite twisted in her posture, but in the dream she was standing upright, holding my arm lightly and walking easily. We went down the entire high street, crossing back and forth to various shops, with Marilyn laughing and enjoying herself the whole time. I was laughing when I woke up and felt a joy in my heart that quickly vanished when I realised it was only a dream. 'If only that could be true,' I thought, sadly. Then I felt God say to me: 'It is true. It's a picture of what I'm going to bring about for Marilyn, but you need to pray it into reality.' I was so excited that I wanted to tell her, but God seemed to say, 'No, just pray.'

Often I found prayer difficult, but this seemed different. It was as if I'd been given a glimpse into his heart for Marilyn, his knowing of what she would love to be able to do. It was a joy to have that picture in my mind as I continued praying, because in reality her back seemed to be getting worse.

Marilyn

We went to Cornwall to do some concerts, and on the way down I felt God saying that I was going to meet a Christian chiropractor who would help me. I wondered if I had misheard, as I felt that an osteopath would be better. But when I asked our hosts, Sue and Peter Richards, they told me a Christian chiropractor, Reg Price, was coming to our concert that night.

Reg took X-rays, and I was amazed when the reason for the back pain was found: the sciatic nerve was trapped and two discs had been damaged. Reg gave me several treatments while I was in Cornwall, and I felt real improvement. Typically, though, this was short-lived. The next concert tour was in Jersey, and the day before we left, I tripped over a bucket and twisted my back badly. Although I was in agony, I knew that I still had to go to Jersey, as I was doing a new recording there: a live album taken from the concerts. During our tour I spent a lot of time lying down between concerts. Lovelight sang with me, and Ian made the recordings. The album was eventually called *An Evening with Marilyn Baker* and had a lovely, homely feel to it that people enjoyed.

But my back was still so painful that, when I returned home, I began to consider giving up travelling. I phoned Reg, who suggested I have more treatment and said he had been praying for me. He invited Tracy and me to stay with him and his wife, Joy, until he could get me back on my feet. He would do the treatments free of charge as an offering to the Lord. I was deeply touched by the love of this couple, who until recently had been total strangers.

Tracy and I flew down and were warmly welcomed by Reg and Joy. The church in Penzance held a healing service for me, which I so appreciated. Reg told me that more damage had been done by my fall and that it may take longer than originally expected for my back to get better, and he wasn't even sure how much his treatment would help, but every day, before each treatment he would pray and thank the Lord for any progress he saw. The treatment was very painful. The nights were the worst, and Tracy read to me for hours. We found some exciting books and became involved with the characters. Sometimes I was in agony and it was hard to concentrate on anything. I think that pain is one of the most destructive things human beings have to cope with. Often well-meaning people said or wrote things like: 'You can spend lots of time with the Lord, Marilyn, now that you're not travelling.' But it didn't work that way for me – I couldn't even think straight.

Tracy

It was awful to see Marilyn in so much pain, but as the days went by, I began to see how present and real God was. He was there in Reg and Joy's sacrificial commitment to helping Marilyn, and in Sue and Peter's prayerful love and care. He was there in the way he enabled Marilyn and me to grow so much closer through this difficult time, and even showed us ways of having some fun. Marilyn said she missed shopping, so sometimes I would catch the bus to Truro and buy her a top or a skirt, take it back and she'd try it on in her bedroom. I also discovered that she was missing having a beer, so I would buy a couple of cans and we'd drink them after we'd said goodnight to Reg and Joy. One funny thing was that our bedroom was right at the top of their four-storey home and there was no toilet. Marilyn couldn't go up and down at night, so Joy put her dad's old commode in the room. The problem was emptying it the next day, as with the combination of the steep steps and my poor balance, it would often splash.

Marilyn

I stayed in Cornwall for six weeks, and during the last week, Carol Franklin stayed with me, as Tracy was going to France. By this time there was an improvement, and I could go for short, slow walks. I was so grateful for that, and even now I say, 'Thank you, Lord, that I can walk.'

My first engagement after the treatment was in Austria with WEC, and I used a wheelchair. Carol Joyce came with me and pushed the chair when there were no strong men available. I was even pushed to the top of an Austrian mountain!

Tracy

I was delighted to see the improvement in Marilyn's back, but it was a few months later that it was brought home to me how much God had done and how important our prayers are. On this particular day, Marilyn and I had gone to Watford to the top end of the high street then made our way down. We were strolling along with Marilyn walking upright on my arm, relaxed and laughing. We'd crossed back and forth a few times when I suddenly had a tremendous sense of déjà vu. This was the dream, exactly as I'd seen it! God had given it to me so that I would pray, and now it was fulfilled. It was as if God was standing there with us in Watford High Street saying, 'You see, all I wanted was for you to partner with me in what I already knew I was going to bring about.'

Tracy

I have struggled personally with an unexpected deterioration in my hearing, sight and balance over the last twenty years. All three areas were supposed to be static effects of the brain damage I sustained through encephalitis, but they've all deteriorated a great deal. At the beginning I used to hear Marilyn in the concerts through a foldback speaker. Now that's impossible, and sometimes I really miss the joy of listening to music or entering into conversations. I've had much prayer over the years, but have seen no change so far. And yet I sense my Father God is so with me; I see him in Marilyn's constant desire to help me know what is going on; I see him in the love of friends who diligently write in notebooks or, in recent years, type on my iPad; like Christine, who comes to many events with the primary purpose of typing what Marilyn shares, so I can follow. I see him in my wonderful hearing dog, Goldie, who brings me so much joy; I see him in the laughs we have at my sometimes inappropriate answers to questions that I haven't heard correctly, for example, Q: What would you like to drink? A: Sausages!

Despite our busy lives, our disabilities can make us feel isolated at times. Without someone helping, it's impossible for me to enter into ordinary conversation. If Marilyn and I want to chat together, we have to sit down with my iPad; we can't just chat while making breakfast. Marilyn can't spot people in a crowd, so has to wait till they come up to her. With only a voice to go by, she doesn't always recognise who is talking, and because she is a singer, people can feel shy, forgetting she can feel lonely or just want fun. The most important thing for all of us is true authentic connection with others. It's what we were made for.

Marilyn

In ministry, when we feel very tired, it's easy to go on autopilot, just doing what we've always done because we know it works but, like the Israelites in the desert, we need fresh input from heaven every day.[2] We've found that only such intimate connection with the Holy Spirit keeps us experiencing his abundance and strength.

Another period of physical weakness happened to me in 1993 when I developed a chest infection. Even though the symptoms died down, I felt exhausted all the time. I tried all kinds of tonics, everything that promised new strength, but to no avail. But I was determined to persevere with our engagements. God was my healer. He would give me the victory in each situation, and besides, all the churches we were due to go to were praying for me, so I certainly couldn't disappoint them. While this was going on, Paul Wood, Tracy and I returned home one night to find I'd been burgled. The house was ransacked, drawers and cupboards emptied all over the floor. It was deeply upsetting, especially as the thieves had taken all my mum's jewellery. It was the sentimental loss that was so much harder to bear. And I felt so weak anyway . . . One morning our friend Sarah, a nurse, popped in and I was shocked when she became angry, telling me that I was in no fit state to sing, and that if I didn't look after myself things would get even worse. I said that I had church events I needed to do. She retorted that my health was far more important and left the room obviously upset. I was upset too. If I gave in to this virus, surely it showed I didn't have enough faith? I talked about it with Tracy. She is often so very wise. She said something that has stayed in my mind ever since and helped me understand God's character much more. She felt Sarah was right and that God wasn't a slave driver, and that he certainly didn't see me as a sausage machine but as his precious child who needed his love and nurture.

We talked to our trustees and they immediately stopped all our engagements, and I went with Tracy to the Trelowarren Retreat Centre in Cornwall. I realised my heavenly Father just wanted me to be real, not striving to fulfil others' expectations or seeing him as a God who is always pushing me to do things. Over the years, especially during our conferences, we've found this is a message people today so need to hear: God does not see you as a sausage machine.

Marilyn

People say how they love the words in my songs, but I actually find words difficult to write. I know that without God's anointing I wouldn't be able to write even one song of any worth. I can't just sit down and write them; I need to feel his inspiration. I was due to do a new album at the end of 1992, but I had no songs at all. We had been very busy and nothing was inspiring me. I began to panic. I would have to let the record company down and break my contract.

Tracy

I kept praying for Marilyn to be able to write and yet, somehow, I felt my prayers were not getting anywhere. One day I lost concentration in my quiet time and started thinking about my friend who'd just told me she was pregnant. I scolded myself, saying I needed to keep focusing on praying for the songs, but the Lord showed me that he'd brought my friend's pregnancy to my mind because he wanted me to think of this new album as a baby being formed in the womb. A baby is unseen at first, yet all the intricate parts are coming together. Could this be how Marilyn's songs would come about? Could I pray in that way? It seemed a bit crazy, but this was how I felt the Lord wanted me to pray.

With a pregnancy, you see a bump, but there were no signs of anything from Marilyn. Then some months later, a whole group of concerts were cancelled. This had never happened before, and for about three weeks the diary became empty. Marilyn said somewhat disconsolately that she would try writing songs, and sat at the piano. After a while, she called excitedly, 'Quick, Trace, find me a tape recorder, a song is coming!'

Over those three weeks she wrote fourteen songs; this was unheard of. I had spent months praying for this 'baby', and now I was seeing the results. It turned out that it was exactly nine months from when I started interceding in this way that the new album *Face to Face* was born. The songs were beautiful, and I felt amazed that God had worked so mightily in our weakness, giving me the way to pray and inspiring Marilyn to write fourteen beautiful songs in such a short time.

Marilyn

Satan has often tried to put a stop to our ministry, and perhaps the most dramatic occasion was in 2009 when I was travelling home from Torch Trust in Market Harborough. I arrived at Tonbridge railway station and got out with Pennie, my guide dog. The platform was crowded, with people standing close to the edge and spreading out over the concourse, making it difficult for Pennie to navigate. The platform was slightly curved and I was on the track side. Suddenly I felt myself falling. I hit the ground hard and realised I'd fallen onto the track and had pulled Pennie down with me. There was an electric rail very close. I couldn't think clearly but heard someone say, 'A train is coming.' Was this my time? I screamed for help.

The next moment I felt strong arms lifting me up off the track. It was two decorators working there who managed to get me back onto the platform. The pain in my back was crippling; I could hardly breathe.

An ambulance was called, and just then Tracy came into the station expecting us to be going home together. She saw someone was hurt but had no idea it was me. When she realised, she was devastated. She came to the hospital with me, and to help my pain they gave me laughing gas. It made me feel rather drunk but the pain was almost unbearable.

After checking me over, I had no broken bones, but tissue damage and extensive bruising. Trace and I proved to the nurses that we could manage with her helping me use a Zimmer frame. Andrew, one of our trustees, took us home, as I didn't want to stay in hospital. Some very dear friends, Maggie and Roy, came over, bringing their recliner chair, which was deposited in our lounge and where I spent many nights, as I could not get upstairs. Trace decided to sleep on a mattress downstairs with me so she could know if I needed help in the night. It took a long time to recover, and amazingly, Pennie, who was a very calm dog, was still able to work despite the shock she'd experienced that day.

Just a week later we had a conference at Brunel Manor in Devon, and a wonderful driver drove us extremely carefully in the van so I would not experience agonising bumps. A wheelchair was hired for me and I wasn't expected to take part in the conference, but I made such an amazing recovery that week with all the love and care from everyone that I was still able to lead worship and do my concert. The experience did make me nervous of travelling, but I knew I would need to get back on a train again if I wanted to travel on my own. Some weeks later, I forced myself to do a journey with Pennie, which was very difficult, but I am so glad I made that effort, as I have to use trains a lot now.

Tracy

We've come to understand, as never before, how Jesus is touched by the feelings of our infirmities. He has promised never to leave us without support, and that has certainly been our experience: that at every point, in our weakness, he is with us ready to help us with his all sufficiency and strength. Sometimes we have been awestruck at the way he's brought about an amazing work of healing or change in someone's life when we've felt completely weak in ourselves, as this following story describes.

One day Marilyn had a call from a friend, asking if we could pray for some friends who were new Christians. 'Sim has Hodgkin's disease again and they're really scared,' Cathy said. 'I told them you pray for people, and they would love you to pray that Sim will be healed.'

Cathy sounded desperate, so Marilyn agreed that we would pray. As the day approached, we both felt nervous. Who were we to offer prayer for healing? How could we say with confidence that God would heal Sim? Suppose he didn't? But we knew that we needed to give hope and comfort to this dear couple.

The night before they came, I still felt full of anxiety. I wasn't even sure how we would go about praying. Suddenly a clear thought popped into my mind: 'Stop focusing on yourself. All I'm asking you to do is to be available. I love Sim and want to touch him with the power of my love. Focus on that and let me do the rest.'

As these words took root, all my anxieties lifted and a joy filled my heart. I went to sleep, and the next day I felt full of confidence in the Lord. Amazingly, Marilyn also felt certain that we should just pray directly for the Lord to heal Sim. God was leading!

Sim and Lou were so friendly, filling Marilyn's small lounge with warmth as soon as they walked in. Yet behind their expressions of gratitude, it was easy to see their anxiety as they explained about Sim's recurrence of the disease. 'I have a scan in a few days,' he said, leaning back in his chair. 'Depending on what that shows, the doctors will decide on the next stage of treatment.'

Lou sat forward. 'Cathy told us you will pray and Jesus will heal Sim,' she said, excitedly. 'Sim, tell them what happened last night.'

'Well,' he said, 'it was something I've never experienced before. Suddenly I had this strangest feeling that I should read a certain Bible verse. I didn't know what to expect but . . .' he paused, and rummaged in his pocket pulling out a sheet of paper. 'This was what I read.'

I took the paper and my heart thumped as I read the words: 'I am still confident of this: I will see the goodness of the Lᴏʀᴅ in the land of the living' (Ps. 27:13).

'How wonderful!' said Marilyn. 'God was showing you what he is going to do. He wants you to see his goodness in this life, not just when you get to heaven.'

'Yes, I really believe he is going to heal you,' I said, full of wonder at how God had spoken to this new Christian. There was no way Sim would have known that verse. Now all we needed to do was to pray along the lines that God had already set.

Sitting by Sim, Marilyn explained that as we laid our hands on him and prayed, God's Spirit would flow onto him in healing power. He nodded and Marilyn began to pray, 'Lord, thank you that you are here and for your love for Sim. Please minister healing to him . . .' As she continued praying, there was an overwhelming sense of the presence of God. Sim relaxed, a look of real peace on his face. I started to thank the Lord for his love for Sim. Suddenly he gasped, 'Something's vibrating in my neck, it's all hot!' We continued praying and worshipping together and then it ended.

A week later we had an excited phone call from Lou. 'Sim's had his scan and guess what, the tumour's completely gone!' she gasped. 'The consultant couldn't understand it and kept asking Sim what treatment he'd had. Sim said, "I had prayer!"'

We were thrilled. We had felt so weak, but God knew exactly what he wanted to do and just needed us to be available as channels.

The humorous but thought-provoking upshot was that about eight months later Sim and Lou's vicar invited Marilyn to sing at their church. Lou was organising the event, as she knew us. Shortly beforehand, Lou told us that they'd been telling everyone in the church that we had a powerful healing ministry and would have words of knowledge.

'Do make time to share your amazing words,' she said. 'Loads of people want prayer for healing.'

We gulped. Didn't Lou realise that Sim's healing had been a one-off? But her excitement was infectious and Marilyn said we just needed to go with it because, after all, it was God doing the work, not us!

When Lou introduced us, I kept getting the giggles because from the way she described us, our names should have been Marilyn Kuhlman[3] Ministries! But I felt God saying, 'Just relax, listen to me and be expectant.' Words of knowledge and prophetic pictures did start to come as Marilyn sang and I wrote them down. Marilyn also shared several words in-between her songs. We had a sense of being lifted up and carried on the wings of Lou's faith and expectancy, and to our great joy, the Lord did work powerfully. At the end, so many people wanted prayer that we were ministering for about two hours. Lou and Sim's excitement had created a 'thin' place where God could work.

19

Humorous Moments

He gives joy

We experience many wonderful things in our ministry, but always alongside the 'glory' are those moments when life goes a little pear-shaped. With one of us being blind and one deaf and partially sighted, with dogs and numerous team members on the road with us, there are always times when we can only laugh or cry. So enjoy these few stories of humorous moments.

In our accommodation...

Tracy

As I settled more into the travelling lifestyle, I began to associate certain types of events with the need to grit my teeth with the expectation of being cold. Many of our concerts took place in traditional church buildings, and while those unloading equipment would get warmed up, Marilyn and I would sit shivering in a cold vestry, trying to prepare.

One night we stayed in a vicarage that felt as if it had never had the heating on, and our hearts sank when we felt the thin duvets. We would surely freeze!

'Are you sure there are no blankets, Trace?'

I decided to get over my fear of hurting the hosts' feelings and ask if we could have extra blankets. 'Marilyn has poor circulation,' I said, by way of justification.

I needn't have feared, the vicar's wife was all bustling concern as she exclaimed, 'Oh, poor Marilyn, I'll get her something.' She came back with an armful of quilts which I knew would slip off as soon as we moved.

'Thank you,' I said. 'That'll be lovely.'

'What on earth did you tell them?' Marilyn asked, when I got back to the bedroom. 'I heard them discussing my terrible circulation. Are they going to put the heating on? I bet that's . . .'

She stopped as a loud thumping, gurgling noise filled the room. Even I could hear it. After fifteen minutes it had showed no sign of settling down.

'Trace!' Marilyn sat up and the quilt slid off once more. 'Go and tell them my circulation's got better, and I don't need the heating on any more!'

Marilyn

Once Tracy was unwell, so another friend travelled with me for the weekend of concerts. We were in separate bedrooms, so she took time to ensure I knew the way to the bathroom and back to my room. But the next morning when I had my shower, I realised that I'd forgotten to find out where my towel was. Cold and dripping wet, I searched around for a towel, but there was nothing. I tried calling but no one heard. Suddenly my hand landed on the toilet roll and I thought, 'I'll have to use this!' Have you ever wondered how much toilet roll you need to dry yourself after a shower?

Concert hiccups . . .

Tracy

At many venues the organisers create a 'stage' out of several hardboard blocks fixed together. We were doing a concert and I took Marilyn to the keyboard while the church leader introduced us. I pulled her chair back for her just as he turned to welcome us. But Marilyn had disappeared! When she'd sat down the chair sank through the cracks between the blocks and she sank with it! The chair had tilted backwards and was fixed fast, so it was quite a struggle, even with the help of two hunky men from the audience to detach Marilyn and get her upright.

Another time, Marilyn asked me, on the way to a concert, if I thought she was refined. I had to laugh, as that wasn't a word I'd use to describe her. When we arrived, we all seemed to be in mischievous moods, so when I saw a pile of soft toys on the stage, I popped one of them onto the keyboard. We came out of the vestry to start the concert and Marilyn put her hands down to play and screamed as she felt the furry toy! She thought Nick Cook, our bass player, had put it there, and she kept referring to him as having 'a base character'! But he was innocent on that occasion. She never guessed it was me.

Later in the same concert she was singing 'He's Alive'[2] and suddenly started to choke in the middle of the song.

'Trace, get me some water, I've swallowed a fly!' she gasped.

Unfortunately, I didn't hear correctly and thought she'd said, 'I've swallowed some phlegm!' I felt cross with her. 'How can she ask me if I think she's refined and then talk about swallowing phlegm?' I muttered. I got her a tiny amount of water to subtly tell her off. By this time, she was laughing with the audience, saying she wouldn't recommend it for starters, and began singing 'There was an old woman who swallowed a fly.' I was mortified to discover my mistake. In fact, the fly turned out to be a daddy long-legs (we saw it on a video of the concert later). It got sucked into her mouth as she took a deep breath to sing.

Dogs...

Tracy

So many places we stay have dogs and, of course, in recent years we've added our own dog stories to the list. In one of the earlier trips, we were staying with a lovely family, and Marilyn and I had been given two separate rooms. I helped Marilyn get familiar with hers and then went to mine. There was no bedside lamp so once I was ready, I went over to the light switch, turned it off and headed back to bed in the pitch dark. Suddenly something small and furry hurled itself at me and started nipping my feet. It was yapping and squealing and so was I! We must have been making such a noise, but no one came to investigate. Hopping and swearing (yes, even after doing a concert!), I eventually found the light switch and managed to get the family Yorkie out of my room. The next day 'Dad' casually said that he hoped I'd not been disturbed as little Bella loved to sleep under my bed and had a penchant for nipping toes!

Another dog incident happened when we were staying one night with a young family. The mum, Becky, said, 'We have a lovely little dog called Snowy, but she runs around very fast, so a friend is looking after her tonight. She'll bring her back at breakfast.'

The next morning, we were all enjoying breakfast when the doorbell rang. It was the friend returning Snowy. 'Here's our lovely little girl,' Becky said, carrying her over to us and thrusting her in Marilyn's face. Marilyn nearly choked as the dog was quite smelly.

Then the dad, Duncan, sat Snowy on the table. Picking up his spoon he filled it with cornflakes from his bowl and offered it to Snowy, and once she'd finished had a mouthful himself then offered Snowy another. I was sitting with my mouth open, hardly able to believe what I was seeing. Marilyn didn't know what was happening and chatted away happily. For some reason, I just didn't fancy the rest of my cereal after that.

Over the years, our own dogs have always been up for raising smiles and bringing blessing to us and our guests. I remember when we were at Brunel Manor, Devon for an Easter house party and the events manager had laid out an Easter egg hunt for early Easter Sunday. But unfortunately I let Marilyn's guide dog at the time, Giles, out for his run earlier still . . .

At our conferences it's always a joy to see how much love and fun our various dogs bring to the guests attending. Here are a couple of stories from those guests, firstly Jill, then Eileen.

I remember one afternoon on the beach with Goldie (Tracy's hearing dog) and Saffie (Marilyn's guide dog), when Saffie buried her ball in the sand and I spent the rest of the afternoon on my hands and knees digging up the sand all around the spot with both dogs helping me, as I desperately didn't want to go back without that ball. We nearly got to Australia in our efforts! Eventually I had to concede defeat and went back without it. However, it turned out great as another of the guests bought her three brand-new yellow balls to replace the dirty old one. I remember Tracy standing up at breakfast the last morning telling everyone the dogs were going home with more than they came with! I also learned a lot from that about having to let go of the old things in order to get the new.

Jill

One very amusing story was when we were enjoying tea having just arrived at the centre and a loose guide dog suddenly rushed into the room, saw the scones on the plate and swallowed them whole like a suction pump. Very naughty but extremely funny.

Eileen

Being disorganised . . .

Tracy

On one occasion, we were at Marilyn's house in Watford doing various jobs there, as it was a free day. We were both dressed extremely casually and Marilyn's hair looked wild, as she'd had important phone calls from the time she woke up, so hadn't bothered much with it. After all, who would be seeing her?

Suddenly at about 2 p.m. there was yet another phone call. I shrugged and got on with more things, only to stop as Marilyn screamed, 'That was John, my minister, we're meant to be at the Koinonia Seniors group.[3] I'm singing to them. It starts now. Help me, Trace!'

We dashed upstairs and I found her a dress that didn't need ironing, but what to do with her hair? It had to be washed, as it was sticking out everywhere. I could dry the front at least. They wouldn't see the back anyway. The plan worked and I managed to style the front nicely before the doorbell rang. John drove us quickly to the church. The elderly audience were already in their seats facing the piano as we rushed in. As soon as I saw it, I started to laugh. So much for all our efforts to style just the front of Marilyn's hair – no one had thought to turn the piano round: Marilyn would be singing with her back to the audience!

Another time at Colwyn Bay, North Wales, Margaret, our hostess, showed us to our bedroom, which was at the end of the corridor on the left of the bathroom. Marilyn went to the bathroom while I unpacked and got ready for bed. Suddenly I heard a scream and commotion. It turned out that when Marilyn had come out of the bathroom and gone into 'our' room, she heard me cleaning my teeth and knew I wouldn't hear if she spoke to me, so she'd found a chair and started undressing. She was wandering around in the altogether looking for her pyjamas, when Margaret came in and cried, 'Oh my dear, you're in the wrong room!' It had been her husband cleaning his teeth, not me! Margaret said, 'I've been married for forty years and he's never had a young lady undressing in his room before!' Fortunately, he hadn't seen anything as his back had been turned, but we kept giggling for ages that night.

It's so easy when you're blind to take a wrong turn.

Concert clothes...

Tracy

We always try to dress up a bit for concerts and have a variety of outfits ranging from smart casual to posh, so we can match the style of the event.

Marilyn

Once, in the nineties, we were on our way to Bristol and were nearly there when Trace shrieked, 'Catastrophe! I've left the hanging bag with our concert clothes!' This was an event needing a properly posh outfit, but we were dressed very casually for the journey. There was nothing for it but to tell the organisers we'd have to go immediately to Marks & Spencer. The more we tried to find something suitable, the harder it seemed. Nothing was quite right. In the end we got an ordinary cream jersey dress for me. It was nice but nothing special. Somehow it got named the 'Glamorous Dress'. It was not glamorous at all, but the girl-friend of our bass guitarist, Nick Cook, was travelling with us, and as she was training to be a beautician, she offered to do my make-up. I'd never had so many coats of mascara and lipstick, and so the dress inherited the name 'Glamorous'!

Tracy

At times, I can take myself a bit too seriously and easily feel a failure or inferior, especially on posh occasions. But I'm discovering that the word 'failure' isn't part of God's vocabulary. Instead, he loves us with a love that always trusts, always hopes, always perseveres and 'keeps no record of wrongs' (1 Cor. 13:4–7). He wants to use those times when we make mistakes to help us grow in our inner security, so that we can learn to laugh at ourselves and discover the joy of knowing we are not called to be infallible!

One of the earliest events I did with Marilyn was a Christian View-point luncheon. These were times of outreach, usually with a meal and an invited speaker. I sat down at a prettily decorated table with Marilyn and several ladies, including the organiser, Karen. They all looked very sophisticated.

We had a nice ploughman's, and just before pudding someone tapped me on the shoulder and a lady smilingly reached forward with a jug. I couldn't hear her, so I presumed she was telling me that it was water for Marilyn. I thanked her and then Marilyn chose a nectarine for her pudding. As she bit into it, she dropped it, scrabbling frantically as it rolled down her front.

'Trace, help!'

'Oh no,' I said, staring at the sticky stain. It looked so obvious against the plain pale blue of her dress. I rubbed it with my serviette but that made it look even worse. I suddenly remembered the jug of water the lady had brought. It was in a china jug which was unusual, but I guessed they'd used all their glass jugs during lunch. Without thinking, I quickly dipped my serviette and rubbed it on the stain. The lady next to me leaned forward and exclaimed, 'Oeh, that was the milk for our cawffee.'

Highly embarrassed, I realised Marilyn's dress was now stained with both juice and milk; we would have to go out to the ladies. How could I have been so silly?

The start of the concert was delayed somewhat as I tried to repair the damage. But whenever I caught sight of the big wet mark, I had to laugh. Marilyn started by introducing Ian and me, taking great pains to say, 'Tracy my assistant is both deaf and *partially sighted*.' The lady who had been upset for her 'cawffee' raised her eyebrows at me, and I felt heat rise to my cheeks. I can *usually* tell the difference between milk and water, but somehow that day . . . So much for trying to be posh!

Marilyn used to wear smart low-heeled court shoes at her concerts. She can't now because of her lymphoedema, which at the time was becoming a problem, so she only wore the 'posh' shoes for the concerts. We were travelling home late after an evening concert, and Marilyn still had these shoes on. She had recently read a book on how shoes can be damaging to our feet: God had not designed feet to fit into tight-fitting high heels.

When we arrived at a service station, we went in for a drink, but Marilyn's feet felt really uncomfortable and without warning she shouted out, 'Why are you making me wear these ungodly shoes?' Poor Nick, sound engineer Alistair and the passers-by looked so startled. Although Marilyn was genuinely upset, we all got the giggles later as we thought of it.

Places to stay and things left behind . . .

Marilyn

Our dear friend and driver, Ron, arrived to take us for a long journey up north. We'd been going for about forty minutes when I suddenly cried out, 'Oh, Ron, I've left my Braille Lite behind!' This was a Braille computer with all my songs, contact details, Bible verses, etc. I just couldn't do the tour without it. So there was nothing for it but to go all the way back through busy traffic to get it. Amazingly, we did make our concert in time but Ron, though very patient, must have found it a real trial! He kept his thoughts to himself and, as always, maintained a most friendly and cheerful demeanour.

As our equipment is quite heavy, we sometimes took along two men to help us, and Ron's friend John often accompanied us. There was one very memorable occasion in Lancashire. The concert went very well and the organiser assured us that she had booked us into a beautiful Christian hotel that was actually a castle. We were excited, but our hopes were quickly dashed because when we arrived after the concert and tried to check in, they'd never heard of us and announced they were completely full. It was late, so we rang the organiser who came and remonstrated with the manager, but there was nothing they could do. In the end Trace and I stayed with the organiser's kind neighbour, squashed into one bed, and Ron and John stayed in a caravan in our host's garden. We called that event from castle to caravan!

When we get grumpy . . .

Tracy

As Marilyn describes in her song 'Refresh Me Lord',[4] sometimes travelling makes us tired and then we can get snappy and grumpy with those around us. Marilyn gets exasperated if I am always rearranging her clothes or suggesting she wears something that feels uncomfortable. I then try to justify myself and we'll start squabbling. One particular day I said to her, 'Stop going on, you're like a Jack Russell,' and as quick as a flash she retorted, 'Well, you're like a Yorkshire terrier!' There was a pause, then we both burst out laughing. We often stayed with hosts that have yappy breeds, so now if we get grumpy we often say, 'Oh, Jack and Yorkie have come!' and start to laugh instead of accuse.

Neither of us are great at making decisions, especially about where we want to eat or go, wanting the other to decide. But in the end, we get tense, and we've been known to have the odd explosion. Once when we were staying near Eve Smith's, we got cross with each other on the slope down to the pier and started arguing silently on our hands, using the deafblind finger spelling. We were 'writing' the letters furiously on each other's hands and didn't think anyone would know as, after all, we weren't speaking out loud. But Eve who was waiting at the bottom said, 'What on earth are you two arguing about?' To our embarrassment, she'd guessed and thought it looked hilarious!

Marilyn

One day when a sermon in the church we were singing at seemed boring, I told Trace a joke, using the hand language. A lady said to us after, 'I know you were not spelling out the sermon to her because you had such a big grin on your face!'

Tracy

We both believe that as Christians laughter and joy should be so much part of our lives. It's the best medicine we can take.

20

Holy Connections

Lord our God, only You are doing wonders

Marilyn Baker[1]

Marilyn

I had always admired the writings of Jennifer Rees Larcombe, and Torch Trust used to publish some of her articles in their magazines. She sounded such a lovely person, though I knew she suffered with the effects of having had encephalitis at least twice. The severity of these illnesses had meant that Jen lost the ability to walk and had been in a wheelchair for the past eight years. She had also developed ME and struggled with constant fatigue as well as pain.

In the articles, Jen shared out the lessons God was teaching her through her difficulties. I found myself praying for her often, longing somehow that she would be healed. In 1990, to my delight I heard that she had indeed received a dramatic miracle of healing.

In 1991, when I found out that Jennifer would be speaking at Gold Hill Baptist Church near where we lived, I was determined to go with all the team. To my amazement she came up before it started and welcomed me as if I was her long-lost friend, explaining that my songs had been a great help to her over the years, especially when she'd been in hospital. I was staggered and remembered how, when I was having the back treatment in Cornwall and despairing of ever being able to live life normally again, a friend gave us Jen's book called *Beyond Healing*.[2] Jen wrote of how God was bringing her deep 'peace-joy' despite still being chronically ill. As we'd read her moving story, I'd felt very encouraged, having a new reassurance that God was working in my life too. How amazing that God had used us both to encourage one another in this way.

Tracy

When the minister introduced Jen, I was eager to hear her story of healing. Marilyn finger-spelled all she said on my hand. She shared how she was speaking one day at a ladies' group and a young lady, Wendy, a new Christian who had experienced much brokenness, suddenly heard a voice saying, 'I want to heal Jen.' She told the pastor, expecting him to then pray for Jen. But he said, 'You need to pray for her, Wendy. It's you God has spoken to and given the burden.'

Poor Wendy had never even heard a prayer for healing, so how on earth could she do it? But the pastor was adamant. So at the end of the meeting, she went up to Jen and very hesitantly shared what she believed God had said.

Jen had been in a lot of pain that day and she hadn't even known what to talk about, but the Lord had given her a vision of filling people's emptiness and that had indeed happened, with many receiving his love. Now when this young lady said that God wanted to heal her, all Jen wanted was to get home as soon as possible. But she smiled at Wendy and said she would love her to pray. Wendy fumbled out a short prayer and Jen described how she then supposed she'd better get up. And she just got up, straight away, without any need of help . . . God had answered Wendy's prayer and healed Jen instantly.

As Jen continued sharing, I felt full of wonder at how lovingly God had brought this amazing miracle about. Yes, he'd wanted to free Jen from her severe pain, but he'd also cared deeply for Wendy and the hurt she'd experienced. How wonderful that God had used her so powerfully. It reminded me of the verse in 1 Corinthians 1:27: 'God chose the foolish things of the world to shame the wise; God chose the weak things of the world to shame the strong.'

God wanted his glory to be made known; the glory of his inexpressible kindness, compassion and grace. I felt deeply challenged and longed to see God's power working more in my own life, and for others who felt inferior to know the joy of God using them.

After the meeting we went to a local pub for lunch and found that Jen and her team were there too. Marilyn and I both felt a real bond with Jen and were so glad we'd gone to hear her.

We kept in touch with Jen and her then husband, Tony, who were taking steps to rekindle their vision to minister to people who had been broken in life. In 1992, they invited us to join them in their first conference at Hothorpe Hall in Leicestershire. The theme was 'Living Through Change' and Marilyn would be leading the worship with Jen speaking and more than a hundred guests, including their prayer team. About three weeks before the conference, Jen and Tony visited us in Watford to pray with us for the guests and their various needs.

Marilyn

When Tony and Jen came, they told us about the people that we would be meeting: many disabled, broken and struggling. I felt overwhelmed. Our ministry was mainly giving concerts, and praying briefly with people at the end, but to get so involved with the guests at a conference was an unknown quantity to us both. I longed that we would be real channels of God's love.

Tracy

As the others talked, I suddenly had a strong sense that one of these guests was secretly ill with anorexia. I couldn't see anything on Jen's guest list relating to eating disorders, but there it was in my heart: 'Someone will be there who has anorexia.' Diffidently I mentioned it and Jen and Tony looked puzzled. 'Let's see if God reveals the person to us when we're there,' said Jen.

We prayed together and experienced a wonderful sense of God wanting to pour out his healing love on all who would be coming.

When we arrived at Hothorpe Hall there seemed to be wheelchairs everywhere and people using walkers, sticks, crutches and even mattresses to lie on in the meeting rooms, as they were in too much pain to sit. One lady, Leah, was about my age and had beautiful dark hair and eyes. She was completely immobilised in a high-backed wheelchair with a neck support. I felt drawn to her but was frustrated because I couldn't hear what she was saying, and as she had no movement in her neck, she couldn't turn towards me. Later we learned that she had been in a terrible car accident causing irreparable damage to her spine. She also developed multiple sclerosis (MS), maybe as a result of the trauma. It was heartbreaking. She was upbeat and spiritual in her responses, but I felt a deep sadness within and was praying for her.

One day in the worship time, Marilyn had a strong feeling she should sing one of her new solo songs called 'Come', which had a haunting melody expressing God's desire for us to draw close and let go of our burdens:

When you are tired and worried,
Your burdens with me you can share;
Yes I will take your heavy load,
Come drink in my love and care . . .[3]

As Leah heard these words she wept, people around her gently praying. She was so weary of trying to be positive and spiritual all the time. She'd felt she'd be letting God down if she expressed her real feelings, but in trying to bury them she'd become exhausted. The pathos of the song opened the door to her letting that burden go and realising that God still loved her, whether she was on the heights or in the depths. Later she wrote a beautiful poem about the freedom of being herself,

Leah, not something permanently shiny that she could never truly live up to.

Marilyn

What a time we had! We saw many lives transformed during that week: the light turning on in many people's hearts. Jen was so personable, everyone viewed her as their special friend. My own heart was warmed and we did our best to play our part. This conference would develop us in ways we could hardly imagine, for Jen was an amazing role model and we were challenged as we saw the tender way in which she made time to listen to people's stories. Everyone seemed to matter, and I saw how those who were shy or depressed came out of their shells when they were with her.

Tracy

The team prayer meetings were very powerful. Humanly, some could do very little, yet Jen and Tony recognised that they were equally God's precious children and heirs.[4] One lady, Janet, had hydrocephalus and could do nothing for herself. Her head rested on her shoulder and she needed a medical hoist to get in and out of bed. Speaking was hard for her and yet she loved to sing and had the most prayerful heart I had ever encountered. She would often bring a song in the middle of the team prayer time and we would all be drawn into God's heart of love.

Another team member, Deirdre Pettitt, was there with her daughter, Ros. They both seemed able-bodied, so Marilyn and I were shocked to discover that Ros was seriously ill with cystic fibrosis. I found it so moving to see the tender way Deirdre looked out for her daughter. She didn't smother her with overprotectiveness but was there for her whenever Ros needed her. I loved Deirdre's caring, prayerful spirit and longed that I might show Jesus' love as much as she did. Tragically, Ros died a few months later, but I was so glad we'd had the opportunity to meet her and her mum. After we moved to Kent in 1995, Deirdre became a wonderful supporter of MBM, too, and a hugely valued member of our prayer team. Sadly, in 2017 she developed cancer and had two years of physical pain and struggle before passing into God's presence in the autumn of 2019, reunited at last with her precious daughter. It's been such a huge privilege to know Deirdre, and we miss her greatly but know she is part of that heavenly cloud of witnesses mentioned in Hebrews 12:1, and we believe she is praying for us and cheering us on.

One of the hallmarks of that first conference, and the many others we attended with Jen and Tony, was the fun and laughter everywhere. At meal times, in the sessions, at coffee breaks and especially on the Fun Night, gales of laughter could be heard all around as guests and team cracked jokes together and shared embarrassing stories. Jen and Tony were a riot at times, as they told us all about the trials of bringing up their six children when Jen was ill. They acted out humorous sketches that had us all shrieking with laughter. Marilyn also brought an item in the Fun Night that nearly had everyone on the floor as she operatically sang 'If You Were the Only Girl (In the World)'[5] acting out the two characters she'd created: Luigi Macaroni and Blodwyn Evans. As Marilyn's voice is naturally low, even I could hear (and see) how hilarious it was as she went up to Blodwyn's falsetto soprano and plunged down again to Luigi's impassioned tenor! Laughter and fun were so healing, a vital part of all God was doing that week.

Near the end of the week, Jen knocked at our door and said with great excitement, 'Oh, Trace, we've found the anorexic!' I'd almost forgotten that word of knowledge as no one had come to light, but now Jen was telling me about a young woman who was there with her mother and who had just confessed that she was struggling with an anorexia relapse. I felt how deeply Father God loved her and wanted to minister to her. Jen and I prayed with her, and it became clear that she felt deep over-responsibility for her mum, who wasn't a Christian. In prayer, she released her mother into God's care and felt an immediate joy fill her heart. Later that evening something amazing happened – her mum gave her life to the Lord. We were all in tears at the tender way the Lord had come to minister to this dear mother and daughter.

Becoming friends with Jen and Tony and having the privilege of being part of their ministry that week and in subsequent conferences was profoundly impacting. Up until then our ministry had consisted mainly of concerts, tours, church weekends and taking part in big events such as Spring Harvest and New Wine. These were all powerful events but there was something missing – the time to really engage with people, to hear their stories, to laugh and cry and pray together. Here at Hothorpe, the greatest impact came through the atmosphere of love, acceptance and the belief that every person mattered and had something important to give. The worship was uplifting, the talks inspiring, the creative times were fun and the prayer ministry appointments brought transformation, but love was the glue that held everything together. Jen and Tony had given us a glimpse into what could be, and we began to feel a real hunger to do more events ourselves where we'd have the time and space to be with the people we were ministering to.

It was soon after that conference that there was a special service at Marilyn's church, SJR, to celebrate Marilyn Baker Ministries' ten years. John and Amanda Duncan came, and to our great surprise so did Tony and Jen. Marilyn sang and we both shared some of the beautiful things that had happened during the concerts and events. The church prayed for us all as a team to be recommissioned, and we felt so validated and supported. Richard and Shirley Harbour came and presented Marilyn with a lovely myrtle bush as a prophetic sign of the Lord's anointing on the ministry to transform the thorns and briars of people's lives into beautiful myrtle as in Isaiah 55:13 (NLT):

Where once there were thorns, cypress trees will grow. Where nettles grew, myrtles will sprout up. These events will bring great honor to the LORD's name; they will be an everlasting sign of his power and love.

This was an amazing prophetic picture of all God was doing through MBM, and we felt excited and full of anticipation about all that he was going to bring about in the coming days.

On a slightly humorous note, most people who know me are aware that I am probably the world's worst gardener as I have a dreadful tendency both with gardens and houseplants to either water them to death or forget to water them at all; or if I do any weeding, to pull up the flowers and leave the weeds. So I am ashamed to say that despite being awed by the myrtle bush's prophetic message, it still fell victim to my hapless gardening skills and very sadly died after a few months. For a while I was terrified that this was a sign of MBM's approaching demise, but time has proved otherwise!

Later that evening we held a celebration concert at Watford Grammar School for Girls. It was an amazing time, and in the middle there was a massive surprise for Marilyn when David Bruce from Word Records presented her with a gold disc for selling more than 50,000 albums. Marilyn's mouth dropped open! She'd had no idea that was to happen and neither had I. The rest of the team had known, but they'd all kept it secret. It was a wonderful validation of God's anointing on her music, and the disc still hangs proudly in her lounge today.

After that first conference with Jen and Tony in 1992 we went regularly with them to their conferences, including holiday conferences in Wales, Corfu and Turkey as well as Hothorpe Hall and Brunel Manor. We've met so many courageous people whose lives have been torn apart by devastating traumas or illness yet continue to hold onto the Lord; people like Peter and Sue who became part of our Brunel prayer team. Peter was only in his twenties when his life was torn apart by a severe stroke, leaving him paralysed down one side and in constant pain. Then our dear friend Gail, so glamorous and passionate in life, despite the brain surgery which left her partially paralysed and unable to see or hear on one side; or grandmother Maud, kind and full of fun, yet who had endured years of ritualistic abuse as a child . . . Somehow as we worshipped and met together in this atmosphere of love, with the Lord being given room to work, amazing doors would open into people's hurts.

In 1993, while helping Jen and Tony at another of their summer conferences, this time at Brunel Manor, Jen asked me if I could lead a workshop on listening to God. I felt a yes in my heart, and as I spent time praying, all the ideas for teaching it came together. On the day, after I shared, people went out or sat quietly in their seats listening to the Lord and writing down the thoughts that came to them. In the feedback time there was a tremendous sense of joy as one person after another shared the beautiful things the Lord had said to them. In fact, so many wanted to share that we had to resume the session after lunch. It was awesome, and I felt full of wonder at how the Lord had enabled people to hear him. Jen had come to the workshop to type for me so I'd know what people shared. She was so excited afterwards and asked me if I could write an article on listening to God that she would submit to *Renewal* magazine on my behalf. Although I was hardly aware at that time, something new and beautiful had been born.

21

Endings and Beginnings

Those who believe will find a love that cannot end.

Marilyn Baker[1]

As 1994 got underway, Marilyn was still making regular trips to see her dad, and sometimes if we were doing events near his home, we'd drop her off to stay with him for a couple of extra days. I always felt slightly nervous of him as he had such a brusque manner. Yet I could tell that he really did love Marilyn: the slight smile when he opened the door, the gifts of meat from his freezer, the way he glanced at her . . . all wordless signs of an affection he couldn't outwardly express.

Marilyn

I knew my dad loved me, but our relationship was never easy. He did not suffer fools gladly, he was an astute businessman and in whatever he did, he was utterly determined to succeed because life had been such a struggle for him. Because of his anxiety for me being blind, he was very overprotective and felt he needed to control everything.

One day in 1994 I was praying about our upcoming tour to Northern Ireland when a clear thought came: 'Your dad won't be going to the holiday home in Wales much more now.' I was shocked. Was he ill? Had something happened? With some trepidation, I rang him and asked if he was OK. He gave his stock answer, 'Yes, fine.' But I couldn't forget it and rang every day just to check. I also started praying especially for angelic protection around him. The following week, his dear friend Mary rang. She said Dad had not wanted to worry me but it was obvious that I had picked something up, and she wanted me to know that he was very ill with an aneurism and needed an urgent operation otherwise he would die.

In the meantime, Carol Franklin and I had been planning a holiday in the summer, but one day, as she was driving past the motorway turn-off that led to Dad's, she had a clear impression that we wouldn't be going on holiday but that she would be helping me clear Dad's house. She didn't say anything to me, but when I announced I wasn't sure about the holiday, she seemed remarkably unconcerned.

Before his operation, I went to see Dad at the hospital. I had hoped he would be happy I was there, and maybe he was, but his manner was terse. He was so afraid he would not make it. I said I would pray for him and he said a simple, 'Thanks'.

The surgery was successful in treating the aneurism, but afterwards the consultant told me that Dad hadn't regained consciousness; however, they still had high hopes for him. Sadness filled my heart. Had I run out of time to reach him with God's love? Paul Wood and Tracy took me to visit him again, and waited outside while I sat and told him how much I loved him, words I had never been able to say to him before, and that God loved him and completely forgave him. Was he hearing any of it? As I was talking, a nurse told me that there were tears in his eyes, but he didn't wake up or make any sound.

Tracy

In the meantime, Paul and I sat outside, praying. Suddenly a picture came to my mind. I could see her dad sitting at a round table with Marilyn on one side and Jesus on the other. Her dad was looking directly at Jesus and then at Marilyn and God said in my heart, 'I am answering all the prayers and turning his heart towards my Son and towards Marilyn.' Deep in my spirit I felt a joy that he was crossing the threshold into heaven's kingdom. I told Marilyn when she came out, and she felt comforted and hopeful but still longed to have proof that her dad really had opened his heart to the Lord.

Marilyn

During our holiday period, Carol and I went to stay at Dad's bungalow instead of going away. We met the hospital chaplain, and as a result, he went to visit Dad and prayed that he would know God's love and be able to release all his worries or regrets into God's hands, including any concerns for me. He said he thought he saw my dad trying to respond as he ended with 'Amen'. Carol and I stayed at Dad's bedside, but in the end, as there was no change, we had to make the difficult choice to switch off his life support. It seemed he was ready to go and died amazingly quickly. Then with the help of my cousin Irene, we had the mammoth task of clearing out the bungalow. It was very dirty and obvious to me that Dad had not been coping for a long time. Carol in particular worked like a trooper. The amazing thing was that she only had those two weeks available, and it made me understand afresh God's incredible timing. I missed Dad more than I imagined I would. I'd been so used to him telling me what to do, and for a time my life felt rudderless.

Tracy

Another ending at that time in 1994 was the era of my sharing rented houses with friends from college and church. I'd been renting ever since my third year at college but in 1994 that pattern came to a natural end when my two housemates, my close friends Judith and Anne, moved away. Marilyn had been living on her own since Penny Cooze left and one day we talked about moving in together. We were hesitant, would it really work? Would we be stepping too much on each other's toes? We were fearful of our friendship being affected, but it would make sense for me to be on hand. It became clear that God had opened the door, and I moved in shortly before Marilyn's dad became so ill. It was incredible timing, as only God could have known what was going to happen and how much Marilyn would need the comfort of someone living with her.

We can truly rest in his love and relax in his care, for he is always working on our behalf.

A prophetic picture for someone

As I've been writing this section, a picture from the Lord has come to my mind of a garden that is in the process of being created. It looks barren and overgrown, but I saw the gardener working with great care, clearing some parts of the garden and planting bulbs in others. He spent time turning the earth and watering ground that looked like bare mud, but he was nurturing the life hidden underneath. He knew exactly what care each area needed: whether it was cutting back or watering. I asked the Lord what the garden represented, and he showed me that it's for someone reading this. You feel very anxious and see your life as barren and a constant struggle, with no expectation of anything good happening. I felt his compassion for you and his longing that you know his loving care. I asked him how he sees you, and I saw a picture of the garden again from his perspective. It was beautiful, with shoots already starting to flower, the bushes and trees in bloom; it had colour and fragrance and the mystery of things yet to be revealed. This is you. You are beautiful to him, and he is always with you to tend and nurture you.

If you've been struggling, let this word encourage you. Just as God helped Marilyn during that time of loss, so he is with you.

For me, moving in with Marilyn was the end of my student way of life and part of me missed that. But Marilyn was such a good friend, and she went out of her way to make me feel that it was my home as well as my workplace. What we didn't know was that moving in together was the beginning of something new – Marilyn and me making our home a place of love and hospitality to all who might come.

One funny but lovely thing also happened around this time. I'd always hankered to own a leather jacket. When I saw other girls wearing them, they looked so cool. I wanted to be trendy too! I'd not long had my colour analysis done and knew that rather than the popular colours of black or grey, I would need to find a jacket in brown or beige. Would it be possible to find a 'cool' brown jacket?

Now Marilyn's back was so much better we often went shopping together in Watford's burgeoning town centre. But as much as I dragged us into shop after shop, I could never find the right jacket; there was always something not quite right. I was especially concerned about the arm length, as my arms are long and I didn't want to look a nerd. Eventually, after trying about fifty jackets I gave up, probably much to Marilyn's relief.

One day Marilyn announced she was going to the Ideal Home Exhibition with our friend Sarah. I was busy so didn't join them. Several hours later, Marilyn returned and excitedly gave me a carrier bag. 'I've got you a present,' she said, all smiles.

I took the bag hesitantly, thinking it must be a saucepan or something. I could see there was leather inside and my heart began to pound. Surely it couldn't be . . .? And if it was, how could it possibly be right when I'd looked at so many? How would Marilyn know the right size? I was dreading pulling it out, as Marilyn looked so happy and I didn't want to disappoint her.

Marilyn

Walking round the exhibition, I'd caught a familiar smell, so we wandered into the Italian leather stall. My hand touched a jacket and Sarah remarked casually, 'That's a nice one, good for someone thin and tall.' It was then I heard it, something so unbelievable my heart nearly stopped: 'This is the one.'

'No, Lord,' I said inwardly. 'It can't be – surely not. I have no idea what she likes; I don't even know what colour she's looking for.' But again, the peaceful thought came, 'This is the one.' I decided to make buying it an improbability as I didn't want to be landed with something Tracy didn't want. The shopkeeper asked how much I would pay. It was well over £100 so I said £40. A long pause followed, and then he simply said, 'Take it.' I was flabbergasted, but knew God must be in it. Nevertheless, I felt nervous as we arrived home.

Tracy

When I saw it, I was amazed. It was a beautiful rich brown and the style was both feminine and cool! Needing it to be feminine was one requirement that had made me reject so many. This jacket was definitely pretty. But surely the size would be wrong? I was so skinny and my arms were so long . . . 'I'll just try it on,' I told Marilyn. She helped pull the jacket round my back and ran her hands over me, testing the fit. It was perfect; I couldn't believe it. What a beautiful gift and how amazing that Marilyn had found it. She said it was a gift from my heavenly Father who wanted to show how proud he was to have me as his daughter. The whole thing showed us how intricately God is involved in our everyday lives and wants to be a real friend to us.

This year 1994 was proving to be full of new things. Just two years after making her album *Face to Face*, Marilyn now had enough songs for a new recording, and in the spring I travelled to Leeds with her to record *By Your Side*. One track resonated with me so deeply, it made me cry. 'Reason for Living' expressed why Jesus had come: to lift our shame, free us from our fears and enable us to walk confidently, knowing that in God we have 'reason for living'.

As she sang the words over and over in the studio and the musicians added their parts, the Holy Spirit worked in my heart showing me that I was his, that God had created me, not to be shamed and rejected but to be loved and have a purpose in my life to reach out to others with that same love. I had tried everything, even as a Christian, to bury the shame of my childhood years, but God was saying through the song that he had already lifted the shame from me and I was totally accepted. The words were powerful and the music exultant.

Jesus Jesus is here,
He wants to comfort, to take all your shame away.
He knows all of your fears,
Sees all the tears you've tried to hide away . . .[2]

God did a significant work in that studio and 'Reason for Living' is still one of my favourite songs. I am so thankful to the Lord for giving Marilyn such meaningful songs and touching my heart so deeply.

As always, it was a great privilege to be part of the 'studio club' and to see how alive Marilyn was as the songs came into being. There is a tremendous buzz as the singers, musicians and techies do their thing. Chris Norton, the producer, was a prolific musician himself, and it was a joy to see him playing some of the piano parts. For this album, we were in a house studio – two converted bedrooms with holes drilled in the walls for the various cables! We would crowd onto a two-seater settee and I would go up and down making drinks for all. Sometimes hours would go by as the backing singers or instrumentalists worked on a small section of a song. Often Marilyn's sense of what was right was different to the rest, and I learned to read her expression and pray if she looked tense because, as the composer, she knew how beautiful she wanted each song to sound. On the other hand, when things went well, Marilyn would be infused with excitement, throwing her head back and laughing. I loved watching the love of creating and music-making in everyone, and I began to long to be more creative myself. I'd always wanted to become a writer and had already experienced the thrill of writing that article on listening to God that Jen had submitted for me. Maybe I could do more like that?

When we returned home I was overwhelmed to find a letter from the publishers Hodder & Stoughton. Unknown to me, Jen had submitted my article to her own editor, and they were interested in me writing a book about listening to God. Joy and butterflies filled me in equal measure. Could I do this? Who was I to think I could write a book and have it published? All the old negative words flooded into my mind. But no, I didn't have to listen to those old lies any longer. Suddenly I realised that I had a choice. I could either go on being imprisoned in the negatives of the past or start to live out of what God said about me. I remembered some verses from Psalm 103 which we often read out in concerts:

> who redeems your life from the pit and crowns you with love and compassion, who satisfies your desires with good things so that your youth is renewed like the eagle's (vv. 4,5).

God wanted to 'satisfy' my buried desires to write. He wanted to renew my youth and enable me to soar. I decided I would accept Hodder's offer, and *The Voice of the Father* was published at the end of 1995.

Not long after moving in with Marilyn, an amazing thing happened. One night I was busy working on the book when there was a ring at the door. A kitchen salesman was there, and as Marilyn was considering having a new kitchen, she invited him in. After a few minutes of 'kitchen talk' he noticed I was at my computer and asked what I was doing. When we explained that I was writing a Christian book, he told us an amazing story – how, as a non-practising Jew, he'd had a serious car accident and was left in a coma. No one had expected him to live, and his family came to the hospital to say goodbye. He told how he could hear them talking as they stood by the bed and had longed to speak, but couldn't, yet they told him later that he looked as if he was crying.

When Marilyn heard those words, she sat up in astonishment. This man was describing exactly what had happened with her dad. They both looked like they were crying. The man described how while in the coma, he'd had a deep encounter with God and asked for a second chance to live his life for him. Marilyn realised that if that could happen to him, then her dad could certainly have had a deep encounter with God too. This was no coincidence. God had sent this man to reassure her that her dad was indeed with Jesus.

We were overcome, realising that God had arranged for this man to come just twelve weeks after Marilyn's dad had died. God wanted to bring that longed-for reassurance to her heart that her dad was indeed with Jesus. Later, Marilyn started to share this story in her concerts, and many people have been comforted and encouraged to entrust their loved ones into God's great mercy and care.

22

A New Home

But in my life I've found something different, my heart's been touched by a wonderful love . . .

Marilyn Baker[1]

In late 1994 Jen and Tony Larcombe made contact. They were moving to Hadlow, a village near Tonbridge, Kent. They had bought a large bungalow that they were planning would become not just their home, but the base for their new ministry. To our amazement, they asked if we would consider moving there too and for our two ministries to become mutually supportive while still retaining their individuality. This would be a massive decision, for it didn't just affect our future but Paul Wood's too. Marilyn had lived in Watford for well over twenty years. All her friends and trustees were based there. Pam Lee, our administrator, would have to leave MBM if we moved. It would take Marilyn a long time to get used to a new house, let alone a new location. There were so many reasons why moving seemed a crazy idea, and yet there seemed a rightness about it that even the trustees felt.

In the spring of 1995, we would be travelling to the USA for about a month of events around Nashville. It was decided that we would continue to pray during that tour, and if there was a general feeling of 'yes', then we would take the necessary steps to relocate our lives and ministry to Kent.

Our trip to the States was organised by Marilyn's first manager, David Payne, and we stayed with him and his wife, Marilyn. The tour included making contact with a record producer in Nashville, and Marilyn would return there later in the year to record a new compilation album called *Changing Me*. The tour was slow to get off the ground, which was frustrating, but I was able to continue writing *The Voice of the Father* and we had some lovely boat trips out on the lakes. Once the bookings got underway the tour proved to be a rich time, and once again it seemed to be in the smaller, personal events that God moved most powerfully.

Throughout the tour we did continue to pray, and by the end we knew that God was in this idea to move to Kent. Paul also felt right about it for himself, which was wonderful. On our return, Tony called and said they wanted to play a game of 'find the house' with us. They took us around Hadlow looking at lots of possible properties. One or two looked quite posh and I hankered after their décor, but somehow none of them seemed quite right.

Over tea with Jen and Tony, we prayed together about the future. That first house hunt hadn't been successful, but we did feel convinced that the move was right.

Soon after that, Marilyn was sent more houses to view and asked Carol Franklin to help her look, as I was with my family.

There was one that Marilyn became particularly interested in: a three-bedroom semi-detached. When Marilyn told Paul and me that she wanted to put an offer on it, we were concerned. We went down to see it a few days later and my initial feeling was negative. It looked smaller than those we'd already seen, and both the front and back gardens were a mass of tangled briars. Paul started to measure up to see if Marilyn's furniture would fit, and to his amazement, everything did. When Marilyn had viewed it with Carol, she'd asked the Lord, 'Where shall I have the keyboards?' and felt him say, 'In the dining room.' It was so clear and specific that Marilyn knew this was his voice and she'd felt a peace within her that the house was right. As Paul measured the possible space for the keyboards, he found to his surprise that it was perfect.

The same thing happened with Marilyn's huge collection of Braille books, housed in Watford in a large, specially made bookcase. When Paul measured an alcove in the bedroom that would be Marilyn's, he discovered it was the perfect size for this bookcase. It seemed unbelievable. Paul also found an affordable room to rent in a house in a nearby village, which was another example of God's wonderful provision. The big hurdle was whether Marilyn could sell her Watford house. But God had it all in hand. A few days later, the man who owned the car valeting business two doors away told Marilyn he'd like to buy her house for his son. Everything was sorted for the move without the house even needing to go on the market.

In 1994, because bookings were changing and we were not so constantly on the road, Marilyn had felt it was the right time to consider having a guide dog again. When life was so busy she'd been relieved not to have a dog, but now she wanted to be more independent. She'd applied knowing that she might have to wait a long time, but it was actually within just a few months that Guide Dogs called to say they had a suitable dog for her and she would need to go to train for a month in November 1995. This would be just three weeks after our move. The timing was quicker than we'd expected, but it proved to be just right.

Both our churches had prayed for our move, and Marilyn's gave her a lovely chiming clock as a parting gift. We felt sad to leave our church families and all our dear friends but knew this was the beginning of a new adventure.

On 15 October 1995, Marilyn, having cooked a final full English breakfast, closed her front door for the last time, and with Penny Misselbrook and two other friends, we headed down the motorway to Kent and our new home in Hadlow.

Paul had gone ahead to oversee the laying of the new carpets and furniture and to ensure the new drive was finished before we all arrived. Hours later, between us and the removal men, the furniture was more or less in the right rooms, boxes were piled up everywhere and we were swimming in cups of tea. Jen and Tony had invited us all for an evening meal, which we were most thankful for. At about 10 p.m.

we waved goodbye to our Watford friends. What brilliant friends they'd been!

The next day we went to Jen and Tony's to join their supporters' prayer meeting, and Jen said that afterwards they would all come back to our house to bless each room. That seemed a fantastic idea, although we weren't sure how fifteen or so people would fit around the boxes! But it was a special time with a lot of laughter, too, as we scrambled to find clear places to stand. Jen's administrator offered to sew curtains for us and Lynn, one of her prayer team, promised to take us food shopping. We felt so touched by everyone's kindness. Later that evening there was a knock on the door, and a couple who lived opposite, Patti and David Hunter, were there to welcome us with cake. They would soon become special friends and supporters of the work, with David becoming MBM's new chair of trustees.

Over the next few weeks, things gradually fell into place. We'd already advertised in the local churches for a new administrator, and Julie Hillary, who lived in Tonbridge, was the one. Julie was so friendly and a very good administrator. Jen and Tony made a space for her to work in their lounge while the new combined office for their ministry and MBM's was erected at the end of their large garden. We still needed to find local trustees and a church, but we were getting there.

Just three weeks later, Paul and I took Marilyn to Redbridge Guide Dogs Training School where she would train with her new dog, a golden retriever – Giles.

Marilyn

Thus it was that the most lovable rogue of all came into our lives. Giles had such a big character and brought joy to everyone. A huge golden softie, he loved to take people's arms gently in his mouth as a sign of his affection, and many other unlikely objects would find themselves in his mouth too. Bars of soap, socks or tights, slippers and all sorts would disappear and turn up rather wet but undamaged. When the doorbell rang, Giles would be as likely to greet the visitor with a piece of my underwear as with a soft toy. He began to make a kind of soft hissing sound whenever he saw something he wanted. I loved this and turned it into a trick commanding him to 'speak', and as time went by, he began to 'speak' all the time!

When Giles first came home with me, we had some difficulties in learning to work together because I was too unfamiliar with my road and the village to be confident in my commands to Giles. I hadn't been out on my own for thirteen years, since giving up Yuma in 1982 when I started singing full-time, so it was a huge thing for me.

My lack of confidence translated itself to Giles, who became unsure, and he developed a fear about crossing a particular side road, sitting unmoving at the kerb. In desperation, thinking I'd have to send him back, I told Jen, and she prayed that Giles would see an angel and be released to work properly. Amazingly, though it took a while, that release did happen, and soon I was rediscovering the joy of going to the village or into town on my own. Giles retained a stubborn streak, and if he had a set idea about a route, he would often dig his heels in if I wanted otherwise.

When Giles was naughty, which was very often, Trace commented on how he always managed to look innocent, as if butter wouldn't melt in his mouth, but he would steal whatever he could find. One day, when we were about to enjoy a delicious Sunday lunch at our hosts' after taking their church service, he found a whole variety of cheeses for after dinner on a low trolley. Wrappings and all disappeared without anyone realising what was happening. Our hostess let out a cry of disbelief when she saw it was all gone! On another occasion when we were singing in Doncaster, he wandered out of our host's house because the lady had left the front door open. We called frantically and searched everywhere, to no avail; I was distraught and said I would not leave the area until he was found, even if we had to cancel concerts. We informed the police and RSPCA and they called back saying he'd been found in a lady's house and was enjoying all manner of treats. As much as I wanted to be cross with him, I couldn't be; I was just glad to get him back.

Tracy

In January 1996 work started to convert the adjoined garage into another room and extend the utility room behind it, adding a downstairs shower. With only three bedrooms, we wanted the option of having more than one person to stay and to be able to have people who couldn't manage stairs. It was a mammoth project and we did get into some muddles along the way, but in the end we were pleased with the result.

About three months after the work was completed, Marilyn, Giles and I were walking up our road when someone tapped me on the shoulder. It was Lilian Wild, who we'd met at Jen's conference at Brunel Manor the previous summer. We were very surprised to see her there. She was planning to move to Tunbridge Wells in September and needed assurance she was hearing God correctly. With no idea of our address, she'd spent the day searching and asking in the village, but no one knew where we lived. She'd been walking up the main road when a bus drew up and we got off; incredible timing! We chatted and prayed with Lilian that day and had tea together before she went home. We didn't know then what a wonderful friend she would become to us and to the ministry. But God was creating strong links with many people who would become close friends and part of our support team.

Julie, our administrator, introduced us to her church in Tonbridge, and after visiting we knew God was leading us to make that our spiritual home. We loved being part of Jen's prayer meetings and quiet days, as well as the bigger residential conferences. It was awesome, too, how the Lord seemed to fit different people's strengths together like a jigsaw puzzle, with Marilyn's songs softening people's hearts and drawing us into worship, Jen's speaking and praying enabling people to take steps into healing and my words of knowledge shining light on hidden needs. Other team members would also contribute their expertise in doing craft or worshipping with banners, which would bring beautiful release to people. Everyone mattered and had something to give. (We were to see this happening again and again when we later took steps to run our own conferences, as people who had obvious weaknesses were empowered to give out in their own unique ways. This is a central part of our ministry today.)

We made friends with Jen's team members, with many of them becoming precious supporters of our ministry, too, like David Stanford-Beale who later replaced David Hunter as chair, Jenny 'Coopie' Cooper who painted my 'tower' vision and Jackie Porter who had great experience in prayer ministry and a naughty sense of humour. Jackie was a 'doggy' person and Giles fell passionately in love with her, and his habit of 'speaking' would reach a crescendo whenever Jackie drew near. One day she was late to a session and Marilyn was already leading worship, with Giles tied to her chair. Jackie tried to sneak in at the back, but Giles saw her, jumped up and, 'speaking' loudly, tried to get to her – through the keyboard stand! Worship that day came to rather an abrupt and giggly end.

As well as drawing us to people who would become part of the ministry, God was also showing us how he loves to heal loneliness and bring the joy of love to those struggling in life.

Dave, for example, wrote to me to say how much my book *Expecting God to Speak to You!*[2] was blessing him. It turned out he was on probation and his life had been in a mess for many years. He had no family and had experienced so much loss, but my book had given him hope. Eventually he moved to Kent and we became friends. His life is not easy, as it is always hard for an ex-offender to be accepted in the community, but he loves to help us in many practical ways. Recently he has experienced a wonderful revelation of God's forgiveness and been filled with the Holy Spirit, which is awesome.

Marilyn

One of the most touching letters we had after moving to Kent was from a Hungarian girl called Ildi. It started, 'Dear Someone'. She had experienced very deep sadness for one so young, having recently nursed her mother until she died of cancer. Earlier she'd lost her brother, and her parents had divorced. Our administrators usually answered our letters, but something told me I should answer this one myself. She was a librarian at the University of Debrecen, and to say she was overjoyed to hear from me was an understatement. We shared a lot in emails and then we tried Skype, which was new for me. I wanted her to feel really at ease with me. Her English was amazingly fluent, and so it was that a precious online friendship began to develop. Tracy also came into the Skype conversations through us all typing. It was great fun and we had many laughs.

Eve Smith, who often went to Hungary, invited us to go with her as the new Kanaan Haz was being built. When I told Ildi, she was so excited and said she could arrange a concert for us in Debrecen. She knew the young people would love it and was determined to get my songs translated so that people could really hear the heart of the Christian message.

Tracy's sister was ill, so Tracy stayed behind for the first part of the trip, and I travelled to Pápa with my dear friend Hilary, who was now widowed. We visited the orphanages with Eve and met some wonderful Christians, enjoyed swimming in the hot pools, and saw how Kanaan Haz was being transformed from a derelict building into a home for needy families. Then Tracy arrived and Hilary went home. We were driven to Debrecen where we met Ildi. I'd kept wondering how it would be when we met 'in the flesh'. We just clicked, as if we'd known each other forever! The students were so keen to be part of everything, all writing in notebooks in English so Tracy could follow conversations, as they didn't want her to be left out. People were very moved, crying in the concert and loving joining in using those translated songs. Everyone was so welcoming, and we tasted some delicious Hungarian cooking.

When it was time to return home, we travelled back to Budapest Airport with Ildi. It was rush hour and the train was jam-packed, but we just managed to get seats. Tracy's attention was drawn to a lady sitting opposite, so she prayed for her and, to her slight consternation, some tender, affirming words began to form in her mind that she knew God wanted to say to this lady. Poor Tracy didn't know what to do, as the lady probably didn't speak English and Trace certainly didn't speak Hungarian! In the end she wrote the words out, explaining that she was a Christian and knew that God wanted to give her this message because he loved her. Tracy then asked Ildi to write it out in Hungarian, and Ildi looked shocked but did so, then quickly left to take a long loo break! Tracy gave the lady the note and she looked surprised but started to read it. The train drew into the next station and it was the lady's, but as she stood up, she looked at Tracy with a big smile and gave a thumbs-up. Trace was so thankful she'd persevered with finding a way to communicate the message. God was at work, despite the language barrier.

It felt like we were leaving family when we said goodbye to Ildi, so we invited her to come for a holiday to England. To my surprise, she kept saying she believed God was calling her to move to the UK. When she came for her holiday, Torch Trust just happened to need a librarian. I went with her for a flying visit to their headquarters and she was offered the job! I knew that working for this caring Christian ministry would help mend her heart. Ildi's confidence grew, and to crown her happiness, she eventually met Craig, and I had the huge privilege of giving her away at their wedding. It has been such a joy coming to know Ildi and to see the deep change God has brought about in her life.

Tracy

Another significant trip abroad, which we made with Paul Wood around 1997, was to Poland. We'd travelled to Poland on at least two previous occasions when it was still under communist rule. In those visits we'd been deeply challenged by the giving nature of the Polish people, who despite having so little, viewed all visitors – including us – as heaven's angels. They would do their utmost to provide 'banquets' for us, which we found so humbling. By this visit, following the end of communist rule, people would have more materially. Would we still be able to reach their hearts with God's love?

We travelled there in our van, and as well as our luggage and equipment, we also took as many crates of unripe bananas as we could carry. We'd be visiting orphanages, and most children would never have tasted a banana. They survived the long journey and were perfectly ripe at just the right time for us to give them out to the children.

The whole tour was very special, as there was an obvious hunger among the Polish Christians, almost a desperation, to know the reality of God's love. We sang in many Catholic churches, and in one memorable concert Marilyn sang her Caribbean song 'Spirit of God' and encouraged people to get up and dance. This was unheard of in these very traditional churches, but to our joy, many did just that, including one lady who, waving her shawl around her like a banner, pirouetted up and down the aisle, tears of joy pouring down her face. A deeply humbling tour, showing that God is always longing to pour out his love.

23

Restoring Lives Through Intimacy with God

Let my whole life be an overflow of worship

Marilyn Baker[1]

In 1996, just a year after we'd moved to Kent, we heard the devastating news that Tony had left Jen. Her marriage was destroyed, yet Jen held onto the Lord and let him hold onto her. The ministry she'd started with Tony couldn't continue, as planned. Through prayer and trust, the Lord resurrected the seeds of the original vision, and eventually in 2008 Beauty from Ashes was born and is still going strong today. Jen is one of the bravest and most compassionate people we have the privilege to know, for she has truly learned to cling onto the Lord and trust him, whatever happens. We've learned so much from her.

Marilyn

When Tony left, Jen needed to step down from doing ministry while she took time to heal, but what would happen to her wonderful conferences? Surely they could not stop? I told her that we would lead her immediate events for her and then run her big annual conferences under MBM's umbrella if she could come and minister. Jen and her trustees agreed. People were amazed, but I felt confident that with Jen there, we would be facilitating it in name only. The next year we did it like that again, but she then began to step back and urged me to take more responsibility. I had seen how she ran the events and very much wanted to follow her pattern. It was through her trust in me that my own ability to lead conferences developed. I would never have dreamt of doing such a thing before meeting Jen. In the end, Jen stepped down altogether in order to develop her new ministry, Beauty from Ashes, helping people get through traumatic loss and change.

We were still doing one-off concerts, church weekends and concerts in care homes, but we'd seen the enormous impact conferences could have and we began to take steps to lead our own in different venues across the country. I was terrified at first, but I had always wanted to be closer to my audiences, as I am a people person. I love interacting with audiences, but I also love meeting individuals and sharing, even if briefly, part of their lives and faith journey. It's such a privilege when people allow us to hear the concerns of their hearts so that we can bring them to our heavenly Father together. Our whole existence as a ministry is to help people connect with God and to find greater intimacy with him, and we believe it is through this closeness their lives will be restored. That is certainly my passion.

Tracy

Just as we were starting to book venues to run our own conferences, Phil and Mo Nowell-Smith began to assist us, as our administrator, Julie, was moving on. They lived in Taunton, so Phil worked from there. Later his daughter, Ruth Dunn, took over the main administration and Rachel Barr became our local administrator. Mo had recently received a dramatic healing from a stroke and had a passion for seeing people restored, so together with her prayer partner Jennie 'Pictures' Metcalfe, she started helping with prayer ministry at our conferences. Phil was an initiator, and under him we launched our new conference ministry, including conferences in Ireland and house parties at both Christmas and Easter. It was at this time, too, at the beginning of 2000, that Paul Wood moved on and wonderful friends like Ron and Val, Lilian, Sylvia (Paul's mum), Jackie, Doug, Val M and Hilary all started offering their time and gifts to support us as a team and bless the guests. It was wonderful to see how God would weave things together in order to touch a hurting person.

Lilian, for example, was really developing her prophetic gifting, and both she and Jennie would share pictures and insights during the worship. Once, Lilian had a picture of a baby learning to walk. It was holding onto a chair leg for security, but needed to let go to take proper steps. Lilian felt that God was calling someone to step out in some area of ministry but they were holding back out of fear.

Mo responded, saying that she knew God wanted her to pray for healing for other stroke victims but she'd been too afraid. Lilian's word encouraged her to step out. There was a guest there who was struggling with mobility because of a stroke. Mo prayed for her and encouraged her to try to walk, and by the end of the day she'd thrown her sticks aside and was going up and down the stairs!

We've also had wonderful speakers join us, such as Tony Horsfall, Norman and Janet Hooks, John Ryeland and Adrian Plass. Tony, a writer and Bible teacher, first made contact after being blessed by Marilyn's song 'The Father's Song of Love' and asked for permission to use it in one of his books. We became friends and Tony spoke at our conferences on several occasions, bringing great blessing to all.

Tony shares

It was such a privilege to be able to share a conference at Brunel Manor with Marilyn and Tracy. It was in the summer months, the time when there are large Christian gatherings all over the country, attracting thousands of people. Here we were, tucked away in a small corner of Devon with about fifty people, many of them disabled, or blind, or needy in some way. I looked around the room. Some were in large motorised wheelchairs. A few had guide dogs. One lady was lying on a mattress on the floor. Yet the sense of God's presence was palpable. Most of these people would never have made it to the larger events, but here was a place of welcome, acceptance and healing. Marilyn's songs brought much healing in themselves, and the theme of 'The King is in the House' was liberating for many. Preaching to this audience was a joy for me, and the fun and laughter throughout the week was an added blessing that seems characteristic of these events.

Tracy

One thing that came out of our contact with Tony was our trip with him to Singapore in 2005. Tony had been ministering there for many years, and it was a joy to travel with him and encourage the churches and individuals there with our singing and sharing. One memorable occasion was when we contributed to a contemplative day that Tony was leading with a group of Singaporean businessmen. I had started doing dance workshops in the conferences, very simple mime movements to Marilyn's songs, and we thought it would be lovely if this group could join in one. The men were quite stiff to start with, as they were unfamiliar with this style of worship, but then they relaxed into the joy of expressing their love to God. Such a precious moment! As well as opportunities to minister alongside Tony, we also loved visiting the shops in Orchard Road in search of silk dressing gowns and sampling the extremely spicy Malaysian and Korean soups.

As well as booking venues to run our conferences, we've had the great privilege of being regularly invited to Christian centres such as The Greenhouse Christian Centre in Poole to lead events, and that is how we mainly operate now.

Crowhurst Christian Healing Centre in Sussex first invited us in 1995, and for many years it became our 'home from home'. There was always such a sense of the presence of God at Crowhurst. I remember one time, while leading a contemplative session called 'Meeting with the Father', where when we placed items around the room – such as sparkly stones, beautiful pictures, a basin of water, a river made by blue and green materials, a royal robe, a wedding ring – an older man was overcome by joy as he held a banner representing God's glory and listened to Marilyn play. At the same session at Brunel Manor, a blind lady who had always longed to be married experienced a wonderful revelation that she was truly the bride of Christ as she put on the wedding ring . . . It's beautiful how the simplest things can become channels of God's love.

Marilyn

Laughter and tears go hand in hand at these events, especially when we add our assistance dogs into the mix. There are plenty of times, too, when we can get a bit fraught, tired or over-bossy, but we're learning that God can use all things, even our weaknesses if we offer them up to him.

Another thing we do is run a regular day at our home, known as an 'Intimacy with God' day. We cook lunch for the group of sometimes up to eighteen people and have times of worship, sharing and a quiet period to listen to God. On one memorable occasion, Trace and I were planning a casserole for the day. I'd decided how we would do it. Like composing, cooking to me is very creative. I don't go with recipes, but think carefully about the flavours I want to achieve. On this occasion, Trace said, 'Shall we add some more seasoning?'

I felt frustrated. Why did she have to interfere? She was being really bossy! Tracy kept suggesting things and I retorted: 'Will you just stop trying to make me do things your way? I know what I want to do, but if you are so intent on changing things, you can get on with it on your own. In fact, you can run the whole intimacy day yourself!'

Trace shouted back, 'Go on, then. I don't want you with me if you're gonna be like that!'

I stormed upstairs and slammed my bedroom door. Flopping onto the bed, I said to the Lord, 'I'm fed up of Trace being so bossy. She never listens to me.' A question came back into my heart; it was gentle but searching and very direct. 'Is Tracy bossy?'

I stopped in my tracks! Who was bossy? I knew that Trace was one of the gentlest people I've ever met. God spoke again, so tenderly: 'Marilyn, this is part of your unhealed heart talking.' I was shocked. It was true. I felt a deep sense of sorrow. 'Lord, forgive me. Please help me to change.' He seemed to say, 'I always listen to you, and so does Tracy, and I have given you to each other as soul mates to build each other up in the ups and downs of life.'

I went downstairs and put my arms around Trace, telling her how sorry I was, and we were able to forgive and laugh together. We shared 'our incident' with the group and incredibly it elicited a real response, as many had had upsets with their husbands or friends and they too needed to put things right. God is able to use even our deepest failings to help others, and he always longs to bring restoration and understanding to people's hearts.

Tracy

In 2014, God opened the door for us to go on a ministry trip to India. Marilyn was singing at the Christian Resources Exhibition (CRE) and met Nancy and Prabhu Rayan who head up the international ministry for the blind and disabled, the India Fellowship for the Visually Handicapped (IFVH) based in India but reaching out into many surrounding countries. They'd long wanted to meet Marilyn, so there was an immediate connection. Out of that meeting the vision was born for a three-week tour to Mumbai, Pune, Chennai and Goa with the two-fold purpose of ministering to the poor and disabled and also communicating to Christian leaders that disabled people are a vital part of God's church and have so much to give. Many families were still hiding away their disabled or blind children, who ended up begging on the streets. We prayed so much that we would have a positive impact.

The whole tour was clearly ordained and provided for by God, from Martin and Sue Relf (UK trustees for Nancy and Prabhu's ministry) accompanying us, to all the needed money coming in for MBM to fund the trip. (I did a sponsored sky dive – a story in itself!) The Lord wove every detail into place. From the moment we arrived in Mumbai at 5 a.m. we were caught up in the cacophony of sound, heat and excitement that is India. We had our first curry at 6 a.m. and then started the three weeks of concerts and talks. Marilyn had stipulated beforehand that she must have a keyboard with a sustain pedal to make the keyboard sound like a piano. Without it the sound would be disjointed, but despite the various leaders assuring Nancy beforehand that this would be no problem, time and again we arrived at the church to find there was no pedal and often only a toy keyboard! It became a running joke, especially one day when the electricity went off in the middle of the event, so not even the toy keyboard was useable. Marilyn asked a blind hand drummer to help on that occasion, and got the audience to clap along while she sang unaccompanied.

It was deeply humbling to see people's hunger for God despite the great hardships many faced. Our enduring memories: riding in the rickshaws, the cows wandering along the main roads, the mopeds with up to three or even four on board, the constant hooting and honking, the cupboard-sized homes made of tin and canvas lining the main roads and full of beautifully dressed children, and most of all, the passion and joy with which people responded to the message of God's love for them. They loved Marilyn singing 'Hollow of His Hand', joining in with great enthusiasm. I cried at one tiny church which, contrary to custom, welcomed the poorest from the (illegally classified) lowest caste.[2] They sat on the floor in their distinctive turquoise dresses signifying their 'untouchable' status. As Marilyn sang and I shared how God had changed me from feeling a nothing to knowing I was a daughter of the King, several of these ladies edged ever closer. When Prabhu gave the appeal, more than forty-five put their hands up – including one who put up both hands!

Nancy's comments

'This is the piano.' But it was a toy piano! We sank in our seats.

To laugh or to cry . . .?

There was no time for anything as the pastor of the church began the meeting.

We saw Marilyn walk towards the table, sit on a chair and her hands felt the piano . . .

Was there shock? Upset?

Her usual composed self with that captivating smile . . . her hands went through the keys as though she was playing one of those Yamaha Clavinovas!

'I am held in the hollow of His hands . . .'[3] the melodious voice rang out the words, captivating the hearts of the people.

Marilyn proved – pedal or no pedal, 'I will sing to the LORD as long as I live.'[4]

24

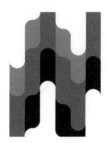

Our Faithful God;
Our Faithful Team

He'll provide all of your needs, there's nothing he can't do
Marilyn Baker[1]

It's been incredible over the years to see how God has faithfully brought people into the ministry at just the right time and with just the right gifts. It was wonderful to have Carol Joyce alongside me when I first joined; with her quiet willingness to help in so many ways, we fitted together like pieces of a jigsaw.

In 1988, very sadly, Ian's marriage broke down and he left MBM. He had been so gifted with sound and building up MBM's PA equipment and was a great spiritual support. We felt concerned about how we would manage. We met some potential applicants but no one was right, so very sadly we went to Scotland for our last tour, and on the way down they dropped me at Ellel Grange for some personal ministry.

I was invited to go out with the young volunteers and noticed a tall man in his thirties.

With my deafness, I didn't usually initiate conversations but suddenly had a strong feeling that I should ask him about his work. With the help of my 'Gossip' notebook, which at that time I always used for people to jot down what they were saying to me (I now use an iPad and external keyboard), I discovered that Robbie Barnes did the sound for Ellel, but would soon be at the end of his contract. Another surprising thought came: 'Ask if he's interested in doing sound for MBM.' Unbelievably, Wee Robbie, as we came to call him, *was* interested, despite never having heard of us before. He came down to meet us all, and then started some weeks later after finishing his contract.

Wee Robbie was extrovert and fun. He loved lighting systems and bought one for MBM, also building a 'coffin' to house it in the van. In his view, the lights had to be set up at every venue even if it was 30 degrees outside. If a concert went particularly well, Robbie would say 'Oh, Wee Marie (as he called Marilyn), that was all because of the lights creating the right atmosphere!'

Robbie had a wicked sense of humour, and one day when he was away in Germany, Trudy, our administrator at the time, came to take us to Sainsbury's. Unknown to Marilyn, Robbie was in the car with Trudy because he'd returned earlier than expected. Marilyn sat in front and when I got in the back, there he was with his finger to his lips. We arrived at Sainsbury's and were queuing to park. Suddenly Robbie leaned forward and said in Marilyn's ear, 'Hello, Wee Marie.' Marilyn screamed so loudly the whole car park came to a standstill!

Robbie had a good musical ear though could not mend equipment, but he developed a relationship with a girl from Bristol whose dad was excellent at repairing and maintaining our equipment. God had provided again!

Carol Joyce left MBM at the end of that year, and in September 1989 Robbie also needed to move on, and Trevor Houiellebecq and Chris Matthews came to join us, followed a couple of years later by Alistair Shenstone and Nick Cook. Trevor joined as road manager and a lovely thing happened: when he met Carol, who was still living in Watford, they fell in love! When they married, we said that MBM should be renamed 'Marital Bliss Ministries'.

Marilyn

God has always impressed on me that whoever helps us in our ministry has been hand-picked by him, and that the time spent working for us is as important for them as it is for us because he uses it to help them to grow as people for whatever he has in store for them in their lives.

This was very apparent when we first met Paul Wood, who applied to join us after Alistair left. He was a wonderful sound engineer and brimming with technical ability, but extremely reserved. Would he be able to cope with meeting so many people? We interviewed another man who was very outgoing, yet Paul kept coming round whenever we had a problem and he could always sort things out. Two of our trustees, Bill and Dorothy, met both men and felt certain that Paul was the one because he felt called by God. We lived by faith and never knew what our resources would be from month to month, and to my embarrassment, his first month's salary could not be paid. How would we tell him? He was so gracious and understanding of our situation because his parents had been missionaries in Zambia, and I remember him saying almost casually that he knew God would meet his needs.

Prior to Paul coming, I worked with wonderful musicians like Nick and Paul and Alison Donnelly and marvellous sound engineers like Ian, Chris and Alistair. We have seen the same pattern with our administrators. Trudy was a wonderful people-loving administrator who sang with me sometimes in concerts. After she and her husband left to lead a church, we met Karen Walker while doing a concert in London. During the concert, Tracy shared a picture of a bombed-out shell of a house and said that someone in the audience felt like that, but that God saw them as beautiful. Several people responded and Karen felt very moved. At more than 6ft and a black belt in judo, she was very unconventional! As well as being a strong character with a great sense of humour, she would never take no for an answer if she felt something important needed to happen. On occasion she would travel with us, and one day when we needed to catch a ferry to Ireland, we missed it because of slow traffic. It was disastrous, as concerts started the next day. Karen decided we would get the night ferry, although they said our van probably wouldn't fit. MBM had just bought a bigger van, but for this tour we were still using the old one. It turned out this smaller van was perfect for the space. Alistair and Karen pushed the car in front in order to squeeze our van on. We made it to Ireland just in time for our first event in Limerick, where eleven members of the same family all became Christians! We were so thankful for Karen's determination and strength.

Pam Lee followed Karen in 1992 and shone at everything she did. As well as organising events, she was an excellent caterer, and then Julie picked up the baton when we moved to Kent in 1995.

Tracy

One night at the end of 1998 after we'd been in Kent for three years, I had a dream. I saw a ship in a harbour, then it pulled up its anchor and sailed across the open sea to another port where it dropped anchor again. I prayed about it because I didn't usually remember dreams, so wondered if this was prophetic. A very surprising insight came to me: that the ship represented Paul Wood and the harbour was MBM. The anchor was God's presence in Paul's life, and he was calling Paul to now put his roots down somewhere else. I was shocked, as Paul had worked for us for six years and had given no indication that he wanted to leave. As I continued to pray, I 'knew' that the time for Paul to leave would come in about a year.

I told Marilyn and she was shocked too. We were all about to have a short sabbatical break, and Paul worked for Torch Trust during that time. When we returned, Marilyn casually asked him how he was feeling about the future.

'I'm feeling I should be moving on,' Paul said. 'I've loved working for Torch and am wondering if God is calling me to join them, maybe in a year, so I can help you sort out what you will do?'

We were amazed at how God had revealed his plans. Of course, we hadn't had divine revelation with every new sound engineer, but things were changing and we were doing smaller, more ministry-based events rather than the old-style big tours. With this new focus, the income level was changing too. We trust the Lord to provide, and part of that comes from ministry gifts from the places that invite us. We didn't have enough big events or resources to justify continuing to employ a sound engineer, and it seemed that God had given that dream to prepare us, as we would now need to become a bigger team using volunteers.

About ten months later, everything was set for Paul to leave us in January 2000 after an amazing trip to Kenya in December 1999 organised by Pastor Francis Wanderi and his wife Mary. It included ministering in Thika at a conference for the blind organised by Torch Trust; taking part in huge nightly meetings in Pastor Francis' church in Kerugoya; and travelling to rural 'tin' churches in the daytimes, where we witnessed the heartbreak of young children with malnutrition and yet families so responsive to God's message of hope. It was a trip full of new experiences: crossing rivers on stepping stones armed with saucepans to ward off the crocodiles, hostesses washing everyone's hands before a family meal of maize, being given a live chicken as a ministry gift, and praying for about 300 people longing to be filled with the Holy Spirit at the end of a concert . . .

We arranged an afternoon at a big Anglican church for Paul to train the new volunteer sound team. It was a diverse group, with Ron Seale in his late sixties, two 15-year-old boys, Philip Bull and Stuart Christie, and Andy Cockerel who at the time was living in Henley and had volunteered when he attended a concert and heard about our need for help. Ron had some technical know-how, but as Paul got more and more equipment out of the van, he was thinking, 'This is too complex for me. I'll have to just drive.' The young lads and Andy understood it, and so we started off with Ron or Andy driving and the lads taking it in turn to do the sound when they weren't at school. Ann Town also drove the van, and later Doug Bentley got involved as both driver and sound person and helped us faithfully for about eight years. Stuart showed Ron the sound system again one day, and Ron realised he could do it after all. Ron is very musical and began to sing with Marilyn, and then Ron's wife, Val, became involved with the conferences. God used Ron and Val's lovely gifts of prayer and loving care to touch many of our guests, who were often struggling with deep emotional pain. Alan and Connie, Bob and Sheila, Roy and Brenda, Marylin, Nicky . . . So many amazing people coming alongside us.

Marilyn

We often met people in unexpected ways as in the case of Hellen Frost, who attended one of our conferences at The Greenhouse Christian Centre in Poole in 2010. She was the youngest guest and very withdrawn. How could we get inside her shell? She was often playing with her phone and seemed 'techy' like me, so I sat down with her one day and started talking about my new iPhone that I was trying to use with its special talking software. We became friends, and I discovered she had not long been a Christian and had come through a great deal of trauma in her life. She was on a healing journey, and I casually said we needed people to help us with driving and sound, as Doug was stepping down. She only lived about forty minutes' drive from us, in Herne Bay, and she welcomed the chance to come and help us. She started to write beautiful, thought-provoking poems describing some of her deep pain and discovery of God's healing presence. As she read these out at events, people would find them incredibly encouraging. She became stronger, but in 2014 experienced a huge crisis in her life and had to stop travelling with us. It was quite sudden, and we had a conference about to start in Norfolk but no driver! It was then that Heather Taylor, who had taken us once or twice before, valiantly stepped into the breach. Heather has also experienced many problems over the years, including depression and anxiety, but just loves driving. The first time we met, Trace was away. I'd just been on a cookery course at Torch Trust and made a jam and cream sponge for Heather to enjoy. She was very impressed and we quickly became good friends. Although Heather cannot do sound, she has grown more and more confident and contributes wonderfully to our ministry. We still keep in touch with Hellen and are good friends. She is going from strength to strength, and we get to see her when we can.

We are blessed by these wonderful friends who give up their time and money to come to help with prayer ministry, or offering workshops, or just to get alongside our guests and serve in any way they can. Many have experienced deep struggles and loss themselves, but have so much empathy for others going through similar things. Over and over we see how the very things that the devil has used to try to destroy them become their strongest area through which they can powerfully minister to others. When we first met her, Lilian was a very broken person, coming from a violent, unloving background. She was experiencing deep depression and loneliness, so we often invited her to our home. Bit by bit God began to do a beautiful healing work in her life, and as well as praying for others, God has given her an amazing prophetic gift which encourages many to experience his wonderful love. She also helps us in lovely practical ways such as with our garden and sewing.

My old friend Hilary, who I first lived with, also became a great support in the ministry after her husband, Dennis, died. She loves to serve our guests in any way she can, and as part of Torch as well as MBM, has a real gift in getting alongside guests with sight loss or other disabilities. Her own experiences of loss and change in her life have given her a wonderful caring heart.

We also love having people with disabilities on our team because, as we ourselves have experienced, we know that God can use anyone who is willing to put their life at his disposal. So we have people with mobility problems, such as Sylvia Wood, who has severely restrictive illnesses but a real evangelistic gift, my blind friends Roger and Margaret Wilson-Hinds, and those with hearing loss such as Marylin Kilsby. Sheila Ames suffers with poor health but has given so much over the years with crafts and running the bookstall . . . We can't mention all, but are so thankful for the love and support of so many amazing friends.

When we run conferences, we love people to feel part of our family. If the team are close and share together, we can pass this down to our conference guests, who often tell us they feel so much love and acceptance flowing that it is like a touch of heaven for them.

For several years after Phil Nowell-Smith and his daughter Ruth Dunn moved on, we had two administrators, Kim Gordon and Rachel Barr, and Rachel is now our longest standing administrator. Rachel is Ron and Val's daughter, so MBM is a kind of family affair! She is so practical in a quiet, sensitive way, but she does struggle getting me to buckle down to doing anything administrative! Once she asked if she had permission to tell me off when I hadn't done something. I gladly said yes! Without people like Rachel, Trace and I would really flounder.

Rachel shares

When I was young my parents used to play Marilyn's music, which I loved hearing. We had one of Marilyn's songbooks, too, which I used to play from at home and sing along to. Marilyn was very instrumental in my making a commitment to follow Jesus. She was singing at a Luis Palau event and her song, 'Can a Mother Forget Her Little Child' really moved me, and I went forward when an appeal was given.

I have been part of MBM for more than eighteen years now. My role has grown over those years, but for the past fifteen I have run the office and done the bookkeeping. I am in awe of the many lives Marilyn and Tracy have transformed with their ministry. I love receiving emails from people when they have been blessed by their time at a concert or conference.

I do love working with Marilyn and Tracy. There is never a dull moment, that's for sure. For a little over three years, the office has been in their home, and I have found myself doing the occasional task outside of my job description. This includes tackling a flying ants' nest that I turned up to one day when Marilyn was at home, but Tracy was away. The whole porch was absolutely covered in these ants, and I could hardly leave Marilyn to sort it out while I carried on with MBM business. I did chuckle to myself, when I was frantically trying to get rid of them, thinking not many jobs would offer me such a varied role!

Testimonies

I have been to several residential conferences and 'Rest & Renewal' days with Marilyn and Tracy over the years, and every one has been a time when I have met with the Lord afresh through their anointed ministries. I've always come away uplifted and inspired. It was also a real privilege a few years ago to have them come to our church for a weekend, and to include a visit to the care home where I was working. Many people, both church members and care home residents, were touched over that wonderful weekend, with one lady in particular coming to a new faith.

Jane

25

God's Transforming Works

The Spirit of God comes like a dove, with gentleness He draws near. He fills our hearts with His peace and love and drives away our fear
Marilyn Baker[1]

Just this week, in March 2020, at least four elderly residents in care homes gave their lives to the Lord after Marilyn did a tour of care homes in Eastbourne, and I heard that a word I'd given at a recent day event had touched someone deeply, helping her to know that God knew and loved her completely.

As Marilyn sings her songs, or as I share in our events and as people listen to the CDs or read the books, we trust that God is doing a work of love in their lives. Sometimes it's clear people are being touched, as we see them crying or they ask for prayer. Sometimes we hear long after the actual event how they've been impacted. We are just weak, ordinary women with our own life struggles and hurts, but as we offer ourselves and follow his promptings, we are so blessed and thankful to see the way he transforms lives and heals deep hurts. We find that the atmosphere of care and acceptance at the conferences is often pivotal to people coming to believe that they are loved and to start to let their guard down. Our lovely friends Kath and Malcolm were in this position. When we first met them, Malcolm had been very ill with a breakdown. But God touched him so deeply . . .

Malcolm shares

Twenty years ago I was blessed by your ministry, Marilyn and Tracy and your team at MBM, in my recovery from a severe breakdown due to work-related stress. You each gave me comfort, strength and encouragement through your sharing of the love and words of our Lord and Saviour. Through song and teaching and joyful witness, you enabled me to return to a Spirit-filled life, which upholds me to this day. My testimony is to the glory of God, that he rescued me through your ministry, for which I am forever grateful.

Sometimes we can't think how to go about a session and feel we're not doing anything worthwhile, and yet God may be working through a song or a reflection to touch someone or even dynamically change them. Our blind friend Roger, for example:

Roger shares

My dad loved me dearly but suddenly died when I was 19. I buried my grief but continued to think about Dad most days.

At one of the Tracy and Marilyn Rest & Renewal sessions, the focus was on Father God, and we were challenged to write a piece about our dads and how memories of our dads helped or hindered us to think of God as our father.

The music from Marilyn and the loving words spoken by Trace just hit the spot emotionally, and I began to write about my dad in a totally new way.

I have never had enough sight to recognise faces, so I don't even know what he looked like. Instead of describing him visually, out flowed a spontaneous list of many smells associated with him and his doings which had been stored away in my brain. The smell of his oily clothes when he came home from the factory; beer on his breath after a works Christmas party; his greenhouse and being given a freshly picked tomato; the list went on and the tears filled my eyes as I wrote it all down.

I had to ask someone else to read what I had written; it was so deep and life-changing. Dad, Father God: Father God, Dad. They both love me, but I have failed to love them as I should. I did love my dad with all my heart, but I don't remember telling him. I realised then and there I had not loved God with all my heart either, but, as he is always with me, there are thousands of opportunities to tell him I love him every day.

So, on that day, the door was opened for me to love and be loved by Father God, and it has remained open. Out walking, on a train, in bed at night, when I am bored in a meeting . . . throughout my daily life I find myself listening to him and pondering things with him, and I know I am never alone, never expected to do things I can't cope with and never fatherless.

Thank you, Marilyn and Trace.

Many have commented on how being included, loved and accepted has had such a big effect on them. Ann Town, a former volunteer driver and friend, for instance . . .

Ann shares

I do not think you fully realise how much you have done for me throughout my time of knowing you both. You will understand the suffering of rejection that has plagued me most of my life. Until you came into my life, there never appeared to be anybody who accepted me as I was/am.

You are delightful people and I have such admiration for all that you both have and do achieve. Both your books and Marilyn's music have been a big part of my life – and long may it continue. When I was invited to your home for prayer and socialising, a great deal of healing took place within me. I loved meeting up with the group. I was accepted.

When we do one concert after another, or struggle to meet a writing/recording deadline, we can forget all God may be doing behind the scenes. It's lovely to receive letters like this one below that show he is always at work:

D & M

One of the highlights for us came at a concert Marilyn gave in London some time in the early 1980s. We invited a very elderly neighbour of ours, who was a churchgoer. She loved the music, songs and ministry, and she committed her life to Christ at that time. That was a real joy.

For us personally, we have been greatly blessed by the words and music of Marilyn's songs over the years. More recently the Lord has also ministered very powerfully through Tracy's books, *Flying Free with God* and *The Father's Kiss*. Marilyn and Tracy are a wonderful team, blessed by God.

We've had so many wonderful people working for us or helping us voluntarily, and it's always a joy to know that the ministry is touching their lives too: Pam was our administrator in the Watford years . . .

Pam shares

My first experience of Marilyn's ministry was when I received the LP *He Gives Joy* from my friend. I also read Marilyn's book *Another Way of Seeing*. The record and book had a profound effect on me and my Christian faith. I had been struck by Marilyn's comment that sometimes people who could not listen to a sermon would be reached through a song; I had listened to some very good sermons, but there was something very special about how Marilyn's music and lyrics touched me.

Some time later, I went to listen to Marilyn at St Andrew's, Chorleywood, and I heard Tracy's testimony. Both spoke about trusting God, in both the little and the big things.

I had to face the question: how much did I trust God?

Some years later, I went to St Andrew's again and collected the weekly news sheet. One item jumped out at me. An administrator was needed for Marilyn Baker Ministries. It was with some trepidation I applied, but to my amazement, I got the job.

There were weekly prayer meetings at Marilyn's home but most of my time was spent alone at the MBM office at St James Road Baptist Church. My greatest struggle was using the ministry's Amstrad computer[2] and this was very embarrassing as Marilyn was brilliant on hers. She loved new technology!

I loved organising concert bookings and time with the team. On occasion, I went on the road and such occasions were memorable. The first time I accompanied Marilyn, we went to an event at Uxbridge. On arrival, I took her arm and walked her to the ladies' room, 'showing' her the toilet and washbasin and adding, 'And there's a nice mirror so you can check your lipstick.' As I uttered the words, I realised how stupid my comment was and started to apologise. Marilyn laughed out loud and told me how delighted she was with what I had said and, yes, we did check her lipstick!

The other amazing thing about the 'work' was hearing testimonies from people who had been touched by Marilyn's ministry. Wonderful letters and calls would be received almost daily. People who couldn't sleep had listened to 'Rest in My Love' and relaxed into deep sleep for the first time in months. There were many who had taken to heart 'God Wants to Give You a Glorious New Life' and were experiencing God's unconditional love for the first time.

One remarkable experience was when Marilyn wanted to visit H Wing at HMP Durham. She and Tracy had been communicating with some members of a newly formed Julian group[3] and all longed to meet. I was asked to organise a concert at the high security wing. Initially I was told it would be very difficult – if possible at all – but swiftly the reply came that the event could go ahead.

One day Tracy asked if she could pray with me. I told her life at home was not easy. My husband seemed very pressured with work. Tracy prayed, as she felt the Lord was giving her insights to do with my marriage. A few weeks went by and I found out that my husband had been contacted by a school friend from thirty years previously. Our twenty-one-year marriage was to end within months. My life was in turmoil and my work with MBM suffered, but I received the most amazing support from the team.

As time went by, I realised I could no longer help move MBM forward. I apologised to Marilyn for my many mistakes and again received the most incredible response. 'We don't think about what you can't do, but delight in you and what you can do.' Never in my life had anyone made me feel valued, and I experienced something of my heavenly Father's unconditional love.

Five years later Marilyn and Tracy were guests at my second marriage, and we were so honoured when Marilyn sang 'The Blessing Song'. That is twenty years ago and was a great preparation for our new life. I had been shown through Marilyn and Tracy and their ministries that I could trust God in the big and little things. He remains with us every step of the way, and we know his love deep within our hearts. Praise God.

Tracy

Sometimes God has given me a word or picture during a concert that seems odd and has a kind of 'So what?' feel to it. One day I saw a picture of someone wearing all black and felt God was saying that he wanted them to wear a red jumper. It seemed such a strange word. Why would God care what colour someone was wearing? I nearly didn't give it but did in the end. No one responded and I wasn't really surprised. Twenty years later, we met a lady who told us that word had been for her. She was a Satanist, and as a Goth, she always wore black. She'd been told that Christians had no power, only Lucifer. It had been her birthday and her aunt, who was a Christian, had given her a red jumper, but she hated it. However, she did agree to go to a concert with her aunt, as she loved her. That was the concert where I stood up and said 'Someone is always wearing black. God wants you to wear a red jumper.' She was overcome with terror, realising that God knew her and was speaking into her life. She ran from the church but couldn't escape from God and became a Christian soon after. When she spoke to us, she was working on the streets reaching out to prostitutes and those caught up in drugs and the occult. An amazing story of how something so inconsequential could be so powerful to transform a life. All I needed to do was speak it out. I didn't have to understand. God did it all.

Every testimony, every example of a transformed life or new hope being given or someone realising they are loved as they listen to a song, is down to him, our amazing God.

Conclusion

Marilyn

Val Muir, a member of our prayer team, arrived at our house one day and told me the Lord had given her a special name for me: 'He says you are "the joy of my heart"', she said. I was staggered. What an amazingly lovely name and so affirming. I realised that was what he wanted to say to all his beloved children, and that when we meet him face to face, we will want to dance and sing that he is the joy of our hearts, too. I decided to put this in a song. It all came together and that is the title of one of two albums I released in 2019. I had not recorded anything new for fifteen years. *Hallelujah Christmas* followed, a jazzed-up celebration of the Christmas season.

Will I do any more? I don't know, but I do know God wants to spread his message of love and acceptance to everyone, for all to know how awesome he is and how real his love is. We have been part of that through my music, Tracy's writing, through what we teach and share, through the events, conferences, hospitality and prayer ministry.

We don't know what the future holds, but as we've looked back, we've realised how God is truly making a beautiful tapestry of all our lives. From the big events to the tiny, seemingly mundane moments, he is drawing all the threads together, weaving them in to create an incredible, ever-growing picture of his love and grace.

Tracy

Since submitting this manuscript in March 2020, the world has been hit by the Covid-19 pandemic. Conferences and events all stopped, and although restrictions are easing now (June 2020), we don't know how things will go for MBM in the coming months because of the problems around holding public events and singing. But whatever happens, we want to be part of all God is doing to restore lives and bring people to know the depths of his love. I long for people who feel isolated and on the fringe of life and full of the wounds of rejection and hurt to be drawn into God's love and know the great value he puts on their lives.

Marilyn

I have a great desire to share with older people too, as both my parents came to faith at the end of their lives. We both long to see people from all backgrounds entering into deeper intimacy with God, and so, whether we resume concerts and conferences or do more online events, we will go on for as long as he calls us, sharing his message of joy.

Marilyn and Tracy

Most of all, we both long to stay close to our Father's heart and out of that closeness, continue to reach out to those around us with his love, working in partnership with him, joined together with those around us.

May an ever-growing, beautiful tapestry be woven in all our lives: the tapestry of God's love and redeeming work in which every thread counts.

Marilyn

We always end our conferences with my 'Blessing Song'[1] and it's our prayer that he will bless you in every way.

> May the blessing of the Lord our God
> Rest upon you day by day.
> May he keep and guide you,
> Every step of the way.
> And may you know his peace,
> Deep within your heart,
> And may his love control all you do and say.

Marilyn and Tracy

Timeline

A timeline of God's amazing guidance and provision from 1979

1979
Marilyn is teaching music in five Watford schools and living with Marjorie. Marilyn now has guide dog, Yuma. Marilyn and Carol Franklin have previously released her first home-produced album *Open Our Eyes Lord* and now Marilyn releases her first studio album, *He Gives Joy.*

1980
Marilyn is invited to do a concert tour in Norway and Hilary accompanies her.
Marjorie, Marilyn's housemate, leaves to go to Bible college, and Penny Misselbrook moves in.

1981
Marilyn releases *Whispers of God,* and a TV documentary called *Marilyn Baker Songwriter* is made and broadcast on many TV channels. Marilyn travels to Holland on her own; a huge adventure. David Payne becomes Marilyn's manager.

1982
Marilyn is asked by David Payne and producer John Pac to consider going full-time into musical ministry and at the end of the summer term 1982 Marilyn leaves teaching. Marilyn has to give up her guide dog, Yuma. Penny Misselbrook gives up her job to travel with Marilyn. One of their first tours is to Australia and New Zealand, an incredible opportunity and reassurance that God will provide.

1982
Tracy leaves London to move to Watford to study for a teaching degree at Hertfordshire College of Higher Education (HCHE), Wall Hall.

1983
Marilyn tours with Prepare the Way to prepare the UK for Billy Graham's Mission England.
She starts work on her third album, *Refresh Me Lord*. Her mum is taken very ill with leukaemia.
At the end of 1983, Penny Misselbrook stops travelling with Marilyn although she is still her housemate. After advertising, Morfudd Bowen joins Marilyn to be her new assistant.

1983
Tracy has to give up her teaching dreams and take a BA degree instead. She becomes very depressed. After a failed suicide attempt, Tracy becomes a Christian in May 1983.

Late 1983–1984
Tracy has an awesome encounter with the Father. From then on, she starts to draw closer to God. Tracy becomes friends with John and Amanda Duncan, who have a massive impact on her life.
In late 1984, Tracy moves out of college accommodation to start sharing the first of several homes with Christian friends, in this instance with Debra, Sian, Daniella and Sarah.

1984
In June, Marilyn's mum's health improves and Marilyn and Morfudd go to South Africa to do a powerful concert tour.
Just a few days after her return from South Africa, Marilyn travels with Carol Franklin to the USA to start the process of making a new album, *Marilyn Baker*. She also visits Disneyland while there and has a wonderful time. On her return home, her mum's health declines sharply. Marilyn shares the gospel very simply with her mum who prays to become a Christian.

In autumn 1984, Marilyn returns to the USA with Morfudd to finish recording the new album. Just before this, Penny Misselbrook moves away and the Lord leads Marilyn to invite her blind friend Penny Cooze to move in with her.

After their return, Ian Valkeith joins Marilyn as sound engineer, and to share in the driving. With Ian's help, Marilyn acquires her own PA equipment, making the concerts much more professional. Marilyn's church realise Marilyn needs more of a management group behind her, formed of representatives from local churches, so Marilyn Baker Ministries Trust (MBM) is formed.

Autumn 1984
Tracy goes with housemates Daniella and Sarah to hear a local Christian singer called Marilyn Baker perform in an Anglican church in Watford.

Winter 1984–summer 1985
Ian's wife becomes MBM's administrator, replacing Marilyn Payne (David's wife). Marilyn's mum's health deteriorates at the same time as Marilyn's travelling schedule accelerates. Marilyn becomes very depressed and has to take a break from doing concerts, and a group called Lovelight take on several of her bookings. Penny Cooze becomes a wonderful prayer support to Marilyn. Marilyn is with her mum when she dies and feels peaceful and certain that her mum is now with the Lord, yet is still devastated by her loss and by her memory of the suffering her mum went through.

Marilyn resumes work in March 1985. In summer 1985, Marilyn goes on holiday to Canada with Carol and has an amazing time. Marilyn realises she is developing serious back trouble.

June 1985
Tracy graduates from HCHE with a BA Hons in English Literature and Education and senses God calling her to work with the blind and deaf. Tracy is accepted to train to become a technical officer for the blind in April 1986 and also to work as a Community Service Volunteer for two

terms at Chorleywood College for Girls with Little or No Sight to get experience with blind people before starting the course.

July 1985
Penny Cooze visits Chorleywood College to speak at the Christian Union and afterwards invites Tracy for dinner. She then suggests Tracy come again to meet Marilyn Baker. Tracy has to leave Chorleywood College earlier than expected because of developing tonsillitis, and sadly is told she cannot go back in September as planned as it is thought she is too deaf for the work. Tracy has dinner with Penny and Marilyn and they become great friends.

July–December 1985
Tracy works on several occasions at Torch Trust. Morfudd decides to move on from the work at the end of 1985 and Marilyn starts looking for a new assistant.
Tracy and Marilyn continue to develop their friendship.

January 1986
Tracy starts to travel with Marilyn, who is still looking for a new assistant. The Isle of Sheppey and Yorkshire tours are life changing for them both. MBM acquires its first van, a Toyota HiAce. Paul and Alison Donnelly start accompanying Marilyn to some events to help musically.

March 1986
God clearly guides Tracy to join MBM as Marilyn's spiritual assistant. Carol Joyce is also employed as road manager.
In summer 1986, Marilyn buys her own keyboard to use in concerts.
Marilyn's back deteriorates and she can no longer walk without severe pain.

April–December 1986
Marilyn, Tracy, Carol and Ian travel extensively across Great Britain and abroad. Trips abroad include Austria, Switzerland, Holland and Poland.

The whole team travel to Jersey with Lovelight to record a live concert – *An Evening with Marilyn Baker* – which Ian arranges and produces. This simple album becomes a great hit.

Spring–summer 1987
Marilyn records a new album, *Close to His Heart* at a London studio. This is under a new label, Word Records UK. Marilyn's back problems accelerate and she has to stop travelling for a while. In the summer, Marilyn and Tracy go to stay at the home of Cornish Christian chiropractor Reg Price and his wife Joy for six weeks, while he prayerfully treats her.

Autumn 1987
Marilyn is asked by Word Records to write her life story, which she does in partnership with author Janet Hall, who writes the story as Marilyn shares her memories on tape.

Early winter 1988
Marilyn Baker Ministries has a three-month sabbatical and Marilyn and Tracy spend it at Emmanuel Bible College in Birkenhead, and while there also become associated with Ellel Ministries in Lancashire. At the end MBM is overdrawn by £7,000 and has one week to replace the money. The team pray together and the full £7,000 arrives through different people's gifts in one week.
Marilyn's life story *Another Way of Seeing* is published.
Tracy starts travelling to Ellel on a regular basis for prayer ministry. Ian's marriage breaks down, and in September Ian makes his last trip with MBM. Tracy meets Robbie Barnes, a volunteer at Ellel and a few weeks later he joins the team as the new driver/sound engineer.

Autumn 1988
Marilyn, Tracy, Carol, and Tim Webb (an old friend covering for Robbie Barnes who was not free) travel to Hong Kong for three weeks of ministry.
This will be Carol's last tour abroad as she is moving on.

1989
Penny Cooze moves away and Marilyn now lives alone. Tracy is still living with friends. Robbie Barnes leaves in September and Chris Matthews and Trevor Houiellebecq join, with Chris being sound engineer and Trevor road manager. They share the driving.

Autumn 1989
Marilyn records a new album *A New Beginning* in Manchester.

1990
MBM is very busy, including annual tours with Lovelight and several concerts each week. Marilyn senses the Lord telling them to restrict it to six (maximum) events a week.
Marilyn, Tracy and Trevor travel to Israel and Egypt as part of a UK group headed up by Bill Hampson who usually organises the tours with Lovelight.

Autumn 1990
Administrator Trudy Wheeler moves away and Karen Walker replaces her. Chris and Trevor also leave and Alistair Shenstone and Nick Cook join, with Alistair doing sound and Nick playing bass and sharing driving. Karen also travels occasionally. There is lots of fun on the road and some hair-raising moments.

1991
Trevor Houiellebecq and Carol Joyce, who is still living in Watford, get married. A wonderful occasion.
Marilyn, Tracy and the team go to hear Jennifer Rees Larcombe share her testimony of healing and a wonderful friendship is born.

Winter 1992
Marilyn records a new album *Face to Face* with Christopher Norton in Lancashire.

July 1992
Marilyn and Tracy go to their first 'Living Through Change' conference led by Tony and Jennifer Larcombe at Hothorpe Hall, Leicestershire. A life-changing experience.

September 1992
Marilyn releases a compilation album for Word called *The Best of Marilyn Baker.*
Karen, Alistair and Nick all move on. Pam Lee (now Maunders) becomes administrator and Paul Wood takes over as sound engineer.

Autumn 1992
MBM celebrates its tenth anniversary and Marilyn receives a gold disc from Word Records for 50,000 albums sold.

Spring 1993
Marilyn and Tracy travel with Tony and Jen Larcombe to lead a holiday conference at a Christian hotel in Corfu.

Summer 1993
Marilyn and Tracy attend their second 'Living Through Change' conference with Tony and Jennifer Larcombe, this time at Brunel Manor in Devon. Tracy leads her first ever workshop on listening to God. Jen asks Tracy to write an article about listening to God, which Jen then submits for her to *Renewal* magazine and also to her own publisher, Hodder & Stoughton, who then contact Tracy to ask if she would be interested in writing a book.

Early winter 1994
Marilyn records a new album *By Your Side* in Lancashire with Christopher Norton. Tracy starts working on her first book. Tracy's housemates move on and Marilyn and Tracy make the decision for Tracy to move into Marilyn's house.

Summer 1994
Marilyn releases a compilation album of her early albums with Pilgrim Records called *Greatest Treasures*.

Marilyn's dad dies after heart surgery and time has to be taken out to clear and sell his bungalow in Birmingham. Tony and Jen Larcombe invite MBM to move closer to their base in Kent to aid their ability to minister together.

Early winter 1995
Marilyn, Tracy and Paul Wood travel to the USA for six weeks of events organised by David Payne who now lives there. Marilyn starts the process of recording a new compilation album, *Changing Me*, for the American market. Tracy finishes her book which is accepted by Hodder & Stoughton and will be called *The Voice of the Father*.

Marilyn travels to Lancashire to record a live concert video which will also be available on CD and tape – *Marilyn Baker: Live in Concert*.

Events are beginning to reduce in number and Marilyn decides to re-apply to have a guide dog, her first since she gave up Yuma. Marilyn, Tracy, Paul and Carol Franklin search Tonbridge to see if a suitable house can be found. Eventually Marilyn makes an offer on a house in Hadlow and sells her Watford house to a local businessman. Marilyn, Paul and Tracy move to Hadlow in October 1995 and Pam Lee leaves MBM. Paul finds rented accommodation in a nearby village.

Three weeks after moving, Marilyn is told a guide dog has been found for her and she travels to Redbridge to train. Giles, a lovely and quite naughty golden retriever, becomes part of the family. Tracy's book is published while Marilyn is away and becomes quite popular. Tracy takes a day event on her own at Mulberry House, Ongar, Essex. Julie Hillary becomes the new administrator and will work in the new combined office being built in Jen and Tony's large garden. A new board of trustees is formed, with representatives from local churches. Work begins in Marilyn's new house to convert the garage into another room.

1996–2000

Marilyn and Tracy become established in Kent, joining a local Anglican church and then moving with the leaders to form a new Christian fellowship. Through the shared events with Jen and Tony, a team of supporters and friends begins to grow around MBM. Lilian Wild, Jackie Porter, Deirdre Pettitt, Val Muir and many others all become close friends.

Marilyn and Tracy acquire a cat, Zoe.

On a trip to Spring Harvest, Marilyn and Tracy meet Evelyn Smith, director of Canaan Christian Centre and a great friendship and mutual ministry support is born.

Jen and Tony's marriage breaks down and MBM takes over the organisational running of Jen's large annual conferences.

Marilyn, Tracy and Paul do a two-week tour of Poland.

Marilyn releases a new album recorded at the ICC recording studios in 1999 called *Overflow of Worship*.

At the end of 1998 Paul senses a call to go to work at Torch Trust and will leave at the end of 1999 to give time to train a replacement. However, God leads in a new way and a team of volunteers begins to come together, Ron Seale, Andy Cockerel, Ann Town and teenagers Stuart Christie and Philip Bull followed a bit later by Doug Bentley. Val Seale, Ron's wife, also becomes a significant team member as MBM develops its own conferences from 2000 onwards.

At the end of 1999 Marilyn, Tracy, Paul and Carol Franklin travel to Kenya for a two and a half-week ministry trip and Paul's last tour with MBM.

2000–02

Cynthia and then Violette do freelance work with MBM's accounts, as Paul used to do this. Jen Larcombe steps back from being involved with the conferences. MBM continue to run them with team support. Tracy leads her first dance workshop and starts to do simple dances in the concerts. Marilyn and Tracy sense God is calling them to develop their own small conference ministry, having been inspired by those they've been part of with Jen.

Marilyn and Tracy become involved with Revd Eric Delve's vision for a local Bible week and are part of the Revival Fire Bible Week's contributing team for several years.

2002

Julie Hillary leaves MBM and Phil Nowell-Smith and his daughter Ruth Dunn take over, working from Taunton. Rachel Barr (Ron and Val Seale's daughter) becomes part-time local administrator, liaising with Ruth and dealing with Marilyn's personal admin. Phil initiates MBM doing conferences at many centres across the UK including Pilgrim Hall in Sussex, Nicholaston House in Swansea, Hothorpe Hall in Leicestershire, Brunel Manor in Devon, Ashburnham Place in Sussex, Crowhurst Healing Centre in Sussex, Scargill House in North Yorkshire, Green Pastures (now The Greenhouse Christian Centre) in Poole, and Cautley House, Hythe. MBM is now a team ministry with many friends such as Lilian Wild, Valerie Muir, Jackie Porter, Alan and Connie Harvey, Ron and Val Seale and Hilary Haines (née Ellwood) plus the volunteer drivers/sound engineers coming regularly to events to give practical and ministry support.

Autumn 2002

MBM celebrates twenty years of ministry with a Thanksgiving and Celebration concert. Marilyn releases a new compilation album to mark the anniversary called *From the Beginning*. Marilyn and Tracy lead a celebratory holiday week in Austria at the Rojachoff Hotel, where they led Christian holidays with WEC in the 1980s.

Penny Cooze is diagnosed with cancer and Marilyn and Tracy start travelling to Watford as often as they can to be with her.

New Year 2004

Marilyn and Tracy go with Eve Smith and friends to the Black Forest for a New Year house party to celebrate Eve's 60th birthday. A longstanding friendship is formed with Len, Phyl, Tim and Debbie who head up the work at Haus Barnabas. One of the guests, Patrick Coghlan, prophesies that Tracy will start writing again and a new publisher will 'fall into her lap'. This is very encouraging because Tracy had lost confidence after *The Voice of the Father* went out of print in 1997.

Spring 2004
Penny Cooze dies in a hospice in Watford with Marilyn and Tracy at her bedside. Many friends from all over the country attend her very moving Thanksgiving Service.
Marilyn and Tracy lead a church weekend at Holy Trinity, Twydall and become friends with vicar Revd Gill Tovar, and her friend and housemate Cathie Aldis. Tracy senses God calling her into ordination and begins a four-year season of going regularly to Gill's church to grow in her understanding of Anglican ministry.

Summer 2004
After their annual holiday at Marilyn's chalet in Wales that Marilyn has inherited after her dad's death in 1994, Giles develops a sneezing condition that causes him to go temporarily blind. Guide Dogs retire him and start searching for a new dog to replace him.
Tracy is asked out of the blue by New Wine Press to write a series of short books about hearing God's voice and experiencing his healing transformation. Patrick Coghlan's prophecy is fulfilled.
Marilyn releases a new album, *All That I Am* with Christopher Norton.

Autumn 2004
Tracy starts a solo sabbatical for a month, while Marilyn continues doing events with the help of friends and also starts training with new guide dog, Pennie. Giles goes to Twydall to live with Revd Gill Tovar and Cathie Aldis for his retirement. Tracy's sabbatical is in three parts: firstly with Gill Tovar, secondly at a retreat centre to attend a silent retreat and thirdly at Marilyn's Welsh chalet.

Early winter 2005
Tracy's first book of this new series is submitted and published in April: *Expecting God to Speak to You!* (Bognor Regis: New Wine Press, 2005).

March 2005
Ruth Dunn steps down as administrator and the admin base returns to Tonbridge. Rachel Barr takes over as general office administrator.

Summer 2005
Marilyn releases *Christmas with Marilyn Baker* featuring her jazzed-up version of Christmas carols and her own songs.
Autumn 2005
Marilyn and Tracy travel for a ministry tour to Singapore with Tony Horsfall.
Kim Gordon starts working for MBM as conference administrator.
Marike Dodd starts working for Marilyn as her PA.

2006–08
Tracy brings out three more books in her series: *Letting God Speak Through You* (Bognor Regis: New Wine Press, 2006), *Encountering God* (Bognor Regis: New Wine Press, 2007) and *Flying Free with God* (Bognor Regis: New Wine Press, 2008).
Three of Marilyn's albums: *From the Beginning, Face to Face* and *By Your Side* are reissued as one triple album: *The Ultimate Collection* and two other albums become one package: *Changing Me/Overflow of Worship* (known in MBM as 'The Double Album').
In summer 2007, after prayer, it is decided to rebrand Marilyn Baker Ministries Trust as MBM Trust with an additional strapline 'Restoring Lives Through Intimacy with God'.
In October 2007, MBM celebrates its 25th anniversary with a special service and concert at Tonbridge Baptist Church. This anniversary also launches the new name and strapline.
Through Phil Nowell-Smith's initiatives, MBM are now established in leading several conferences a year in venues across the country, including Easter and Christmas house parties. They still lead one larger conference a year at Brunel Manor, which Ron, Val and team help them to host and other speakers like Tony Horsfall, Adrian Plass and Norman Hooks greatly contribute to. Many lives are deeply touched.

In 2008, Tracy is turned down for Anglican ministry and her visits to Holy Trinity, Twydall come to an end.

2009
Marilyn has a serious accident when she falls onto the railway line at Tonbridge station and badly hurts her back.

2010–11
Doug Bentley, who has been the primary volunteer driver/sound engineer for some time, retires from MBM and, just at the right time, Marilyn and Tracy meet new Christian Hellen Frost at a conference at Green Pastures (now called The Greenhouse Christian Centre) in Poole, and Hellen starts doing the majority of the driving and sound.

Tracy is told by Hearing Dogs for Deaf People, who she applied to for a hearing dog seven years before, that they have a suitable dog for her. Tracy goes to train with Goldie, a 'goldador' (Labrador/golden retriever cross) in November 2011.

2012
Pennie (guide dog) is diagnosed with cancer and immediately retired but will live out her days at home with Marilyn. It looks like Marilyn will have a long wait for a new dog but then is paired with Saffie, a 'goldador' (Labrador/golden retriever cross), aged 4, whose owner has died. There are now three dogs and a cat sharing the home. Pennie dies after ten happy months in October 2012.

Autumn 2012
MBM celebrates its 30th anniversary with a special service of thanksgiving at St John's church, Hildenborough.

2014
Hellen becomes ill and stops working with MBM. Heather Taylor, a local friend, takes over the majority of the driving, and MBM start using the equipment in centres and churches instead of their own, as they no longer have a sound engineer.

Marilyn and Tracy go to India for a three-week tour accompanied by Martin and Sue Relf, travelling with and sharing the vision of Prabhu and Nancy Rayan.

Tracy returns for two further retreats at Loyola Hall, Merseyside (now closed) and senses God speaking to her about writing a new book about the Father's love.

Autumn 2015

After ten years' excellent work as conference administrator, Kim Gordon leaves MBM. Rachel becomes sole administrator, moving the office into Marilyn and Tracy's home and turning the garage conversion that they had built in 1995 into Rachel and Tracy's combined office.

2017

Tracy completes her new book *The Father's Kiss* and submits it to Authentic Media in 2018.

2018

MBM employs freelance marketing expert Kevin Campbell to help them become more visible on the internet. MBM's website and Facebook page and various groups are all developed.

The Father's Kiss is published in September and receives many wonderful endorsements, kicking off with a lovely launch celebration at Christ Church in Tonbridge.

2019

Marilyn draws together many of the new songs she's been writing and releases her first new album for fifteen years, *Joy of My Heart*, produced by Classic Fox Records.

Saffie, now 11, is retired and goes to lives in Broadstairs with a friend, Peter Such. Marilyn is now without a guide dog and can no longer go out independently. Goldie is now the only dog.

Tracy writes forty-day devotional *A Desert Transformed* for her previous publishing contact Tim Pettingale, who now has his own publishing company, River Publishing. *A Desert Transformed* is published in June 2019.

Marilyn has a big launch concert for *Joy of My Heart* in June at Tonbridge Baptist Church, also celebrating her forty years of songwriting.

Autumn 2019
Marilyn's second Christmas album, *Hallelujah Christmas* is produced with Classic Fox.

Marilyn and Tracy are asked by Authentic Media to write the joint story of their lives and ministry.

2020
Marilyn and Tracy complete *A Beautiful Tapestry*.

Covid-19 sweeps through the nations bringing Great Britain to a halt for months. Due to being unable to do public events, Marilyn and Tracy start to develop online workshops and events.

Marilyn, Tracy and MBM are in prayerful trust in the Lord for the future.

About MBM Trust

MBM Trust's strapline is: 'Restoring Lives Through Intimacy with God' and this is the heart of Marilyn and Tracy's ministry. They believe their calling is to encourage and build up individuals and fellowships, helping people draw closer to God and be transformed in their inner lives. As well as doing concerts and taking church services, they run workshops, and Rest and Renewal residential and day conferences to help people develop new depth in their relationship with the Lord. Many people experience God's healing touch through Marilyn's songs and are greatly encouraged through Tracy's writing, teaching and prophetic insights.

If you are interested in knowing more about MBM Trust or Marilyn and Tracy's resources, please use the following contact info:
MBM Trust
PO Box 393
Tonbridge
Kent
TN9 9AY
Tel: 01732 850855
Email: info@mbm-ministries.org
Website: www.mbm-ministries.org
Facebook Page www.facebook.com/mbmtrust/
Tracy's Author Page www.facebook.com/tracywilliamsonauthor/

Marilyn's songs

Throughout the book, lyrics have been quoted from many of Marilyn's songs. Often the original albums are no longer available but see the Notes to discover details, as many songs have been put on compilation albums.

Available CDs may be purchased from your local Christian bookshop, online retailers or our website at www.mbm-minstries.org. Different outlets may stock different titles.

Many of Marilyn's tracks are also available to watch on YouTube or various online music platforms.

Tracy's books

The Voice of the Father is out of print.

The following books are generally available from Christian retail outlets, online stores and MBM:

The Father's Kiss

A Desert Transformed

The following are primarily available through MBM although they can be bought online and may be found in some Christian retail outlets:

Expecting God to Speak to You!

Letting God Speak Through You

Encountering God

Flying Free with God

Notes

Foreword

[1] Extract taken from the song 'He Gives Joy' by Marilyn Baker, Copyright © 1982 Authentic Publishing (Adm. by Integrity Music, part of the David C Cook family, songs@integritymusic.com). On the album *Marilyn Baker Live in Concert*.

1 Beginnings

[1] Extract taken from the song 'Where Can I Go from His Spirit?' by Marilyn Baker, Copyright © 1987 Marilyn Baker Music (Adm. by Integrity Music, part of the David C Cook family, songs@integritymusic.com). On the album *From the Beginning (The Ultimate Collection)*.

2 Chorleywood College

[1] Extract taken from the song 'Do You Know the Difference?' by Marilyn Baker, Copyright © Authentic Publishing (Adm. by Integrity Music, part of the David C Cook family, songs@integritymusic.com). On the album *From the Beginning (The Ultimate Collection)*.

[2] Leslie Weatherhead, *The Transforming Friendship* (London: Epworth Press, 1930).

[3] Publishing details not found.

3 The Sighted World

[1] Extract taken from the song 'Abraham' by Marilyn Baker, Copy right © 1985 Authentic Publishing (Adm. by Integrity Music, part of the David C Cook family, songs@integritymusic.com). On the album *From the Beginning (The Ultimate Collection)*.

[2] New language – speaking in 'tongues', a sign of the baptism in the Holy Spirit, as taught in the New Testament – see 1 Corinthians 12:10 and 1 Corinthians 14.

4 Stepping into God's Plans

[1] Extract taken from the song 'God Has a Plan for You' by Marilyn Baker, Copyright © 1988 Authentic Publishing (Adm. by Integrity Music, part of the David C Cook family, songs@integritymusic.com). On the album *From the Beginning (The Ultimate Collection)*.

[2] Extract taken from the song 'My Love Will Never Fail' by Marilyn Baker, Copyright © 1985 Authentic Publishing (Adm. by Integrity Music, part of the David C Cook family, songs@integritymusic.com). On the album *From the Beginning (The Ultimate Collection)*.

[3] Extract taken from the song 'Jesus You are Changing Me' by Marilyn Baker, Copyright © 1981 Authentic Publishing (Adm. by Integrity Music, part of the David C Cook family, songs@integritymusic.com). On the album *Changing Me (Changing Me/Overflow of Worship)*.

5 Rest in My Love

[1] Extract taken from the song 'Rest in My Love' by Marilyn Baker, Copyright © 1982 Authentic Publishing (Adm. by Integrity Music, part of the David C Cook family, songs@integritymusic.com). On the album *Changing Me (Changing Me/Overflow of Worship)*.

[2] Extract taken from the song 'Rest in My Love' by Marilyn Baker, Copyright © 1982 Authentic Publishing (Adm. by Integrity Music, part of the David C Cook family, songs@integritymusic.com). On the album *Changing Me (Changing Me/Overflow of Worship)*.

6 The Curveball

[1] Extract taken from the song 'All I Ever Do is Love You' by Marilyn Baker, Copyright © 1982 Authentic Publishing (Adm. by Integrity Music, part of the David C Cook family, songs@integritymusic.com). On the album *Marilyn Baker Live in Concert*.

7 Mixed Memories

[1] Extract taken from the song 'Where Can I Go from His Spirit?' by Marilyn Baker, Copyright © 1987 Marilyn Baker Music (Adm. by Integrity Music,

part of the David C Cook family, songs@integritymusic.com). On the album *From the Beginning (The Ultimate Collection).*

8 Tough Times

[1] Extract taken from the song 'I Am the Way (Can Anybody Find)' by Marilyn Baker, Copyright © 1982 Authentic Publishing (Adm. by Integrity Music, part of the David C Cook family, songs@integritymusic.com). On the album *Changing Me (Changing Me/Overflow of Worship).*

[2] Elinor M. Brent-Dyer.

9 God at Work

[1] Extract taken from the song 'Even Before Time Began' by Marilyn Baker, Copyright © Authentic Publishing (Adm. by Integrity Music, part of the David C Cook family, songs@integritymusic.com). On the album, *A New Beginning.*

10 A Huge Life Change

[1] Extract taken from the song 'He Gives Joy' by Marilyn Baker, Copyright © 1982 Authentic Publishing (Adm. by Integrity Music, part of the David C Cook family, songs@integritymusic.com). On the album *Marilyn Baker: Live in Concert.*

[2] Falcon Books.

11 A Divine Encounter

[1] Extract taken from the song 'All I Ever Do is Love You' by Marilyn Baker, Copyright © 1982 Authentic Publishing (Adm. by Integrity Music, part of the David C Cook family, songs@integritymusic.com). On the album *Marilyn Baker: Live in Concert.*

12 A Growing Friendship

[1] Extract taken from the song 'Constantly Amazed' by Marilyn Baker, Copyright © Authentic Publishing (Adm. by Integrity Music, part of the David C Cook family, songs@integritymusic.com). On the album *Face to Face (The Ultimate Collection).*

13 Our First Concert

[1] Extract taken from the song 'Resources of Heaven' by Marilyn Baker, Copyright © 1994 Marilyn Baker Music (Adm. by Integrity Music, part of the David C Cook family, songs@integritymusic.com). On the album *By Your Side (The Ultimate Collection)*.

14 The Isle of Sheppey

[1] Extract taken from the song 'The People That Do Know Their God' by Marilyn Baker, Copyright © Authentic Publishing (Adm. by Integrity Music, part of the David C Cook family, songs@integritymusic.com). On the album *Close to His Heart*.

[2] See Matthew 23:33.

[3] See Isaiah 61:1–4 and Luke 4:18.

[4] Nehemiah 8:10.

15 Off to Yorkshire

[1] Extract taken from the song 'Wonderful Father God (Seek and You Will Find Me)' by Marilyn Baker, Copyright © 1982 Authentic Publishing (Adm. by Integrity Music, part of the David C Cook family, songs@integritymusic.com). On the album *Changing Me (Changing Me/Overflow of Worship)*.

[2] James Alfred Wight (1916–95), or James Herriot, was an author and a vet who wrote a series of books about the life of a vet among people and animals in the Yorkshire Dales.

[3] Extract taken from the song 'Whenever You're Lonely' by Marilyn Baker, Copyright © 1982 Authentic Publishing (Adm. by Integrity Music, part of the David C Cook family, songs@integritymusic.com). On the album *Marilyn Baker*.

16 The Joy of the Bible Festivals

[1] Extract taken from the song 'He is the Rock' by Marilyn Baker, Copyright © 1992 Authentic Publishing (Adm. by Integrity Music, part of the David C Cook family, songs@integritymusic.com). On the album *Face to Face (The Ultimate Collection)*.

[2] Extract taken from the song 'God Has a Plan for You' by Marilyn Baker, Copyright © 1988 Authentic Publishing (Adm. by Integrity Music, part of

the David C Cook family, songs@integritymusic.com). On the album *From the Beginning (The Ultimate Collection)*.

[3] 'He Called My Name' by Marilyn Baker. On the album *From the Beginning (The Ultimate Collection)*.

[4] 'My Heart is Now His Temple' by Marilyn Baker. On the album *From the Beginning (The Ultimate Collection)*.

[5] Emmanuel Bible College had originated in the Methodist/Holiness movement but was now interdenominational. The college closed down in the early nineties.

[6] A memorial medal in memory of the founder of the institution at Koszeg, the Nagy Laszlo medal 1919–88, presented every year to someone special chosen by children and staff.

17 Hearing the Father's Heart

[1] Extract taken from the song 'Whispers of God' by Marilyn Baker, Copyright © 1985 Authentic Publishing (Adm. by Integrity Music, part of the David C Cook family, songs@integritymusic.com). On the album *From the Beginning (The Ultimate Collection)*.

[2] Tracy Williamson, *The Voice of the Father* (London: Hodder & Stoughton, 1995).

[3] See 1 Corinthians 12:8.

[4] John 10:16,27.

[5] 1 Corinthians 2:16.

18 In Times of Weakness

[1] Extract taken from the song 'Lord in All Your Gentleness' by Marilyn Baker, Copyright © 2019 Fox Music A Division of Classic Fox Records/Kobalt Music. On the album *Joy of My Heart*.

[2] Exodus 16:4,5.

[3] After Kathryn Kuhlman (1907–76), the famous healing evangelist.

19 Humorous Moments

[1] Extract taken from the song 'He Gives Joy' by Marilyn Baker, Copyright © 1982 Authentic Publishing (Adm. by Integrity Music, part of the David C Cook family, songs@integritymusic.com). On the album *Marilyn Baker: Live in Concert*.

[2] 'He's Alive' Copyright © Lou Lewis. On the album *From the Beginning (The Ultimate Collection)*.

[3] Koinonia group, a fellowship meeting for the seniors in the church.

[4] 'Refresh Me Lord' by Marilyn Baker. On the album *Refresh Me Lord*.

20 Holy Connections

[1] Extract taken from the song 'Who is Like You?' by Marilyn Baker, Copyright © 1990 Authentic Publishing (Adm. by Integrity Music, part of the David C Cook family, songs@integritymusic.com). On the album *A New Beginning*.

[2] Jennifer Rees Larcombe, *Beyond Healing* (London: Hodder & Stoughton, 1986).

[3] Extract taken from the song 'Come' by Marilyn Baker, Copyright © Authentic Publishing (Adm. by Integrity Music, part of the David C Cook family, songs@integritymusic.com). On the album *Face to Face (The Ultimate Collection)*.

[4] Romans 8:15–17.

[5] Published in 1916 and republished in 1946. Music by Nat D. Ayer (1887–1952) with lyrics by Clifford Grey (1887–1941).

21 Endings and Beginnings

[1] Extract taken from the song 'Sacrifice' by Marilyn Baker, Copyright © 1994 Marilyn Baker Music (Adm. by Integrity Music, part of the David C Cook family, songs@integritymusic.com). On the album *By Your Side (The Ultimate Collection)*.

[2] Extract taken from the song 'Reason for Living' by Marilyn Baker, Copyright © 1994 Marilyn Baker Music (Adm. by Integrity Music, part of the David C Cook family, songs@integritymusic.com). On the album *By Your Side (The Ultimate Collection)*.

22 A New Home

[1] Extract taken from the song 'Seeing is Believing' by Marilyn Baker, Copyright © 1998 Marilyn Baker Music (Adm. by Integrity Music, part of the David C Cook family, songs@integritymusic.com). On the album *Overflow of Worship (Changing Me/Overflow of Worship)*.

[2] Tracy Williamson, *Expecting God to Speak to You!* (Bognor Regis: New Wine Press, 2005).

23 Restoring Lives Through Intimacy with God

[1] Extract taken from the song 'Overflow of Worship (Lord I Want to Tell You)' by Marilyn Baker, Copyright © 1998 Marilyn Baker Music (Adm. by Integrity Music, part of the David C Cook family, songs@integritymusic.com). On the album *Overflow of Worship (Changing Me/Overflow of Worship)*.

[2] The caste system which classified the poorest in society as outcasts or untouchables was abolished in the mid-1990s but was still evident in the way people related to and treated one another, especially in rural India. Similarly, those with disabilities were still viewed as being a source of shame in the family with disabled or blind children frequently being hidden away or pushed out of the home to beg on the streets. (Sourced in conversation with Prabhu and Nancy Rayan.)

[3] Extract taken from the song 'Hollow of His Hand' by Marilyn Baker, Copyright © 1987 Authentic Publishing (Adm. by Integrity Music, part of the David C Cook family, songs@integritymusic.com). On the album *From the Beginning (The Ultimate Collection)*.

[4] Psalm 104:33, ESV UK.

24 Our Faithful God; Our Faithful Team

[1] Extract taken from the song 'To God You are So Important' by Marilyn Baker, Copyright © Authentic Publishing (Adm. by Integrity Music, part of the David C Cook family, songs@integritymusic.com). On the album *A New Beginning*.

25 God's Transforming Works

[1] Extract taken from the song 'Spirit of God' by Marilyn Baker, Copyright © 1994 Marilyn Baker Music (Adm. by Integrity Music, part of the David C Cook family, songs@integritymusic.com). On the album *By Your Side (The Ultimate Collection)*.

[2] This was 1992!

[3] Christian contemplative and meditation group.

Conclusion

[1] Extract taken from the song 'May The Blessing of the Lord' by Marilyn Baker, Copyright © 1986 Authentic Publishing (Adm. by Integrity Music, part of the David C Cook family, songs@integritymusic.com). On the album *From the Beginning (The Ultimate Collection)*.

The Father's Kiss

Living in the reality of God's love

Tracy Williamson

Many of us experience crippling wounds through events in our childhood. The Father heart of God longs to heal these wounds and bring joy and freedom in their place. But how do we learn to trust and love a heavenly Father when we have been hurt by our earthly fathers?

Tracy Williamson honestly shares the insights and lessons she has learnt on her own journey to freedom. With a unique mix of practical teaching, personal stories, poems, prophecies and questions for reflection, this is a life-changing resource for all who carry the wounds of rejection.

Experience the reality of the Father's deep affection for you and start the adventure of a lifetime.

978-1-78078-988-0

Blood, Sweat and Jesus

*The story of a Christian hospital
bringing hope and healing in a
Muslim community*

Kerry Stillman

What is a Christian hospital doing in a remote Muslim area of
Cameroon?

Kerry Stillman shares her own experiences of working as a physio-
therapist in a sub-Saharan village hospital. A vivid impression of
daily life is painted as the team deal with the threat of terrorism, the
attitudes of local people towards Western medicine, their patients'
health issues, and the challenge of sensitively sharing the gospel in a
different culture.

Passionate, intriguing and uplifting, this is a colourful interweaving
of cultures, beliefs and the power of prayer alongside modern
medicine.

978-1-78893-148-9

Salt Water and Honey

*Lost dreams, good grief
and a better story*

Lizzie Lowrie

Reeling from the disappointment of a failed business venture, Lizzie Lowrie's life takes a nightmarish turn as she suffers miscarriage after miscarriage.

Written from the messy middle of life, where there are no neat or cliched answers, Lizzie honestly shares her pain and the fight to find God in her suffering.

Providing a safe space to remind people that they're not alone, it's okay to grieve and their story matters, this is for anyone who has lost their dream and is struggling to understand their purpose when life looks nothing like they hoped it would.

978-1-78893-095-6

Though I Run through the Valley

A persecuted family rescues over a thousand children in Myanmar

Pamela Johnson

Amid decades of war and political strife in Myanmar one family fights back with their weapon of choice – the Bible.

Three generations of Emmerline's family have been living out their love for God by rescuing children who have been orphaned, abandoned or made destitute by their country's upheaval. Theirs is not a story of merely evading the enemy and surviving, but instead one of seeking out the vulnerable and teaching them how to thrive.

Daring to trust God against all the odds, this is the powerful story of one family's sacrifice to provide a home for orphans so that the children of Myanmar could hope for a better future.

978-1-78893-160-1

Authentic

We trust you enjoyed reading this book
from Authentic. If you want to be
informed of any new titles from this author
and other releases you can sign up to the
Authentic newsletter by scanning below:

Online:
authenticmedia.co.uk

Follow us: